RANDOM HOUSE

NEW YORK

THE MAN ON
MAO'S RIGHT

THE MAN ON MAO'S RIGHT

From Harvard Yard to Tiananmen Square,

My Life Inside China's Foreign Ministry

Ji Chaozhu

For Wang Xiangtong

CROSSING THE YELLOW RIVER
TO CLEAR RIVER DISTRICT

My boat adrift on a vast river, heaving
water spreading into far shores of sky,

sky's deep swells break suddenly open
and a city's ten thousand homes appear.

Further on, I glimpse the markets again,
hints of mulberry and hemp out beyond,

then gaze back to my homeland: a flood
brimmed boundless into cloud and mist.

—WANG WEI, eighth-century Chinese poet

Preface

Books that purport to tell the inside story of China's recent past range from wrenching tales of suffering during the Cultural Revolution, to speculative or even salacious biographies of Mao, to serious works of history. My story is none of those, yet it includes aspects of all of them.

Yes, my family and I suffered during the Japanese aggression, the civil war between the Communists and the Nationalists, the Anti-Rightist Campaign, the Great Leap Forward, the Great Proletarian Cultural Revolution, and all the political purges and economic upheavals that swept China as it struggled to define its role as a sovereign nation in a modern world.

And it is true that I witnessed or was privy to much of the political and personal machinations that took place behind the scenes as certain leaders of our government jockeyed for power and privilege.

And finally, I was an eyewitness to an astonishing number of historic events, rubbing shoulders and sometimes becoming casual with a long list of world leaders, including six presidents of the United States.

But, unlike some biographers of Mao, I decline to pass judgment. Let the facts speak for themselves. Mao was indisputably the father of modern, independent China—our country's George Washington, except he was truly godlike in our hearts. While he was a populist who led a people away from thousands of years of feudalism and foreign domination, his catastrophic mistakes and failures have been well documented.

Unlike many credible and moving accounts of our long, dark decade—the Cultural Revolution—I can only report my experience as this terrible epoch wove itself into the fabric of my daily life and career. However, I think it serves history well to see this period through the eyes of one who experienced life inside the crucible.

I am unqualified as a true historian. Rather than studying China, I spent more than four decades in its service, advancing from a note-taking translator at the negotiating table during the Korean conflict to my final posting as an under secretary-general of the United Nations.

Even if I had wanted to make a historical record of my years in government, keeping diaries and journals was discouraged, especially in the Foreign Ministry. I have relied largely on recollection; the excellent memory and superior intelligence of my wife of fifty years, Wang Xiangtong; and the observations of the many colleagues and acquaintances with whom I worked or crossed paths.

I sometimes think of myself as having been a flea on the collar of events—both historically momentous and profoundly human. In telling this tale I have also relied on others, such as Henry Kissinger, whose friendship I continue to enjoy, as well as numerous other historical sources that I deemed reliable or objective. Where appropriate, I have noted those sources, but I have tried to avoid weighing this story down with ponderous footnotes and strings of exotic-sounding Chinese names and places.

This is the story of an ordinary man on an extraordinary journey during a pivotal period in world history. What may be most surprising to many readers is how much China and the Chinese people—geopolitics notwithstanding—have in common with the rest of the world.

—JI CHAOZHU
Beijing, 2008

Contents

Author's Note

The book you hold in your hands began with a near-death experience, one of many I survived during my four-plus decades in government service. I had just completed five years as under secretary-general of the United Nations, four years as China's ambassador to the Court of St. James's, and thirty-six years working with China's top leaders. I had logged millions of air miles crisscrossing the globe, meeting kings, presidents, and prime ministers of every political stripe and color.

Having reached my sixty-seventh birthday, I was looking forward to putting all I had learned to work, in some new capacity. Before I left New York, I had to decline with regret offers from friends and private think tanks to stay and enjoy a comfortable semi-retirement. I was flattered, but no enticement could dissuade me from returning to the nest.

I arrived back in China eager for a new assignment or challenge. But none presented itself and I grew frustrated. The sudden transition from center stage—one of my last speeches was before an audience of six thousand at the Kremlin—to inactivity was dispiriting. But I had my old comrades, some of whom had already mustered out from long careers as ambassadors, and we saw one another frequently.

One day I was having lunch with one of them, feeling a bit low, and agreed to have a beer. It had been years since I'd indulged. Apart from a glass of wine now and then, I never acquired a taste for liquor. Happiness to me is a tall, frosty, chocolate milkshake. An hour later, I had stabbing pain in my gut and had to be rushed to the hospital, where I fell into a coma.

I awoke nine days later, having narrowly survived an attack of hemorrhagic necrotic pancreatitis, generally a fatal illness. After a nine-hour surgery and six months in the hospital, the doctors sent me home with instructions never to touch another drop of alcohol.

When I was well enough, I began to receive and accept offers to serve as an adviser or in a leadership role in several nongovernmental organizations. I also received a number of interview requests from authors and documentary filmmakers working on historical projects.

Before I'd gotten sick, my wife, Xiangtong, had written a biography about me, published in 1997 in my home province, Shanxi. It sold modestly well—ten thousand copies in two printings. Books by retired government officials had become popular, with entire sections of bookstores stocked with them. There was great interest in the details of the Mao period that were just becoming public.

Xiangtong encouraged me to fill my free time by writing my own book, which was published by Beijing University Press in 1999. By that time, there were many more such memoirs in print, Xiangtong's book had apparently satisfied the curiosity of the Chinese public, and the country had become preoccupied with imagining and building the future. My book sold about three thousand copies.

The person who connected the dots for this book was Ray Dalio, a financial executive from Connecticut. He was visiting China with his teenage son Matthew, who had attended a year of primary school in Beijing while homestaying with a mutual acquaintance. We were introduced, and when Ray learned about my career he immediately offered to help me get my story published in English.

Through an intermediary, he recruited Foster Winans, an experienced author and ghostwriter. Foster agreed to take my somewhat disorganized and Chinese-specific manuscript and help rework it into a compelling narrative that would appeal to a non-Chinese audience. My goal was to demystify China and the Chinese people—to explain in human terms how we got where we are today and what makes us tick.

After a hundred or so hours of interviews, two months of research in China, and extensive historical readings, Foster succeeded in bringing the story to life. He guided me through the process of recruiting an enthusiastic and prestigious literary agent, Al Zuckerman of Writers House, who in turn guided me to an enthusiastic and prestigious publisher, Robert Loomis at Random House.

I am indebted to all these good people for taking such care with my legacy and helping me open a window into the soul of modern China in a way that I hope will bring us all closer together.

—JI CHAOZHU
Beijing, 2008

Introduction

One of my favorite anecdotes about the two decades I spent working alongside China's Premier Zhou Enlai comes from the first formal words he exchanged with Henry Kissinger in 1971, at a top-secret meeting in Beijing. After more than two decades of war and threats of war, it was the first time that a senior representative of each of these great nations had sat at the same table.

The moment could be considered the birth of modern relations between my native land, China, and the land where I spent much of my childhood, America. The stakes couldn't have been higher. It was my duty to interpret both for the premier and for Dr. Kissinger, who had been smuggled into the country on a delicate mission to negotiate the first-ever visit to the People's Republic by an American president, Richard Nixon. Although the premier understood English quite well, he rarely spoke it, preferring to take advantage of the interpretation pauses to compose his thoughts.

Kissinger, looking a bit tense and anxious, shuffled his papers and, peering through his glasses, began to read from prepared remarks that he would later admit were "slightly pedantic." At one point, he read, "Many visitors have come to this beautiful and, to us, mysterious land."

The premier raised his hand. Startled, Kissinger stopped in midsentence. His aides shifted in their seats and exchanged glances. Smiling slightly, the premier said, "When you have become familiar with China, it will not be as mysterious as before."

Kissinger permitted himself a fleeting, abashed grin of relief, set aside his sheaf of papers, and they began to get to know each other as two men seeking common ground for their respective nations.

The Western world has certainly warmed to China in the thirty-six years since those first meetings, but there remains a great deal of befuddlement in the West about who we are as a nation and what we care about as ordinary people. China is too often portrayed in the Western press as a threat when, in fact, the Chinese worldview is traditionally inward-looking and defensive rather than imperialistic.

It is my goal in these pages to help demystify China and the Chinese people, through the narrative of my life as a son of China—including my youth growing up in the United States—and through the events that I was privileged to witness and participate in during my career.

Much about the Chinese character can be gleaned from the sayings with which we season our daily discourse—our favorite clichés. For example, someone who is in a hurry to pocket a profit—as is now happening more often in our burgeoning economy—is said to be killing chickens to get eggs. When embarking on a great undertaking, we remind ourselves that a journey of a thousand miles begins with a single step. Both sayings speak to a central element of a shared subconscious that has evolved over five thousand years of continuous history. We embrace time as seamless and ceaseless. This makes us persistent and patient.

One of our most revered ancient parables illustrating this idea was popularized by Mao Zedong a few years before the birth of the People's Republic of China. It strikes me as a fitting metaphor for my people, my nation, and my career as an English translator, interpreter for Chairman Mao and Premier Zhou, ambassador to the Court of St. James's, and an under secretary-general of the United Nations.

This parable, entitled "The Foolish Old Man Who Removed the Mountains," was invoked by Chairman Mao in a speech designed to fire up the troops in 1945 as the People's Army found itself fighting both the Japanese and a civil war against the American-backed forces of Chiang Kai-shek. Mao wanted to inspire his followers with the conviction that the liberation of the Chinese people was inevitable, no matter how long it took.

The fable tells of an old man who lived long ago in northern China. His farm lay in the shadows of two great mountains that blocked the life-giving sun from reaching his fields. One day he decided to remove the mountains. He summoned his sons and, with hoes in hands, they began to dig and carry away the earth.

A nosy, gray-bearded neighbor strolled by. When he was told the purpose of all the digging, he scoffed, "How foolish you are, old man! It is quite impossible for you to dig up those two huge mountains."

The Foolish Old Man replied, "Yes, you are right. I will not live to see it done. But when I die my sons will carry on. When they die, there will be my grandsons, and then their sons and grandsons, and so on, to infinity. High as they are, the mountains cannot grow any higher. But with every shovelful we remove, they will be that much lower. Why can't we clear them away?"

We Chinese may choose from time to time to withdraw from the field of battle, but we never give up. From childhood, this was the message I received at my father's knee. The metaphor Father chose to make his point was the persistence of an ant trying to climb a flight of stairs. The ant may fall back again and again trying to ascend the risers, he told me, but it does not give up until it succeeds, or it dies trying. This, Father assured me, is the secret of a life honorably lived: Always do your best, and never give up.

THE MAN ON
MAO'S RIGHT

CHAPTER 1

Our Long March

On this last day of our innocence and privilege, my older brother and I rushed home from school, trembling with outrage at the effrontery of our teachers.

"They can't do that to *us*!" Chaoli blustered. He marched down the center of the packed-earth street, his skinny, ten-year-old arms swinging with purpose. The chill gusts blowing down off the mountains billowed the hem of his quilted robe into a blue sail. I skipped to keep up as we hurried past clutches of people bent under the weight of overloaded shoulder poles or pulling carts piled with household belongings, old women, and babies. They were all hurrying in the opposite direction.

Several days had passed since the last time enemy planes swooped down and dropped their bombs on Fenyang, my family's ancestral town. The respite had an ominous air as a growing stream of refugees from the advancing battlefront shuffled and clattered past our schoolroom windows. Our teachers said they were fleeing the Japanese, whom my father cursed as "the little devils."

In the way that a child knows without comprehending, I understood what was happening: like the ancient Mongol hordes I had read about in my schoolbooks, our enemies threatened us from the north. But for the moment my eight-year-old mind was preoccupied with the ultimatum we had just received at school.

"Father will tell them," Chaoli said. "He's the chief! They must obey him."

In the gathering chaos of the bombings and the rumors of imminent invasion, the number of empty seats in our classrooms had grown and the number of tuition coins chiming in the palms of our teachers each morning had begun to shrink. Increasingly worried, our teachers had told us to warn our parents: any child who failed to attend classes would be expelled forever.

I was a conscientious student and it gave me great pleasure to hear my parents' praises when I brought home good marks. School also allowed me to play a role I relished: that of the young lord. Because I was a member of a wealthy, educated, landowning family, my teachers never dared scold or discipline me. If one of the other children arrived late, the teacher rapped his knuckles with a bamboo switch. But never me. Both the teachers and the other children kowtowed to Chaoli and me. As a result, I had no friends in school, or anywhere else for that matter. This was the world I'd known since I could walk or speak, a world of privilege and deference, and I was comfortable in it. Everywhere Chaoli and I went, we were treated like princes. I was a happily spoiled brat.

The teacher's expulsion threat left me worried that my mother and father might actually keep us home. I also felt rather smug—we were not cowards like the children whose families had run away or were hiding in their homes like mice. *My* father was not afraid of the little devils. He was important—a law professor, the commissioner of education, and a friend of the warlord governor of Shanxi Province, General Yan Xishan, who sent us birthday gifts of toys carved from sandalwood.

I revered my father for being a Chinese patriot. He was too old and gray to be a soldier, but he knew Mao Zedong, as well as the other leaders of the People's Army valiantly fighting the Japanese on one side and waging a civil war against the Kuomintang—Chiang Kai-shek's Chinese Nationalists—on the other. Before we moved to Fenyang, my father had a bodyguard who rode on the running board of his chauffeured car, a big pistol hanging from his belt. No lowly teacher could possibly keep me away from school unless Father agreed. Chaoli was right, and we princely tattletales couldn't wait to get home.

Chaoli was practically running. "Just you wait till Father hears about this! Hurry, Wah."

Small for my age and chronically ill, I was soon exhausted by the effort of keeping up with my big brother. I struggled to catch my breath. "I wish Fuhai was here," I moaned.

Fuhai would have let me ride his shoulders, as he had in Taiyuan, the provincial capital where we had lived until recently, before my father retired from his government and university posts. Fuhai had been my friend and playmate, as well as my protector—one of our nine servants. I was delicate, a constant worry for my parents. Fuhai's job was to protect me and keep me comfortable, nurse me when I was sick, and walk me to and from school.

He was a gangly, good-humored, illiterate young peasant. He catered to my every whim, and I adored him. We had often walked to the ancient city wall, where I climbed on his shoulders, brandishing a stick, while he snorted and pawed his sandal-clad feet like a horse. I was a great Han general in gleaming armor, riding into battle against the murderous tribes from the north!

Before I learned about real life, I was well acquainted with war, fascinated by military heroes and English knights. I had been born into a world of cruel conflicts: provincial warlords fighting one another; Communists against Nationalists; the little Japanese devils against us Chinese. I heard about war constantly, but until 1937, when I was eight, I had yet to experience it. That's when the Japanese, who had already invaded Manchuria, in the north, began dropping bombs on Taiyuan.

To escape the danger, we abandoned our large home in the center of the city, with its two courtyards and staff of servants, and drove for many hours over dirt roads to Fenyang, a small market town. We moved in with my ancient widower grandfather in the house where my father had been born, near where all our ancestors were entombed. In that dry region, my grandfather owned much of the arable land, which he rented to tenant farmers who paid him in crops of millet, corn, and wheat.

Though prosperous, my grandfather's house was smaller than the one we left in Taiyuan. With our future uncertain, my father said that we had to leave the servants behind, including dear Fuhai. The Japanese, he explained, would have little interest in a peasant town far from the provincial capital. We would be safe there until the fighting was over. But after a few months the Japanese planes began bombing Fenyang, too.

The raids were always preceded by the sound of clanging gongs in the streets and shouting—"Enemy planes! Enemy planes!" Chaoli and my little sister, Chin, sat frozen with fear on the raised sleeping *kang*—the traditional earthen platform warmed in cold weather by the heat from the cookstove, which was built into the base. Having been born with a fearless streak, I usually bolted for the door. I always wanted to watch.

"Wah!" my mother shouted. "Come back here!" A distant *whump* interrupted the drone of the bomber engines, followed by a fresh wave of shouting and gong clanging.

My mother ordered me to lie down on the tiled floor with the rest of the family, next to the massive kang. I remember my poor grandfather letting out a deep groan as Father helped him out of his chair to lie beside us. I felt Chaoli trembling beside me. Chin softly whimpered in my mother's arms each time someone in a neighboring house screamed in fear. My heart pounded in my ears. Would this be the day a bomb landed on us? I counted the *whump*s and listened to the roar of the engines grow louder, then slowly fade.

When the last muffled explosion died away, someone nearby shouted, "All clear!" I got up and sat on the edge of the kang. Father pulled on his coat. "I'm going to have a look," he said.

I again bolted for the door. Again my mother's stern voice stopped me in my tracks. I begged and cajoled and stamped my feet, which nearly always worked whenever I was displeased or wanted something. My parents were endlessly indulgent with poor sick Wah, the nickname I had earned by being so small and frail.

This time they were unyielding. "Do as your mother tells you," Father ordered, lifting his long gray beard so that it lay outside his coat. So I climbed a ladder into a second-story grain loft to watch him walk down the street and out of sight. The houses I could see were all intact, but in the distance above the rooflines rose a pillar of black smoke.

Father returned with his face as tense as a fist. "We don't even have Chinese soldiers here!" he spat out, cursing the Japanese raids. "Just innocent people being slaughtered like meat on a cutting board." The image made me shiver.

While war had arrived on our doorstep, it had not yet touched my brother and me personally. We had continued to enjoy the perquisites of self-importance and rank. As a result, when our teachers threatened that day to expel us if we skipped school, we were incensed. My brother was loudly declaring his complaint to my father when I reached the threshold, wheezing. A pot of noodles boiled on the stove, and the humid, yeasty air soothed the burn in my throat.

Father glanced at me from his comfortable reading chair and stroked his beard as Chaoli, hands on his hips, leaned over him repeating what our teachers had said. ". . . And Madame Chiu was disrespectful, Father. She made us leave our slates at school and said we could not take them home anymore, as if we might steal them. Imagine stealing a stupid slate!"

Mother's eyes were fixed on Father as she pulled flakes of dough from a yeasty ball and dropped them into the steaming pot. "The other children are not going to school?"

"That's right, Mother," Chaoli said. "Fewer and fewer every day."

"They are cowards!" I declared.

Over his reading glasses Father returned Mother's gaze and held it for a long moment with a cocked eyebrow. Then he slowly closed the book in his lap and sighed.

"Father, they can't keep us out of school, can they?"

"Help your mother, Wah," he said. "Chaoli, go and wake Grandfather."

In my limited experience, I had no doubt that Father had good, wise reasons for everything he did and said. I knew that I could eat whenever I was hungry. I knew that in the courtyard of our house in winter there would always be a frozen puddle for skating, and that my mother would come out on those cold days and give us children a sliver of smoked duck as a treat. I knew that I hated being sickly—I wept with frustration whenever I was ordered to bed during one of my extended illnesses. I knew the powerful warmth of my mother's and father's love. All this I took for granted.

War, on the other hand, I found intriguing and romantic. At mealtimes my father frequently told stories about the Long March, during which the brave People's Army overcame all odds to escape destruction by Chiang's Kuomintang army. "It will be remembered one day as a great epic of military history," Father said, "along with Hannibal crossing the Alps, or Napoleon's retreat from Moscow."

He often spoke of my eldest brother, Chaoding, who had gone abroad before I was born. I'd never met him but often heard of his exploits. Halfway around the world, he had earned a doctorate in economics at Columbia University. As a secret Communist, he was living in New York City while pretending to work for the Nationalists, whom he secretly opposed. He had even married an American named Harriet, a loyal Communist whose Jewish parents had fled Russia. Father was fiercely proud of Chaoding, and we kids were all brought up to admire him for his courage. If he was exposed, Father warned us, he would certainly be killed. "Never talk about this outside the family," he said. "Every wall has ears."

Father explained the war to Chaoli and me simply: "The little devils want to make us a people without a country, a nation of slaves." I promised myself that, in the tradition of the warrior heroes of our ancient past, I would one day help drive the little devils from our land.

But on this night Father had nothing to say about our beloved China, the war, or my heroic brother in America. While I stirred the pot of noodles, Mother and Father disappeared into their bedroom and closed the door. I strained to hear, but I couldn't make out even one word from the low murmur of their voices. When they emerged, we sat down to eat. Father barely spoke, his forehead furrowed in thought. Mother sharply scolded me for eating too fast, and they both ignored my questions about whether we would go to school the next day. After supper, we children were sent straight to bed.

The next morning I woke up shivering from the chill. The kang cookstove was cold and the air smelled of gun oil. Father sat at the table cleaning his pistol, and Mother was stuffing clothing into sacks. "We're going on a trip," she said brusquely, her small hands fluttering like a pair of sparrows as she worked. "Hurry and get dressed."

Things happened so fast that I forgot my fear of being expelled from school until we were in the back of a truck bumping along a road out of town. We had joined the stream of refugees fleeing the Japanese.

The truck wound its way through the rocky, mountainous countryside between two columns of people with sacks roped to their backs, wobbling under the weight of shoulder poles, or pulling handcarts. The crowd had to step aside to let our truck pass. Chaoli and I sat in the back on a hard bench, watching the lines of peasants behind us step back on the road to resume trudging in the cloud of red dust that had gathered in our wake.

When the road narrowed to a cartway, the truck stopped. My bottom ached. It felt good to get out and stretch my legs. Next, Father hired two mule carts from a local farmer, who helped us reload our belongings. Chaoli and I climbed on one cart and my mother got on the other with my grandfather and my baby sister, Chin. Thus we began the next leg of the journey, the farmer and one of his sons leading the carts.

The wagons lurched over rocks and holes for *li* after *li*.* "This is boring," Chaoli groused. "I don't see what all the fuss is about. What do the Japanese care about us? I don't see why we shouldn't just go back home. We're missing school!"

I didn't know if the Japanese would hurt us, but I accepted Father's wisdom that they might. I preferred to think of this journey as a great adventure. In my mind, I connected the stories I'd read about China's glorious past with my father's stories about the struggle for China's future. I had now become a soldier in a great army of patriots, eluding the clutches of the enemy.

The cartway narrowed to a pockmarked trail. Again, we unloaded and my father sent the mule carts back. We hired a man with a sedan chair suspended on poles between two donkeys. "Grandfather is too old and Chin too small to walk so far," Father said. "They will ride together. The rest of us will walk until we reach the Yellow River." Our belongings were tied to the back of a pack mule. The hired man led the donkeys carrying the sedan chair, then my mother and father led the pack mule. Chaoli and I followed last.

---

*A *li* is five hundred meters, or just under a third of a mile.

We plodded along like that for a week, over a great mountain range. Dry, barren slopes gradually gave way to grass-covered hills and streams, with small villages huddled along the banks. For the first time I understood the vastness of China, a country of poor rural peasants with big hearts who welcomed us into their homes at night.

We had to share sleeping kangs with smelly strangers, and eat our meals on the dirt floors of their tiny cottages, shooing away the dogs and chickens that pestered everyone for scraps. No one in our family had ever known anything less than privilege and prosperity. I could see in my parents' exhausted faces the toll this was taking, but they remained stoic through the inconveniences and discomforts. I took my cue from them. When Chaoli whined about the corn gruel and the watery soups served by our hosts, I said nothing. I hated the food, too, but acting strong and silent like my father and mother made me feel superior.

Chaoli and I walked behind the mule all day long. To break the monotony, Chaoli sang the "March of the Volunteers." The popular patriotic war tune put a spring in my step, so I asked him to teach it to me. He sang it over and over, until I knew it by heart. Marching south toward the Yellow River, we sang at the top of our lungs:

> Arise all ye who refuse to be slaves!
> With our flesh and blood, we will build a new Great Wall of China.
> The Chinese nation has arrived at its moment of greatest danger,
> We are all forced to call out with our last breath,
> Arise! Arise! Arise!
> United as one and braving the enemy's fire, we'll advance!
> Braving the enemy's fire, we'll ever advance!

We marched from dawn to dusk, stopping only to eat and tend to the animals. Then, one afternoon, we crested a pass and there, stretching from horizon to horizon, shimmered the broad Yellow River. We had arrived at the southwestern edge of our province, Shanxi, where the Yellow turns sharply east. Thin columns of wood smoke rose from the riverbank, where hundreds of people camped, waiting to cross. On the other side was a small town. The shriek of a locomotive whistle echoed in the valley.

At the riverbank, we joined a crowd outside the garrison commander's office getting their papers checked. Two soldiers with rifles slung over their shoulders guarded the ferry landing.

"Are they Long Marchers?" I asked.

"Quiet, Wah," Father said. "You must learn to hold your tongue among strangers."

When it was our turn, Father presented his papers to the guard, who carefully unfolded the thin rice-paper documents covered in Chinese characters and red stamps. "This permit is for a pistol," the guard said. He held up one of the papers and gave my father the once-over. "You must surrender it before you cross." He held out his hand.

Father nodded, reached under his robe, and produced the holstered gun, handing over the last vestige of his once unquestioned authority. I gawked in stunned disbelief. A fleeting grimace crossed my father's face. The guard bowed as he accepted the pistol. I remembered stories I'd read of the gallant English knights and how, once defeated, a warrior surrendered his sword. It was a quick, quiet ceremony that filled me with regret and with new respect for my father. He was losing his authority, but the guard had let him keep his face—the term the Chinese people use to describe dignity.

Ahead of us, across the broad, silty river, lay several more days of travel before we reached Hankow, a bustling industrial city on the middle reaches of the Yangtze River, China's longest. Hankow would be our new home, far from the bombs, where Father could work as a lawyer and we could safely go to school.

In spite of the harsh traveling conditions, it had not yet fully dawned on us boys that we were no longer the pampered children of a wealthy family, entitled to have our way. As we waited our turn for the ferry ride across the Yellow River, a chill wind blew off the waves. Chaoli shivered and announced that he wanted some fruit drops.

"There is no more candy," my mother said. "You kids ate it all."

Chaoli made a face. "Can't you get some more?" he whined. "I want something sweet. I'm sick of peasant food. I hate this place! When are we ever going to stop walking? I'm so tired. What's wrong with having a bit of candy?"

Chaoli carried on for a few moments more until a dark scowl crossed Father's face. He raised his hand and with a lightning-fast blow struck Chaoli hard across the cheek. Chaoli stumbled backward, mouth agape, eyes like plums. I gasped. My scalp crawled with fear.

I had never seen my father raise his hand in anger. He rarely scolded us, let alone punished us. He was both genteel and gentle. He had once accepted an invitation to join some important friends on a hunting expedition. For me, this had been an exciting new way to see Father, going out the door brandishing a brand-new rifle. But when he returned he told Mother that his first kill left him feeling so mournful for the little bird that he threw the rifle away. He never hunted again.

As the commissioner of education, Father had once defied the orders of his boss, General Yan Xishan, to direct soldiers to fire live rounds into a mob of protesting students. Instead, he had them herded onto trucks and driven to the edge of the city so that they could cool off on the walk back into town. He undoubtedly saved the lives of many young men.

He once cut a little hole in our doorway so one of the alley cats that had adopted us could come in and get a bit of food when it was hungry. He had a Buddhist sensibility; I had seen him alter his stride to avoid stepping on an ant.

The slap Father delivered to Chaoli roared in my ears. Chaoli rubbed his inflamed cheek and stared at his feet through silent tears. I stood frozen in disbelief.

"You children must behave from now on." Father's voice was as cold and commanding as I had ever heard it. "Once we cross this river, I'll have lost all my powers. From now on you must earn the respect of others, not expect it. Everything has changed, and you must change also."

Chaoli stomped off to sulk on a rock.

CHAPTER 2

To America

On that afternoon in 1937, although it was Chaoli's face that stung, I, too, felt the blow. The world I had always known ceased to exist. We had left behind our ancestors, the five houses my father had built for his children, and our high rank in society. Nothing was the same. Nothing ever would be.

In Hankow* we would be safe, Father explained, because it was now the capital of China. Also, we would be joined by my brother Chaoding. He had written Father that he was returning from New York to confer with Mao Zedong and Zhou Enlai, two of the top leaders of the Chinese Communist Party and the People's Liberation Army.

Chaoding and Zhou Enlai, my father told us proudly, became friends as teenagers, when they both joined the Party, at its very beginnings. It was the Party's decision that Chaoding should go to America to further his education, while Zhou would stay behind to lead the People's Liberation Army in its fight against the Japanese and the Kuomintang. Our lowly status as refugees was now tempered by the sense of purpose I saw in Father's stern demeanor.

A long train ride left my siblings, my mother, and my grandfather ill with motion sickness. Father and I were unaffected. I spent much of the trip running up and down the aisles, or staring out the window at the changing landscape. Having spent all my life in an arid zone, I was mesmerized by the carpet of green covering the land, and the glinting

*Hankow merged with two other cities (Hanyang and Wuchang) to become Wuhan in 1949.

rice paddies dotted with peasants stooped at their work. It was late autumn, 1937.

At Hankow's noisy railroad depot, a friend of Chaoding's met us and took us to our new home. It was not much bigger than Grandfather's house in Fenyang, but, wonder of wonders, it had Western-style toilets. I took to them instantly, vowing never again to use the awful squatter holes I had grown up with.

Soon after our arrival in Hankow, Chaoding arrived from America. He'd returned to collect material for his research on China's economy for the Kuomintang, to make secret reports to Zhou Enlai, and to help his family. I liked Chaoding from the moment we met. He smiled easily, was round and soft and affectionate, and acted in every way as I thought a big brother should: always showing concern for us kids, always playful. He made funny faces and strange noises, played the bogeyman, and carried us about on his shoulders, which my dignified old father would never have considered.

One of the first things Chaoding did to endear us to him was treat us to our first, heavenly taste of ice cream. At our new home, he arranged for an iceman to deliver chunks of ice to fill our wooden pail. Then, the iceman would put the precious bars of vanilla-flavored ice cream, in their paper wrappers, into the pail to keep them cold until we were ready to eat them. This became a daily ritual that I greedily anticipated.

Chaoding had been abroad for fourteen years. He often walked Chaoli and me to school, enthusiastically telling us about the impossibly tall buildings in New York ("Taller than the tallest pagoda!") and the strange foods Americans ate. He had left behind Harriet and their infant son, Emile. Chaoding was twenty-six years older than I. His mother, my father's first wife, had died giving birth to Chaoding's younger brother. Father's second wife had died as well. Mother was his third wife, and she was born on the same day of the year as Chaoding, so they celebrated their birthdays together.

At first, life in Hankow overwhelmed me. I was enrolled in primary school, and instead of kowtowing to me the other students regarded me with scorn, mocking my provincial Shanxi accent. The teacher was just as abrupt and strict with me as with the other students.

I remembered well Father's admonition on the banks of the Yellow

River. I hid my displeasure, and tried to appear humble at all times. I made sure always to arrive on time, to stand when the teacher entered, and to bow to her with all the other pupils. I dared not fidget and learned to appear to be listening intently to the teacher's droning voice, pretending now and again to take notes.

Doing all this was not enough. The class bully quickly sniffed me out. He waved his little fist at me on the first day, and I shrank into a corner like a frightened rabbit. I must have presented such a small target that he decided it wasn't worth the effort. I escaped unharmed, though mortified by my cowardice. I had learned my first lesson in survival diplomacy.

From the half-pint tyrant I had been in Fenyang, I became a mousy, bullied kid trying my best to avoid other half-pint tyrants, as well as the attention of my teachers.

Our living circumstances had plummeted, too. Our family kept mostly to ourselves at home, a small one-story house with three rooms. Hankow was cosmopolitan by comparison with Fenyang. The streets were choked with cars competing for space with rickshaws and bullock carts. Knowing almost no one, we ventured out only to go to school.

I paid close attention to Father's many long conversations with Chaoding. One day Chaoding revealed that Father had been offered a high government post. Chiang Kai-shek had sent a message asking him to be the deputy attorney general of the Nationalist Chinese government. Father laughed. "One spy in the family is enough," he said.

Chaoding brought home reports that the war was going badly for the Chinese. The Japanese had committed horrific crimes against the citizens of Nanking. At school, I heard stories of bayoneted babies and of people being scalded alive in locomotive boilers. And then, one day, the Japanese began daylight terror-bombing raids in Hankow. Once again, we were under siege.

Chaoding assured us that we were safe from immediate danger because we lived in a section of the city that had diplomatic immunity. Many cities in China had these zones, called concessions. These diplomatic zones date back to the first British concession in 1861, where the business zone of the foreign settlement was built. Obtained from the Chinese authorities by a lease in perpetuity in the Crown's favor, the British concession was followed in 1895 by a similar concession to the Germans, and this was then followed by concessions to France and Russia.

We lived in Hankow's French concession and Father rented an office nearby, where he practiced law. Although the country was at war, the Japanese honored the neutrality of the diplomatic zones by using their weapons elsewhere. As spectators, we watched the bombs land with dull thuds on distant neighborhoods. Some days, in the skies over the city I saw the telltale smoke trails of aerial combat. On one occasion, many of us were out on the street watching the aerial bombardment and the Chinese anti-aircraft batteries firing at the Japanese planes. Suddenly a jubilant shout was heard, and we all looked up to see a smoking Japanese plane crash to the ground with a spectacular explosion. We cheered.

My grandfather, who, at eighty-four, had managed to travel all that distance with us to Hankow, began to suffer from chronic constipation and was soon bedridden. He complained about the Western toilet. Grandfather said that he could move his bowels only over the old-fashioned squatters. His condition worsened, and one day he called me to him. Patting me on the head, he muttered, "See how sick your grandpa is. I am going soon." A few days later, he died.

People came to our home wearing the white robes of mourning. They wept and bowed to Father and Mother. Our whole family was also dressed in white mourning robes. We kids were forbidden to see Grandfather. Only grown-ups went into his room to pay their respects. Then his open coffin was carried out of our house and everyone wept, especially my poor father and Chaoding.

I wanted to see inside the coffin, but it was being carried too high and, in that solemn moment, I dared not ask. My parents led the men who carried Grandpa's remains out of our house and into a car waiting outside.

Our family's ancestral tomb was far away, back in the countryside in Shanxi Province, near Fenyang. Grandfather's coffin had to be entombed in Hankow, thousands of li from my grandmother's coffin. Because of the little devils, we were unable to observe the tradition of taking food and flowers to the family tomb, burning incense, tidying up, and kneeling to kowtow. Father sank into a deep funk, burying himself in his law books and his teaching duties at a law school.

The news from back home was equally grim. One night Father read a letter from a cousin to the assembled family. It told how the Japanese troops had arrived in Fenyang right after we fled, and rushed to Grandfather's house looking for Father. Upon finding us all gone, the Japanese officers said, "We know that Mr. Chi Kung-chuan* is a famous scholar, and we have come here to pay our respects." The officers then removed their hats, bowed three times, and left.

My father had studied law in Japan for six years and was fluent in the language. He had been in Japan in 1911 when China's Republican Revolution overthrew the last of the Qing dynasty. His scholarship ended. The Japanese offered to subsidize the rest of his legal education, but he declined and returned to China. He was thirty years old and, in addition to distrusting the motives of his Japanese benefactors, he wanted to start a family. Years later, he did return to Japan, where he earned his full law degree.

My father was not only well known to the invading Japanese; he had been a high provincial official. He would have made quite a prize had they "persuaded" him to be their puppet governor. "That would have been the end of us," Father told Chaoding. "Our own long march saved our necks."

From Taiyuan came word of atrocities. Women, children, and the aged who were able had fled to the hillsides and hidden in caves, concealing the entrances with brush. After hunting them down, the Japanese burned them alive in the caves with flamethrowers.

A pall fell over our family. The harsh forces of nature and man loomed over us in every direction we turned. Zhou Enlai sent word to Chaoding asking him to bring the family to Yan'an, the distant redoubt to which Mao's People's Army had fled Chiang's Nationalists. Mao lived there with his remaining troops and senior staff, in rooms carved from the sides of cliffs. Reaching Yan'an would be a long, arduous, and dangerous journey, but Chaoding was eager to try.

Meanwhile, by land and from the sea—steaming up the mighty

---

*My father's name in the English used in those days.

Yangtze River from Shanghai—the Japanese army was fast approaching Hankow. There was only one route to Yan'an: through the wartime Chinese capital of Chongqing, 850 miles west, up the winding Yangtze River. We could have gone by boat, but the journey would have taken weeks and the Japanese were sending waves of bombers up the river valley. No Chinese man, woman, or child was safe. If they couldn't find a military target, the Japanese were notorious for strafing civilians.

One bright morning I woke to find my parents and Chaoding gathering up our belongings. We were again on the move, leaving the house and walking through the city streets to the banks of the mile-wide river. My heart leaped with joy to see a beautiful, shiny seaplane anchored in the water. I looked at Chaoding and he winked. My first airplane ride!

I gazed with awe at the silver machine bobbing on the river surface, gleaming in the reflected light. I trembled as I stepped into the small launch that carried us out to the plane. The pilot and the copilot helped us board, one by one. The plane was small inside, just big enough to hold our family and our luggage.

The pilot turned the engine over, and as the propeller roared to life river water sprayed against the windows. I couldn't see a thing. The plane gathered speed, bumping hard on the waves, then finally floated up off the water. The windows cleared and, like a blooming flower, a panoramic vision of green fields, forests, and thin columns of smoke from cook fires unfolded. How beautiful China looked from the air!

Our flight was supposed to be nonstop, but partway up the valley the pilot stuck his head out the window and looked up. Suddenly, he put the plane into a sickening dive. "Japanese planes!" he shouted. "Probably on a bombing run. Still, they could shoot us down just for practice!"

He skimmed the river surface until he saw a good spot to land. He taxied to shore and we scrambled out the door and leaped off the pontoons onto a sandy beach. Expecting any moment to hear the roar of a Japanese plane and the chatter of a machine gun or the shriek of a falling bomb, we dashed from the riverbank into a shaded graveyard; the burial mounds under the trees provided good cover. Our pilot told us to lie flat to avoid being spotted. The droning Japanese bombers flew slowly past, high overhead. We waited and listened until the sound of the engines disappeared, and then completed our flight.

We rested in Chongqing for about a month, and witnessed bombing attacks with increasing frequency. We lived on a hillside away from the city center, so we appeared to be safe, but we were herded into shelters whenever the sirens and gongs announced an approaching raid.

One day Chaoding awoke with a stomachache so painful that he was rushed to Chongqing's hospital. It was appendicitis. My brother had already been diagnosed with diabetes, and his recovery from surgery took so long that the opportunity to go to Yan'an and meet with Mao came and went. When Chaoding came home, he had his wormy-looking appendix in a jar of formaldehyde to show Chaoli and me.

"This little devil changed my life," he said. It would be many years before I understood his full meaning.

While Chaoding was recuperating, Zhou Enlai came to Chongqing to meet with him and my father. A world war was coming, he told them, and although the Communists and the Nationalists had made an uneasy truce to join forces against the Japanese, China needed friends abroad and money for weapons and other supplies. Furthermore, the Americans were giving all their aid to Chiang's Nationalists. Chiang had converted to Christianity, and the Americans hoped that, when the war was over, the Nationalists would defeat the Communists and China would become a Christian democracy.

It was decided that Chaoding would be more valuable in the States helping raise money and secretly looking out for the Communist cause. Also, Zhou told him, "you should take your little brothers with you to New York and get them a first-class education. When they are grown, they can come back and help build the new China."

New York! Chaoding had regaled us all with stories about the wonders of New York, of enormous buildings that pierced the clouds, streets clogged with automobiles, and every imaginable flavor of ice cream. "In New York, there is nothing a person could want that cannot be found," he told us. So we packed again and flew south to the Vietnamese border, landing in the city of Kunming, made famous by Marco Polo's storied thirteenth-century visit.

I was too young to grasp the historical significance of what we were experiencing. But the farther we fled from Shanxi Province, the more I sensed that something momentous was happening to both my family and our nation. Our journey was defining my impression of China, and of myself as Chinese. Traveling with my revered father and my heroic brother, I was in the company of patriots, and therefore I was a patriot myself. We were not fleeing a fight but withdrawing to fight another day, just as the People's Army had, just as the great Han generals of the past had done, to deceive the enemy into complacency. It all made perfect sense.

The next leg of our journey took us in a bigger plane over the high mountains, extensions of the Himalayas. The plane had seats for a dozen people, and all the passengers got airsick except Father, Chaoding, and me. I ran about inside the plane, carefree as a butterfly.

Kunming was crowded with refugees. We stayed just long enough to catch a train from the Chinese border south to Saigon, on a route that wound through a dramatic mountain range. Chaoding teased me by screaming at the top of his lungs each time the train plunged into a long, dark tunnel. I screamed back, and then we both collapsed with laughter.

In Saigon we boarded an oceangoing ship for the short voyage to Singapore. There we embarked on the Peninsular and Orient Steam Navigation Company's SS *Corfu* and sailed across the Indian Ocean, through the Red Sea, the Suez Canal, and the Mediterranean to Marseille, France.

I loved shipboard life. The *Corfu* was no luxury liner and we were traveling second class, but it had a pool on deck and I swam most days. It was midwinter at home, but the ship sailed through tropical waters. The food was fresh, delicious, and plentiful. "It's like a birthday party every day," Father chortled.

The captain gave each of us children certificates declaring us a "Band of Little Travelers," with my name written backward as Chao-Cho Chi. The certificate declared, "His name has been entered in the Book which stays in the ship, and will be there for all time." It even had a wax seal at the bottom. We were living a more privileged and exotic life than anything we'd known in China.

From Marseille we took a train to Paris, where I freely indulged my obsession with ice cream and gawked at the tall buildings. While awaiting the next leg of our journey, we took long walking tours.

From Paris, we rode the train to Cherbourg, on the Atlantic coast. We boarded the SS *Aquitania,* a monstrous four-stack Cunard liner that had been a troop- and hospital ship during World War I (and would become a troopship again in the next war). Including a stop in Southampton, England, the crossing took a week. My seasick mother, Chaoli, and Chin stayed in the cabin near the toilets, while Father, Chaoding, and I walked the decks watching the mountainous waves roll beneath us.

As we neared New York, the pace of shipboard life quickened. Bags were packed, immigration papers retrieved and organized, and passengers crowded the railings to catch a first glimpse of the skyline. Chaoding, returning home to Harriet and his baby son, was more animated than usual, smiling broadly. He eagerly pointed out the Statue of Liberty, emerging out of the foggy rain. "Do you see that big, tall, beautiful lady holding the torch?" he said. "She is here welcoming us to the United States!"

The ship towered over the tugboats and other harbor traffic as the vibration of the engines faded, and the massive *Aquitania* glided serenely up the Hudson River. The city looked just as it had in photographs, a giant castle with skyscraper ramparts touching the undersides of the heavy cloud cover. I could hear a chorus of beeping car horns. It was February 3, 1939.

I stood next to Chaoding as the ship inched toward the dock, and we looked down on an undulating sea of black umbrellas and upturned faces. Suddenly he burst out shouting and began waving madly. "Harriet! Harriet! Emile! Emile!" I searched the sea of faces looking up at us until Chaoding pointed out his wife and my little nephew in her arms.

My parents wore beaming smiles. Our long and difficult two-year journey, filled with perils witnessed and feared, was finally over. They had been downcast over leaving Shanxi and burying my grandfather, but Zhou Enlai's instructions that we go to New York had given our family a sense of high purpose. Our new work was about to begin.

In the chaos of disembarking, Chaoding wept freely as he hugged Harriet. We passed easily through customs and the immigration officers waved us on with smiles, unlike the sober scowls that had met us in Europe, where every nation was bracing for war.

After a short taxi ride through a steady rain, we emerged on the sidewalk in front of our new home on East Twelfth Street, on the Lower East Side. I looked around in astonishment at a canyon of dull, stained tenement buildings, and at the trash in the streets.

Chaoding led us up the front steps and into a dark corridor that smelled of rancid grease. We climbed up and up and up—six flights! Finally, he opened a door and we tentatively and wordlessly entered a dilapidated apartment with a few battered pieces of furniture. Enormous cockroaches scuttled away into the dark corners.

My illusions were shattered. After the luxury and drama of traveling on ships, trains, and airplanes—after all the exotic landscapes I had seen and the gleaming cities we had passed through—I couldn't believe this was the country represented by the beautiful tall lady in green holding aloft the torch of freedom. As far as I could see, America was poor!

CHAPTER 3

Poor Little Chinese Refugee

Our railroad-style apartment—four rooms in a row—was on East Twelfth Street between Second and Third avenues. This was just a short walk from New York's teeming Chinatown. That first night, we had barely unpacked our belongings and settled into our new home when Father summoned Chaoli and me to the wobbly chairs at the scarred kitchen table. Chin napped in one of the bedrooms. The sounds of clattering dishes and voices speaking English floated in through the air-shaft window.

"Tomorrow you will start school," Father began.

Mother sat on a stool by the stove with Father's overcoat in her lap and a small knife in her hand. She ripped stitches out of the lining seams, then fished inside the folds and pulled out—one by one—tiny bars of gold. These she slipped into an old sock with a clink. I remembered thinking how odd it was that Father had always had his coat with him, even when walking the decks as we sailed through warm climates. He'd smuggled his money out of China on his back!

"Wah! Pay attention," Father scolded. "You boys and Chin will be going to different American schools where you will be the only Chinese students. You are to learn perfect English, and you must stay away from other Chinese people. From now on, as long as we are here, you will make your friends among Americans."

I'd never had a friend. When we lived in Shanxi Province, children of high officials such as my father were never sent out to play with the neighborhood kids. Except for school and family visits, we mostly stayed inside our courtyard-style villa. Across the street was an old palace built in an era when it was considered bad luck to leave by the same door through which you arrived. We lived on the side of the palace where guests departed, and where they would mount their horses.

Before the Japanese chased us from the provincial capital to rural Fenyang, I sometimes went outside the house, but always with my servant, Fuhai. Now, at the age of nine, I was excited about making friends, Chinese or not. During our long journey to New York, we'd been surrounded by foreigners on boats and trains who had fawned over us poor little Chinese kids fleeing the bloodthirsty Japanese. When we passed through immigration at the dock, the American officers patted us on our heads and pinched our cheeks.

On our journey, Chaoding had assured us that Americans loved the Chinese. It was American generosity following the Boxer Rebellion that had allowed Chaoding to study at Columbia University. When the Chinese government paid the American government for damages to their legations during the rebellion, the Americans—unlike the other aggrieved foreign nations—gave the money back in the form of scholarships and stipends for promising Chinese students. Chaoding had been one of those selected. At fifteen, he was fluent in English. At Columbia he wrote his doctoral thesis on the Chinese economy.

"Another thing," Father said, pulling on his stringy gray beard. "You must never go to Chinatown, and you must not discuss our affairs outside this house. First of all, the Chinese here mostly speak Cantonese, so you wouldn't understand them. But they might understand your Mandarin.

"Most important, Chaoding's work is secret and you must never speak of it. No Chinese, no family gossip! There are Kuomintang spies everywhere. You must always remember that. It could be a matter of life and death. Do you understand?"

In sober unison, we answered, "Yes, Father." I felt so proud to be Chinese, sitting in that tenement kitchen in Manhattan. Like Chaoding, I would study hard, earn excellent marks, and one day return to China a patriot.

We celebrated our arrival in America with our first Chinese family-style meal since leaving Hankow. Chaoding had arranged everything in advance, and Harriet had stocked the apartment with wheat flour, cooking pots, a teapot, cups, chopsticks—everything we needed.

I helped Mother by doing a simple chore that I loved, and one at which she had made me an eager expert: kneading the flour. I was impatient in most things, but in that one task I was focused. I took great pleasure in kneading until all the lumps had been worked out according to my mother's rule of the "three cleans." "The kneading is done when you find your hands are as good as washed and all the flour has gone into the dough," she'd taught me. "Second, the flour should come out of the bowl, leaving it completely clean. And third, the dough should be very smooth, free of all lumps."

Chaoli showed no interest in such chores. But I rejoiced in this work, because it gave me a chance to earn my mother's praise, which I craved. I learned how to knead the dough and roll it into a thick rope, then hold it over a pot of boiling water, pinching off thumb-size flakes and dropping them in. These were not noodles in the traditional sense, long strands of dough, which my mother sometimes made—"longevity noodles," she called them. But we called all forms of boiled wheat dough noodles.

In Shanxi Province, the making of certain noodles has long been an art form: shaved off the ball of dough with a knife into foot-long strings; curled around a finger into little funnels that can be stuffed with bean curd or other fillings; or endlessly pulled, twisted, and stretched into a mass of threads, like a skein of creamy white wool.

When the noodles were done, my mother ladled them into a large bowl and mixed in vinegar—a condiment used in almost all dishes from our region—and a sprinkle of sesame oil. Sometimes she added bits of vegetables and small scraps of meat and served the dish as a soup. That first night in our new home, we had plain noodles. As luxurious as our diet had been while circling the world, no smell evoked such intense feelings of comfort as the steamy, yeasty cloud released by a pot of freshly made noodle dough boiling on the stove.

That night Chin and I slept with my mother and father in a cramped little bedroom at the end of the apartment, behind the living room. In Chinese tradition, it was common for entire families to sleep in the same bed, especially during the winter, when the only comfortable place was the raised clay sleeping *kang*. Because I had always been a sickly child, my mother still kept me close by at night, to keep an eye on me. Since we left Shanxi Province, however, my diet had grown protein-rich and my health had steadily improved.

Chaoli slept in another room off the narrow corridor, and that first night Chaoding stayed with us, sleeping in the living room. I drifted off to the voices of our neighbors floating up the air shaft, the hum of the city, the distant sound of sirens, and the rumble of cars passing on the street below.

The next morning Chaoding fixed us an all-American breakfast of oatmeal with sliced banana, milk, and honey. I had become a dairy fanatic. Milk, cheese, especially ice cream—I craved them all.

Chaoding and Father walked us to our new schools. The weather had cleared and turned brisk. I pulled my knitted cap down over my ears and opened myself to the sights, sounds, and smells of my new world.

Because I was small for my age—thanks to the starchy diet on which I had been raised—I was enrolled as a seven-year-old. Born on July 30, 1929, I was nine and a half when I arrived in the States. But I was instructed always to say that I had been born in 1931. My father worried that if I started out as the smallest kid in my correct age group, I might present an easy target for bullies.

"Besides, having to learn English will take you time," Chaoding added. "An extra year or two will help you catch up. People will say you are very smart for your age."

As we crossed Third Avenue, we could see soaring above Fourteenth Street the tall, columned pyramid on top of a skyscraper that Chaoding said was the gas-and-electric company—Consolidated Edison. Giant clocks on each of the four sides could be read from far away.

As we walked farther west, more trees grew out of the sidewalks and we passed immaculate town houses with gleaming brass door handles and tall windows with lace curtains through which I caught glimpses of sparkling chandeliers. By the time we crossed Fifth Avenue, I had figured out that America was not poor, but we were.

A short walk farther and we climbed the steps into an 1850s-era town house to enter my new school, City and Country, on West

Twelfth Street between Sixth and Seventh avenues. Chaoding and Harriet had arranged for Chin to be enrolled with the very young children, and I was enrolled with other children around my "new" age of seven.

I was a leaf floating down the stream, making nothing of the gibberish being spoken over my head as Chaoding guided us through the introductions and the registration.

After being shunted here and there, beamed at and petted like a foundling puppy, I was taken to a seat at a table in a small dining room. A bowl of steaming white rice appeared in front of me. I made a face and glared at the aproned woman who'd just set it down. She beamed as she handed me a pair of chopsticks and said something in English.

With all the princely outrage I could muster, I pushed the bowl away, folded my arms defiantly, and declared in my Shanxi dialect, "We Chinese *never* eat rice!" Her smile melted into a frown.

Rice, indeed! Had our family been chased out of China and halfway around the world to be served lowly rice, food fit only for inferior southern Chinese? We privileged northerners, living in an arid zone where rice could never grow anyway, never ate it. My mother always served wheat products—the more bleached the better. Only the wealthy could afford such luxury.

But, even if she had, I wouldn't have touched it. I disliked rice then, and never developed a taste for the stuff. I had also established a lifelong distaste for other Chinese staples, such as garlic, as well as any spicy foods. I had arrived in America with a decidedly un-Chinese palate. I sat there with my arms crossed, prepared to starve to death before a single grain passed my lips.

Finally, the bowl of rice disappeared and in its place arrived a steaming plate of roasted potatoes and onions with bits of beef. The aroma was heavenly. I snatched up the chopsticks and tucked in, to the gentle chuckling of hovering adults. I might be a poor little Chinese refugee, but I could still be a spoiled brat when it came to my taste buds.

There were a dozen or so students near my age, mostly eight-year-olds—a year younger than my real age and a year older than my stated age. They were all friendly, curious, and eager to teach me English. The lessons were like nothing I'd experienced in China.

City and Country founder Caroline Pratt was a sprightly septuagenarian who was nearing the end of a long career as a controversial school reformer, one of the leaders in a progressive-education movement that emphasized experience over memorization. She is credited with the introduction, in the early 1900s, of wooden building blocks as a teaching tool for young children.

To teach geography, she took us down to the waterfront to look at ships riding at anchor. We drew pictures of the national flags fluttering from their masts and went back to school to look up the countries in the encyclopedia and the atlas. We learned mathematics by running a little store the children had built from cardboard and scrap wood, selling pencils and pads. We pretended to be Indians and fur traders, and learned about American history. Some of the older children operated a printing press on which they published the school menus and school currency that could be spent in the little store.

Chaoding and my father had given Chaoli and me impromptu English lessons now and again during our long exodus, so the language came quickly to me. School had been a passion of mine in China. In the free-spirited atmosphere of America, the flame burned even brighter. There was always someone friendly to play with, and the lessons were adventures rather than chores. Everywhere else except home, I was isolated by language and culture, so I often stayed for after-school activities as well. I especially loved painting and drawing, an art form so vital to Chinese history that we must have a gene for it.

Written Chinese has been in continuous use and evolution for four millennia. The scholars of today can read and comprehend the scholars of ancient times. The language is made up of intricate symbols—sometimes inaccurately described as pictograms or pictographs—requiring a delicate brush, a dab of ink, and a hand as light as air.

Writing and drawing in America was fun. We were encouraged to experiment, and I typically drew battle scenes I had imagined, or aerial dogfights I had seen over Hankow, or my favorite subject of all: kings and queens in their castles watching heroic knights on snorting, armored steeds galloping off to dispatch the barbarians.

From my first day, a clutch of new friends made me their mascot. No one questioned my age. I was still small for a seven-year-old, and my halting English also made me seem younger. So instead of being the wiser older boy who had fled war and escaped death, I became the poor little Chinese refugee who, my classmates decided, needed their protection.

My guardians and guides comprised a gang of boys—many of them children of secular Jewish families—who shepherded me through the days. They competed with one another to show me every little thing, from how to drink from a water fountain to the correct way to eat an animal cracker—*always* head first, I learned. At day's end, they showed me off with pride to their parents and siblings. The next day, many of them came to school with boxes of cookies and candies that their mothers had sent for me to take home. I was as happy as a dog with two tails.

Many of the teachers were unmarried women, dedicated to the principles of progressive education. They all loved FDR as president. Most City and Country parents were middle-class journalists, professors, doctors, or teachers. My good friend Peter Reich's father was a doctor, his mother director of Bank Street School. John Sonneborn's mother ran a children's bookstore at Bank Street School. Pierre Epstein's father was a journalist, professor, and activist for Social Security. He was frequently attacked in print by the Communist Party. At this school we learned folk songs and some anti-Fascist songs like "The Peer Boy Soldiers."

I enjoyed the simple games we played at recess in the backyard behind the three town houses that made up the school. But when spring arrived I was introduced to one of the few activities that truly terrified me: baseball. I avoided outright refusal to play by hiding behind a tree. The ball was a deadly missile that I could never catch and that would surely knock my brains out if I was struck in the head, which I was certain would happen sooner or later.

Basketball was less treacherous but too ridiculous to comprehend, let alone play. Soccer was the only sport that stirred me, but I was a terrible teammate, given to chasing the ball and kicking it just for the fun of it. The teachers let me spend organized sports time doing something I enjoyed, and often I simply lay on the gym floor practicing the relaxation techniques we'd learned.

The New York World's Fair opened in April of my first year in America. One Sunday soon afterward, Father and Mother took us all to see it. It was a sleek, forward-looking city-within-a-city, a sparkling, dazzling world that stretched as far as you could see in every direction. But what I found most enthralling was the dinosaur exhibit. Outside the entrance was a picture of the skull of Peking man—*Homo erectus pekinensis*. The famous ancient skull—believed to be hundreds of thousands of years old—had been discovered in China in the 1920s. The dinosaur hall had a replica of my fierce-looking, heavy-browed ancestor. I told my parents that I would meet them later outside the hall and trotted off to buy a ticket.

Admission cost a nickel, and I'd already spent four of the five nickels my father had given me—one for the subway ride to the fair and three others on ice cream. I would need the last nickel for a subway ride home. I bought the dinosaur ticket anyway, and became so absorbed that I lost track of time. When I finally emerged, my parents weren't there, and I was sure they had given up and gone home.

I waylaid a kindly old couple resting on a bench with my biggest little Chinese smile and, in halting English, communicated my dilemma. They smiled and dropped a dime into my palm. "Thanks you too much!" I shouted, and they burst out laughing as I dashed off to the station.

When I got back to Twelfth Street, I was gently scolded for begging, but my parents showed no other sign of concern. They had grown used to my wanderings. On our long voyages, I had often disappeared for whole afternoons, exploring the hidden compartments where the crews lived and the machinery hummed. By the time we reached New York, I had become a seasoned and eager traveler: a half-pint man of the world.

After the first couple of days of escorting Chin, Chaoli, and me to school, my father sent us off on our own. We three made a tiny slant-eyed convoy sailing through a sea of round-eyes, but we always felt safe and welcomed. Nearly everyone smiled at us, and occasionally stopped to pass a comment or pat our heads. We loved the attention.

My parents' confidence in me also reflected my steadily improving health: I was no longer a sickly child over whom my mother needed to hover. The good food I'd been eating since leaving China had fueled my body's rapid growth and unleashed my natural childish energy. I'd been starving for years, and was catching up fast. I still loved my mother's noodles at night, but breakfast and lunch became all-American: orange juice, cereal drowning in milk and heaped with sugar, hamburgers, hot dogs, spaghetti with meatballs, peanut butter and jelly sandwiches, ice cream.

Among my new friends, I discovered that I had a talent as a class clown. I had a rogue tooth that jutted forward at an odd angle. If I twisted my lips a certain way, the tooth protruded so comically that I could always make the other kids laugh.

Weekends were often spent at the homes of classmates, sometimes in the city, sometimes at their country houses. I was a popular guest, the poor little Chinese boy who'd cheated death and found safety and freedom in America's bosom. As my English improved, I found that I could hold an audience with tales of diving for cover on our flight up the Yangtze River to Chongqing to escape the Japanese.

But I rejected the notion of myself as a refugee. I was merely following in the footsteps of my patriotic elders. My father had gone to Japan to study law and had returned to China to use his education for the good of the country. Chaoding had gone to America and was doing the same. Now it was my turn.

CHAPTER 4

My Movie Star Dad

Always in the back of my mind was my father's voice exhorting me to excel in my studies, to prepare for the day I would return. Coal mining was the main industry in Shanxi Province, so Father suggested that I become a chemist. "We will need scientists to modernize our mines and factories," he said.

In my child's mind, the years ahead stretched to a fuzzy horizon; it would be more than a decade before I could earn a doctorate and return to China. I would need the determination of Father's exemplary ant, and the patience of the mythic foolish old man who tried to remove the mountains. School and friends kept me distracted much of the time, but, even as I was rapidly assimilating, there were constant reminders of our family mission. Each day Father brought home from his office the latest news about the ebb and flow of battle between the Japanese and the Chinese resistance.

By the time our family arrived in New York, Chaoding had publicly and duplicitously renounced his Communist sympathies and now held a high position with the rival Nationalists as the top adviser to the minister of finance, Kong Xiangxi. Chaoding was helping arrange loans and other aid from the Americans.

He returned to China in 1940 on an official mission to inspect the Burma Road, a "back door" supply route from that British colony to China that had recently been carved out of the mountain jungles by an army of Chinese laborers. The Japanese controlled the Chinese coast, rivers, and major inland cities, so the new Burma Road was a vital lifeline.

My father had made it clear since our arrival that Chaoding's work was dangerous and secret. I later learned just how nerve-racking it was. He was under constant suspicion from every quarter. He could not disclose to his friends and associates in the Communist Party that his renouncement was for show, so they began to distrust him.

Chaoding's Kuomintang superiors, meanwhile, knew well that his friendship with Zhou Enlai, one of the three top leaders of the Chinese Communist Party, stretched back to when they were teenagers. My brother and Zhou had met following the historic uprising of May 4, 1919, which came to be known as the May Fourth Movement and is today celebrated in China as Youth Day. Considered the moment of conception of the Communist Party in China, it began when thousands of Peking University students stormed Tiananmen Gate to protest the military regime's concessions to foreign powers as part of the Versailles Treaty settling claims from World War I.

As young men, Zhou and my brother had both spent time in Europe hobnobbing with leading Communists. Chaoding had been active in the Communist movement in the States from 1925 and officially joined the Chinese Communist Party in 1927. In 1928, in Moscow, he attended conferences with Communists from around the world. The international Communist movement was convinced at the time that the demise of capitalism was inevitable and just over the horizon.

But during the fifteen years he'd spent in America—getting his degrees, writing his Ph.D. thesis on the Chinese economy, marrying and settling down—Chaoding had grown increasingly wary of running afoul of the immigration authorities. His activities became more clandestine, and when he wrote for American Communist publications he used the pseudonym Richard Doonping.

By 1940, Chaoding's new role in the Kuomintang Finance Ministry, his perfect English, and his intimate knowledge of economics and international finance made him the number-one candidate to serve on a new Chinese currency-stabilization committee with representatives of the United States and Britain. During the war, he played a leading role in facilitating U.S. support of the Chinese resistance, working directly with the U.S. Treasury Department.

The Japanese attack on Pearl Harbor elicited a mixture of indignation and jubilation in our family. As horrific as it was, we weren't surprised; we knew well just how treacherous and barbaric the Japanese could be. But the import for China was monumental. The attack meant that the United States was now actively in the war, and that the Japanese were ultimately doomed. I decided that before I went to college I would become a fighter pilot and do my part.

In 1942 my father—a writer comfortable in English and Japanese as well as Chinese—was offered a stipend by the U.S. Office of War Information to translate American war news and publish it in Chinese. He was interviewed for security clearance that November. The investigators asked him what he knew about Chaoding's attending an international Communist gathering in Moscow in 1928. My father prevaricated, claiming that during Chaoding's many years abroad he rarely wrote home.

The day we could all go home—and how—was a frequent topic of conversation in our household. How long would the war last? Could we go back as a family? Or must one of us go first and send for the others? As time wore on, Mother, Chaoli, and little Chin became less enthusiastic about going back. With the exception of my quiet mother, we were all forming friendships among our peers. Life in America was comfortable and peaceful, and there were those lovely Western toilets.

I enjoyed the luxuries as much as my siblings. But nothing would ever convince me to abandon my goal. I would stay only as long as it took to earn my Ph.D. in chemistry, not a moment longer. Until then, I was happily settling into an all-American childhood.

My father—who had grown up in a prominent intellectual family and had a long career in law and government—found himself with time on his hands and a world away from his beloved and extensive library. He was almost sixty, too old to start over. Besides, he, too, expected to return to China as soon as it was safe. In the meantime, he had Zhou Enlai's instructions to do what he could to encourage support in America for China's fight against the Japanese, and to quietly advance the Chinese-Marxist cause.

The hope was to counter the advantage that the Nationalists had established. Chiang Kai-shek—the self-proclaimed generalissimo of the Nationalist Army—and his American-educated wife had appeared on the cover of *Time* magazine in 1937 as its Man and Wife of the Year. Madame Chiang, as she was known, was popular and persuasive in America because she spoke perfect English, having grown up in the States and attended Wellesley College, in Massachusetts.

She was a favorite of the First Lady, Eleanor Roosevelt. When World War II broke out, Chiang was by default the head of state who represented China as one of the four Great Powers (along with the United States, Britain, and the Soviet Union) leading the fight against Fascism. In February 1943, Madame Chiang was invited to address the United States Senate, where she was introduced as "the wife of the generalissimo of the armies of China." She declared, "The traditional friendship between your country and mine has a history of 160 years."

My father channeled his energies into becoming something of a minister-without-portfolio. The principal vehicle he chose emerged from the Chinese Hand Laundry Alliance, an organization that had been formed a few years earlier to protect the rights of Chinese immigrants in New York, thousands of whom worked in hand laundries. The workers had banded together in 1933, when the city passed a burdensome tax aimed at Chinese laundry workers.

With Tang Mingzhao, a Chinese-born graduate of the University of California and one of Chaoding's friends and peers, my father launched a Chinese-language newspaper. The *China Daily News* debuted on the streets of Chinatown on July 7, 1940, the third anniversary of what in the West is known as the incident at the Marco Polo Bridge outside Beijing, marking the beginning of the full-scale Japanese attack on all of China. The Japanese provoked a military confrontation at the bridge as an excuse to invade the rest of China, setting in motion the events that forced us to flee for our lives.

Tang Mingzhao had moved with his family to San Francisco when he was a child. In 1927, he returned to China to attend high school and then to study English at Tsinghua University in Beijing. He came back to the States in 1933 a committed and underground member of the Chinese Communist Party. In New York, he met and married an American-born Chinese girl named Constance, who had spent time studying in China.

Soon after he and my father started the newspaper, Tang Mingzhao and Constance became the parents of a baby girl whose Chinese name was Wensheng but whom they called Nancy. Tang Mingzhao was the Party representative, and my father was editor in chief. The Tang family became one of the few Chinese families we socialized with.

Because the office of the *China Daily News* was in Chinatown, I almost never went there. "Too many eyes and ears," Father said. "And no place for a kid. There are hardly any women and children there. All men, and some of them no good."

The newspaper's clandestine agenda was to promote the cause of China and the Chinese Communist Party, and to form alliances with American leftists—without appearing to take sides. Father had been doing this for years, so it came naturally to him: the Chinese art of disagreeing while appearing to agree.

He had one foot planted on each side of China's civil war. On the one hand, Father was trusted enough by Chiang Kai-shek that Chiang had tried to recruit him into the Nationalist government. Furthermore, the Kuomintang government issued him the travel papers that allowed us safe passage out of China and into French-controlled Vietnam. Without them, we would have had a very hard time getting transit papers from the French so that we could travel to New York.

But my father's sympathies lay with the Communist cause. He, Chaoding, Tang Mingzhao, and others helped raise money from sympathetic Chinese-Americans and American Communists to buy supplies for Mao's People's Army. Although the Communists and the Nationalists had declared a truce in order to unite against the Japanese, it was inevitable that the true struggle for China's future would resume as soon as the invaders had been expelled.

Although I was still rather young, I made it clear to my father by my questions and my attentiveness to his work that, unlike Chaoli, I shared his zeal for China's future. As a result, he took time now and then to describe recent Chinese political history and explain why the Communist Party would ultimately bring about the new Chinese nation.

The Kuomintang drew its support from the urban, wealthy élite and military strongmen—known as warlords—who before the Japanese invasion had governed their provinces by force, Father explained. They financed their activities through onerous taxes, profiteering, and, worst of all, the opium trade.

Opium killed my second-oldest brother. He died when we were in the United States. "Opium is what destroyed China a century ago," Father said. "And feudalistic warlordism will never lead to a united China. Stale rice won't bind, no matter how hard you squeeze."

My father had been the commissioner of education in Shanxi Province in December 1935 when General Yan Xishan, the Shanxi warlord and a Kuomintang ally, ordered him to send soldiers to fire on a mob of students. They were in the streets protesting the Kuomintang's pursuit of the civil war against the Communists at the expense of China's defense against Japan. Father refused the general's order and resigned in disgust.

I admired my father for that, among other things. He had been brought up in a wealthy, privileged family and had been a wealthy landlord himself before we fled. Yet here he was, contentedly eating my mother's simple noodles at a wobbly secondhand table in a tenement apartment in one of New York's poorer neighborhoods, eking out a living as an editor and publisher. He set a powerful example.

Once full-scale world war had broken out, Father's newspaper began to publish reports of U.S. criticism of runaway inflation in China, a series of bungled military campaigns, and official corruption. Chiang's army traveled like conquerors, not liberators. "Honey-mouthed but dagger-hearted," Father said. When the Nationalist soldiers entered a village, they helped themselves to food and lodging while rooting out Communist sympathizers for torture and execution.

Mao's Communists, on the other hand, were organizing the downtrodden rural peasants who made up the lion's share of China's five hundred million people. Their loyalty was neither extorted nor bought. The Chinese Communist credo was to "serve the people." Mao issued strict orders that People's Army soldiers were never to enter the homes of villagers. They were to sleep in the streets and refuse to take food from the peasants' tables. They were to honor the women and were not allowed to mistreat prisoners of war. Everywhere the People's Army went, disenfranchised Chinese were being recruited to the Communist cause by small acts of decency.

"Chiang will be able to fool the world for only so long," Father predicted. "One day he will become a kite with a broken string."

Our relative poverty meant that there was no money for luxuries or entertainment. I went to the movies only if my school friends invited me and paid my way, which they were eager to do after some of them came to our apartment and saw where we lived. I especially liked war movies and was overjoyed when my father was invited to play a role in one.

The film was based on the true story of the first-ever bombing raid by the American army on Japanese soil in 1942, led by the famous aviator Jimmy Doolittle. Sixteen bombers took off from a carrier in the middle of the Pacific, on a daring, one-way mission to drop bombs on Tokyo and three other Japanese cities, then continue on into China. Their goal was to reach the Chinese-controlled airfield in Chongqing, but if they ran out of fuel first they would bail out and try to avoid capture by the Japanese.

The actual raid did little damage, but, coming less than five months after Pearl Harbor, it rallied the country. It also further endeared us Chinese to the Americans, because many of the surviving pilots were rescued and doctored by my countrymen. My father was cast as one of them: Old Dr. Chung. The character was exactly what the name suggests: a wise old country doctor with a heart of gold. And Father was perfectly cast, right down to the terrible teeth with which we Chinese have been cursed. The producers sent him a train ticket to go to California for his scenes with screen legends Van Johnson and Robert Mitchum.

"All I did was stand around and look wise and nod my head knowingly," he reported upon his return. "I didn't have to say a word." My father said that everyone on the set cried when a chorus of Chinese children sang "The Star-Spangled Banner" in Chinese.

My school chums were impressed when I went with them to see

Thirty Seconds over Tokyo the day it opened in November 1944. Spencer Tracy played a secondary but starring role. The film was riveting, with astonishing special effects, and incorporated actual footage taken during the raid. When the American planes dropped their bombs on the Japanese factories, the theater erupted in cheers and shouts.

Finally, more than halfway through the film, my chubby old dad appeared in the doorway of a rural Chinese hospital and walked down a stairway. "That's him!" I shouted. "That's my father!" The packed theater responded with a chorus of shushing.

He had only two lines in Chinese, but he was on-screen in many scenes, tending to the injured pilots or standing around looking wise and kind in his quilted vest, long gown with wide sleeves, and thin gray hair and beard. I already worshipped my father. Seeing him in this noble role, showing him off to my friends, my chest swelled with love and pride.

The film played up the gratitude and warmth the Chinese felt for their American allies, which in every way reflected my own experience in New York. The Chinese and the Americans were good friends with a common goal. I was too young to have experienced the anti-Chinese discrimination that had existed in America from the 1880s into the 1930s. I was also too naïve to understand that this goodwill might be fragile. The film described how I felt about my life. I loved both of my countries, and wanted them to love each other.

Right after the children's chorus sang "The Star-Spangled Banner" in Chinese, Old Dr. Chung, through another actor playing his son, presented a wounded pilot, played by Van Johnson, with a gold bracelet. "It has been in our family since the fifteenth century," the son explained. "Father begs me to tell you that beauty deserves beauty, and he wishes you to present it to your wife."

When the Americans prepared to leave the hospital to escape the approaching Japanese, Old Dr. Chung remained behind. His son explained, "My father feels he must stay with his people." Then the entire screen filled with a long shot of just my father's sad, wise face, silently watching the aviators depart. I felt the respect of everyone in that theater flowing toward Father's image. Tears streamed down my cheeks.

The film moved me in another way, too. I was shocked at how little I understood of the Chinese spoken in the film, of which there was quite a lot. I had been living in the States for almost six years and, as my father wished, I was fluent in English. Even at home, Father encouraged our family to speak English in order to sharpen his own skills. I felt a twinge of guilt about my lost tongue, but there was no imperative to study it yet. There would be chance enough when I got to college, before my return to China.

CHAPTER 5

Me and Mrs. Roosevelt

By the time the Japanese surrendered in September 1945, our little family of world travelers had wandered off on individual adventures. Father was busy with the newspaper and had begun to think about returning home. Just as he had predicted, the string of the Nationalist kite was beginning to fray. Renewed civil war was brewing and, in the U.S. press, it was clear that Chiang was starting to wear out his welcome. *Time* magazine referred to him irreverently as "the Gissimo," and in one dispatch described his attempt to form a government from a ragtag group that included Tibetans, Catholics, and the offspring of the Chinese Republic's founder, Dr. Sun Yat-sen. Chiang was portrayed as a ringmaster in a clown circus.

Zhou Enlai was quoted speaking for the Communists, who were having none of a regime headed by a Christian convert being propped up by the very same Great Powers that had been exploiting and abusing the Chinese for more than a century. There was no doubt in our minds—Father's and mine—that Mao would be China's next leader, and soon.

Chaoding had been to China several times during the war, and when it ended and the Nationalists began losing support he had trouble persuading Harriet to move to Beijing with him and their two sons. Her focus was naturally on the best, and safest, place to rear her children. Chaoding had managed to dance with the devil for many years without getting burned. But what would happen if the family was in China in the middle of a civil war?

My eldest brother was ambitious, much sought after, and eager to be a part of the historic events that were now unfolding at an accelerating pace. China needed his knowledge of international banking and economics to help with reconstruction and nation-building.

Chaoding faced an impossible, Solomon-like choice. He loved his family, but returning to China with an American wife at a time of feverish nationalism might lead to political complications. He loved America and, if he stayed, America would have loved him back with a shining career in academia, government, or banking.

But his patriotism and a blossoming relationship with a longtime colleague in Beijing won the day. To her credit, Harriet tried. She took the boys to Shanghai to be closer to Chaoding. He was always busy or traveling, though, and she found herself isolated in a rowdy port city in an impenetrable culture that was in the grip of a violent revolution. After a few months, she returned to New York and the marriage quietly ended. She and my nephews remained a part of our family in New York, but we were all saddened by the way things had worked out. In America, people like to say that family is everything, but, at the time, for us loyal Chinese everything was China.

Meanwhile, Chaoding's Nationalist cover was growing thin. When he had been in China in the Nationalist capital of Nanking during one of his visits, his boss, the Nationalist finance minister, Kong Xiangxi, telephoned him late one night and asked him to come at once. Chaoding had a warm, professional relationship with Kong, whom he called Uncle, the term by which the Chinese often address respected elders, related or not.

When Chaoding arrived, Kong, rather than greeting him with a handshake, remained seated and blurted, "Chaoding, tell the truth. Are you a Communist?"

Chaoding told us later—when he returned to New York for an international economic conference at Bretton Woods, New Hampshire—that he thought he had finally met his doom. Chiang Kai-shek commonly had Communist agents jailed, tortured, and executed. Without skipping a beat, Chaoding replied, "Uncle, I have followed you these many years. You know all about me. Do I look like a Communist to you?"

"No, I suppose you don't," Kong muttered, waving a hand. "It was just a rumor."

Chaoli was in the final years of high school and would soon be going off to college in California. He had no interest in politics or in returning to China. Chin had a limited social life and spent a good deal of time at home with my mother, who had never learned English. My mother had a few Chinese friends, but she used her free time to paint Chinese art, which she occasionally sold. Both Mother and Chin were quite content to stay in New York, although Mother often talked about missing her family back in China.

In 1944, the year that I officially turned thirteen but was actually fifteen, I graduated from City and Country and began attending Horace Mann–Lincoln, a hard-left-leaning experimental high school associated with Teachers College at Columbia University. The school was named for Horace Mann, the nineteenth-century educator in Massachusetts considered to be the father of American public education, and for Abraham Lincoln.

I became a commuter. The school was on the Upper West Side, on 123rd Street. The subway was faster, but I usually gave myself enough time to take the bus. I enjoyed being able to look out the windows and see the life of the city.

At Horace Mann–Lincoln, I was no longer the poor little Chinese immigrant. I was just another American teenager who loved hamburgers, milkshakes, and war movies. I quickly found myself a circle of friends. There were three of us, just like the Musketeers, only we called ourselves the Holy Order of Knoodchi—a word made up of letters from our last names.

Ralph Knoph and I were the radicals, quoting Marx and writing slogans at the bottoms of our letters and school papers: "Death to the capitalist exploiters!" "Come to the revolution or be hanged!" Nicholas Wood was our token reactionary capitalist, who made sure that we always had something to criticize and revolt against.

What bound us together was our mutual love of ridiculous humor. Our bible was Edward Lear's nineteenth-century classic, *A Book of Nonsense*. The British writer and illustrator popularized the limerick form of poetry ("There was a young lady from Wales . . .") and was a master cartoonist of funny- and odd-looking people, which appealed to my artistic interests. Lear also wrote "The Owl and the Pussy-Cat," described recipes for dishes with ridiculous names like Crumbobblious Cutlets, and assembled a botany guide to such species as *Bottlephorkia spoonifolia* and the *Manypeeplia upsidownia*. We were always reading aloud or quoting from it to one another, and making nonsense rhymes out of our daily lives. We laughed our way through high school.

Humor aside, I was quite serious about my politics. It was well known in high school that I was a Communist. I often drew caricatures on the blackboard while we waited for our teachers to arrive. I made unflattering portraits of Chiang Kai-shek, and scrawled Communist slogans. My teachers merely shrugged. Most of them were leftists, too, and the culture of the school was to encourage learning through self-expression.

China was regularly in the news, as the world waited to see who would inherit the future. There was another Chinese student who was a Nationalist. We were the human face of a drama taking place halfway around the world, so our teachers decided that it would be interesting for us to have a debate.

We had never discussed our differences. We were polite to each other, but it would have been quite un-Chinese to be confrontational. However, we agreed to a civil discussion before our fellow students and the faculty. In our youthful enthusiasm, we missed the bigger picture. He talked about how the horrible Communists were slaughtering landlords, and I talked about how the horrible Nationalists were slaughtering the poor Communists. Sadly, history proves both of us correct.

I always took my studies as seriously as I did my politics. I threw myself into everything I did. I loved history and historical novels. By the time I got to the end of a meticulous reading of Tolstoy's *War and Peace,* dictionary at my elbow, I felt fully competent in English. My favorite authors included Shakespeare, and I was intrigued by everything connected with medieval Europe. American history held little interest—it was too short to be much of a history.

My grades were consistently among the best in my class. I was undistracted by the sorts of things my classmates did with their free time.

My time was spent getting to school, attending school, studying, or working. In high school, I washed dishes and took other odd jobs to earn extra money for some of my minor expenses. There, as at City and Country, my tuition had been underwritten by a generous scholarship.

My social life was limited to visits to the homes of my Holy Order of Knoodchi brothers, and the occasional party. I was the only one to arrive at such gatherings by public transportation, and I owned not a stitch of clothing that could be considered "dressed up." But I never felt out of place and no one commented on my shabby appearance, even when I attended a formal dance and was the only student wearing street clothes.

My dates were all casual school-related relationships. I was keenly aware of the heartache Chaoding and Harriet had suffered as a result of their cross-cultural relationship and, as much as I loved America, I had no interest in putting down roots there. Still, I was ambivalent about the prospect of marrying a Chinese girl. Chinese women were raised to be servile and obsequious. I wanted a strong partner for life.

During several summer vacations, I worked on farms outside the city, in Connecticut. One summer, I lived and worked on a small farm owned by a retired couple who treated me like family. He had been a colonel in the army and was sympathetic to the Chinese cause. They were interested in all my stories about fleeing the Japanese, but I thought it best to keep my political views to myself.

Another summer, I lived on a larger, commercial farm whose owner was always cranky. He was furious when, on my first day, I came back from a field holding a young corn plant that I had pulled up thinking it was a weed. I worked with two other field hands, one of whom took a look at my unusually dark skin (made even darker by the sun) and declared that I was a "nigger." I corrected him, and his attitude instantly changed from hostile to friendly.

The farmer treated me like a servant—a new experience. "Clean that up! There's a spot you haven't swept yet!" I was being paid and I needed the money, so I kept my mouth shut. "Look," he said to me one day. "You're quite stupid, but I see you do want to do good work. I suggest you forget about all this college nonsense and go to a trade school where you can learn something useful." I laughed up my sleeve, but to his face I remained polite. "Yes, sir!" I said. "That's a very good idea, sir!" He had two grown daughters who often came to visit and were kind to me. When their father was discourteous, they would come to me afterward and say, "Don't bother about him. He's an old fogy."

Living far from the city, isolated from my friends and family, was a big adventure. When I wasn't spending time with the other farmhands or with my employers, I'd hitchhike into the local town to walk around, and sometimes I caught a country fair. Everywhere, people were happy to give me a lift.

During Christmas break in December 1945, my father announced that he had been invited by Dr. Hu Shih, the president of Peking University, to return to China and become the dean of the law school. It was a visible, prestigious position—one for which my father was both highly qualified and eminently suited by virtue of his background and his political skills. He decided to accept.

My mother now faced a Solomonic choice of her own. She was happy that Father had been so honored: better to return the wife of a respected educator than that of an unemployed lawyer. But she had hoped the family would stay together in New York. As much as she missed her mother, life in America was easy and safe. Chaoli and Chin were also determined to stay. Father and I were determined to return.

My mother could have returned with my father and left us kids behind to finish our schooling. I was sixteen years old, and Chaoli was eighteen. Chin was no longer a baby. We all had scholarships and could take care of ourselves. A sympathetic family could have been found to provide us with a place to call home while we finished our American education. But she was a mother first, and the idea of leaving her children behind was unthinkable. Father would return to China and Mother would remain in the United States until we were grown up.

On Sunday, January 20, 1946, we piled into a taxi to take my father to Pennsylvania Station, where he would board a westbound train to begin the long journey back to China. Reading *The New York Times* in the taxi, in between articles about war-crimes trials in Germany and Japan, I found a story about a vast project to restore the Yellow River to its former course. There was a map of China, showing how the river had changed course in 1938, when Chinese troops dynamited some dikes to flood the path of the advancing Japanese army.

The story described widespread famine and disease in the affected region, with estimates of 130,000 people having died. So many people were starving that "Chinese were staggering into coffins lined up in ranks by a charitable Buddhist organization, then lying down to await death . . . [to be] . . . sure of burial." I decided not to draw attention to the article with my mother in the car. She had enough to fret about.

Saying goodbye to Father was a predictably emotional scene. I was both saddened and envious. Ahead of me lay many years of schooling before I would be able to return. My father was sixty-three, and although he appeared healthy, he would be past seventy before I finished my studies. The thought that he might reach the end of his life before I could join him in China was unbearable.

"Remember the ant," Father said, shaking my hand. "Do your best at all times."

"Yes, Father," I answered, coaxing the words from my aching throat. "May your journey be peaceful."

We were a somber and quiet group on the way home. When we got back to the apartment, I picked up a printed booklet Father had given me that morning: a collection of English-to-Chinese translations he had made of some of the speeches of the late President Franklin Roosevelt. Father greatly admired the Roosevelts, and one of his final instructions was to make sure the booklet was delivered to Mrs. Roosevelt, who lived not far from us, on Washington Square Park. He had written the address on a slip of paper, along with a note in English explaining what it was all about.

I walked through the bitter cold, found the address, and knocked on the door. I was shocked when it swung open to reveal the tall and imposing Mrs. Roosevelt herself.

"Yes? What is it, son?"

"I'm . . . I wish to present you with this book of my father's," I said. "He has translated the president's speeches into Chinese."

I must have cut quite a pathetic figure: skinny Chinese kid with unkempt hair shivering against the icy wind in my threadbare overcoat. She invited me into the kitchen, where she poured me a glass of milk and set out a plate of cookies while I explained that my father had been the editor of the *China Daily News* and that the booklet of speeches had been distributed among the Chinese in Chinatown.

What she said is lost in the fog of time, but she was gracious and made me feel completely comfortable in her presence. She thumbed through the booklet and asked me a couple of questions about which speeches were included. I didn't know, which embarrassed me. I was Chinese, but I could not read the language.

The whole episode lasted just a few minutes. Then I ran home to tell Mother. I felt so proud of Father, and so delighted to have been able to personally deliver his work to this great lady we admired so much.

Now that World War II was over, one of the hot debates in the United States at the time revolved around military demobilization. Many American troops were still deployed abroad, and political pressure was mounting to bring all the boys home, especially from Europe, where the western European allies worried about Soviet domination. The next day, the papers carried a report from Washington that would prove to be a harbinger of things to come. The headline read:

COMMUNISTS ACCUSED
IN GI DEMONSTRATIONS

The House Committee on Un-American Activities claimed that Communist agitators were behind demonstrations by U.S. soldiers in Germany who were protesting delays in being sent home. An official of the committee claimed there was a "well-laid Communist plot" to stir up the homesick soldiers by distributing pamphlets critical of American foreign policy. Any news about Communism interested me, but what was happening in Europe at that moment hardly seemed relevant to my future.

Five months after Father left, Chiang Kai-shek made headlines by promising to destroy the People's Army in three months. He failed, so the United States began selling him surplus military equipment and then arranged to transport half a million Nationalist troops to the northwest, closer to Communist-held territory. On Christmas Eve that year, a Chinese student reported being raped by an American marine. Word of the alleged attack spread, sparking anti-American demonstrations and general protests. A million students poured into the streets, and Chiang sent troops to club and shoot them. I never bothered to translate these news stories for Mother. I was doing enough worrying about Father for both of us.

He had left me several books to study, telling me to start with *Red Star over China,* by Edgar Snow. Snow was an American journalist who had reported from China for more than a decade, and had spent several months in northwestern China at Mao's headquarters. Published in 1938, his book about the experience was the first comprehensive report on the development and growth of the Communist movement in China as seen through Western eyes. The book was transporting and transforming. The vivid descriptions of people and places made China come alive for me. What was happening to my homeland suddenly became three-dimensional. I understood the interaction of the forces driving China toward a new, and inevitably Communist, future.

I learned the names of the great generals of the People's Army, such as Zhu De and Peng Dehuai, and paid close attention to the military tactics outlined by Mao. I was particularly intrigued by the notion that, when preparing for battle, a plan of retreat was as important as a plan of attack.

Snow described Mao's strategy of warfare: a series of attacks and organized retreats to confuse the enemy into making mistakes, "to lure the tiger down from the mountain." Armies should go into battle only when they are certain of victory, Mao said, or, when outnumbered, to gradually exhaust the enemy through frequent hit-and-run skirmishes. My favorite tactic was: "Pretend to attack the east while attacking the west." A great student of China's past, Mao borrowed strategies from its long history of surviving repeated invasions and occupations, but he used modern insurgent tactics and weapons.

I was shocked to read that there had been a coup d'état in the Nationalist leadership in 1936. Chiang Kai-shek's guards enabled him to escape his hotel, but he had been caught in a cave by rebels a short while later: barefoot, cowering, shivering in his nightgown. At this point, even Chiang's own commanders had grown fed up with his failure to mount a unified defense against the Japanese. "Shoot me and finish it all," Chiang told his revolutionary captors. He was taken into custody to await his fate.

A golden opportunity had landed in Mao's lap. There was talk of a people's trial—a reading of Chiang's atrocities before an angry mob—which would certainly have been followed by a public execution. Chiang had it coming. Although atrocities had been committed by both sides, it was Chiang who committed true war crimes, tricking the Communists in 1927 into a false alliance in Shanghai and then ordering that thousands be rounded up and executed in a grisly fashion. Some had been thrown into locomotive furnaces to be burned alive. The episode came to be known as the White Terror, borrowing from the Russian Revolution's tag for the czarist forces—the White Army—who were defeated by the Soviet Red Army.

Chiang's loyalty clearly lay with himself and his corrupt cronies. He and his charismatic wife had pandered to the same Great Powers that had exploited China for a century. And, while China was being looted and its women raped and murdered by the Japanese, Chiang had picked a fight with his fellow Chinese, who happened to be Communists.

Chiang's fate appeared sealed in 1936. But Stalin, the Communist "pope," who had played both sides of China's civil war at one time or another, decided it would be better for China to be united in its war against Japan. He sent word to Mao that Chiang was to be spared. Mao was in no position to defy Stalin, so he had to let Chiang go. Attack and retreat.

The Red Army had been hemmed in in northwestern China. The Soviet border lay behind it to the north, from which came Soviet guns, supplies, and money. In front were the Nationalist forces and the Japanese. Mao knew that any shift in the balance would be disastrous for his army.

Snow's book showed me that all Communists were not created equal. Stalin was supposed to be Mao's ideological ally, but that had only been since the 1920s, and the alliance was an uneasy one. The Russians had exploited and abused the Chinese along with the rest of the world. Since ancient times, it had been from the north that the

Mongol hordes periodically came to loot and pillage our cities. In 1938, with a world war looming, it had been in Stalin's interest to keep China's factions busy fighting the Japanese and one another—two fewer threats for him to worry about.

My father also gave me a copy of *Report from Red China*, by Harrison Forman, a journalist who had spent more than a year with Mao's People's Army during World War II. The book described his experiences in detail, including the Communist practice of having soldiers sleep in the streets rather than impose on the peasants. These accounts whetted my appetite to know more, fueling my determination to get back to China as soon as I could.

It was frustrating to be young and eager yet so far from the action. All around me, America was celebrating its returning heroes. I wanted to prove my heroism on behalf of China's war of liberation. I was growing up, but inside there remained the little boy riding on the shoulders of Fuhai at the city wall in Taiyuan, pretending to be a great Han general while Fuhai scuffed his sandals like a mighty steed.

For China and for me, 1949 was a year of momentous change. In January, Chiang Kai-shek resigned as head of the crumbling Nationalist government. The next day, the Chinese People's Liberation Army—previously known as the Red Army—captured Beijing without firing a shot. I later learned that it was my brother Chaoding and my father who persuaded the Nationalist general to peacefully surrender the city of Peiping and his two hundred thousand troops. The negotiations had taken place in the house my father had purchased when he returned, directly across the wide moat surrounding the massive wall of the Imperial Palace.

The leader of the beleaguered Nationalist garrison was General Fu Zuoyi, also from Shanxi Province, who, in spite of their political differences, knew and trusted my father to be an honorable, level-headed man. This was a reputation Father had cultivated his whole life. As a law student in Japan in 1910 and 1911, during the uprising that dethroned the last of the Manchus, my father had expressed support for the student movements and made many friends. But he consistently refused to join any political party.

He once explained to me, "I knew that if I joined the 'Preserve the

Empire' Party, I might lose face. If I were to join the Revolutionary Party, I might lose my head. I decided it was wisest to keep both." Thus, after he had refused the order of the Shanxi warlord General Yan Xishan to have soldiers fire on protesting students, he simply resigned his position as education commissioner and moved our family away from the provincial capital of Taiyuan. In this way, he both kept his honor and saved his neck.

The Red Army generals in charge of liberating Beijing in 1949 had instructions to avoid destroying the city's antiquities and cultural landmarks. Chaoding was a great lover and collector of Chinese antiquities. He spent all his extra money buying anything that was truly old and caught his fancy. Together, he and Father were recruited to help persuade the Nationalists to peacefully give up, if not for their own necks, then out of respect for China's heritage. It worked, and the Nationalist troops became part of the People's Liberation Army. The general who surrendered later joined the new government in a largely ceremonial role.

Chiang was on the run, having made off with an estimated $300 million in gold and other valuables. President Truman was being accused by the Republicans of having lost China to the Communists. *Time* magazine ran a cover portrait of Mao. It was hard to concentrate on my schoolwork knowing the new China was finally blossoming on the other side of the globe.

CHAPTER 6

My Short Harvard Education

That spring, 1948, I was admitted to Harvard University, a dream come true. I did my best to appear modest among my friends, but privately I enjoyed a bout of smugness. It gave me a powerful feeling of accomplishment; I had washed ashore just ten years earlier, an impoverished, sickly, bucktoothed, swarthy-skinned, nerdy refugee brat knowing no English. I wrote to my father, flush with purpose: "The insignificant ant has reached another step of the stairs!"

As high school seniors, we were asked to draw caricatures of ourselves for inclusion in the yearbook. I drew myself seated in the lotus position and split down the middle, with the right half dressed in a Western suit and the left half in the robe of a Buddhist monk. Behind me I drew half the Empire State Building joined to half of a pagoda.

This was the picture I presented to the world: a man of two cultures. But the unseen mind and heart were completely Chinese. My motto for the yearbook: "I am wealthy in my friends." I felt richer than the richest of my many wealthy classmates. I had experienced more than my share of human drama and kindness.

That kindness continued even after I graduated from Horace Mann–Lincoln. Because I could not have survived without it, the school provided me with a continuing scholarship while I was at Harvard. Along with a stipend I received through Harvard, I was able to squeak by. Horace Mann–Lincoln made sure none of its students went hungry or homeless.

One of my roommates was a Jewish boy from Larchmont, a well-to-do suburb of New York. Herb Levin seemed especially delighted to be sharing space with me. When we met, he told me, "I wrote on my application that I wanted to be put in with people as different from me as possible. A Chinese Communist! How perfect is that?" We got along well, and he showed great interest in my explanation of why it was incorrect to lump the Chinese Communists in with the Soviets. "The Russians and the Chinese have never been true friends," I said. "In Russia they tell their kids to be good or the nasty Chinese will come and eat them."

On the wall of our room, I taped a map of China on which I used pushpins to mark the progress of the People's Liberation Army. When news came that the PLA had reached my old hometown of Taiyuan, I insisted that my roommates and I share a bottle of wine to celebrate.

As I had in New York, I initially avoided other Chinese students. But one day soon after classes began I was visited in my dorm room by Pu Shan, a doctoral student born in China and a member of the Chinese Communist Party. He and his older brother, Pu Shouchang, also a doctoral student at Harvard, knew my family and were actively organizing like-minded overseas Chinese.

Pu Shan invited me to join a semi-clandestine Chinese Communist student reading club whose members read Mao, Marx, and Lenin, and then met to discuss their works. "I'd like that very much," I said. "But my Chinese is terrible. I can't read it, and it's even become hard for me to understand it spoken."

Pu Shan found someone to translate for me, a woman named Daisy Chan. At my first meeting, I sat next to Daisy and she periodically whispered in my ear what was being said. The leader of the group scolded us: "If you have something private to discuss, wait until after the meeting!" Daisy and I laughed and blushed. "She's interpreting for me," I confessed. "I've been in America too long."

We focused on Chairman Mao's writings, which were just becoming widely available. The thread weaving itself through all our discussions was how and when to go back to China, and what to do once we got there. More and more, it sounded so uninspired to explain, "I'm going to get my Ph.D. in chemistry and go work in Shanxi's coal industry." It didn't sound nearly as patriotic as I felt.

The historic moment we had all been waiting for arrived on October 1, 1949, when it was reported in all the world's newspapers: Mao Zedong and my brother's old friend Zhou Enlai announced the founding of the People's Republic of China. Mao was chosen chief of state and chairman of the Party. Zhou was designated premier and foreign minister.

In his first official speech, Mao declared, "Ours will no longer be a nation subject to insult and humiliation. We have stood up." I wept with joy.

At our next reading-group meeting, one of the students read Mao's proclamation aloud and we all clapped. I was especially struck by several passages:

The imperialists and the domestic reactionaries will certainly not take their defeat lying down; they will fight to the last ditch.

After there is peace and order throughout the country, they are sure to engage in sabotage and create disturbances by one means or another and every day and every minute they will try to stage a comeback. This is inevitable and beyond all doubt, and under no circumstances must we relax our vigilance.

As long as we keep to our style of plain living and hard struggle, as long as we stand united and as long as we persist in the people's democratic dictatorship and unite with our foreign friends, we shall be able to win speedy victory on the economic front.

Let the domestic and foreign reactionaries tremble before us!

Let them say we are no good at this and no good at that.

By our own indomitable efforts we the Chinese people will unswervingly reach our goal.

The heroes of the people who laid down their lives in the People's War of Liberation and the people's revolution shall live forever in our memory!

Hail the victory of the People's War of Liberation and the people's revolution!

Hail the founding of the People's Republic of China!

The USSR immediately recognized the new Chinese government. In December, Chiang and his remaining loyalists fled the mainland for the island of Formosa (now called Taiwan), Chinese territory that had for decades been isolated by Japanese occupation. Now, the final step would be to finish off Chiang.

Members of our reading group disappeared one by one as leading intellectuals like the Pu brothers were summoned back to China to play important roles in the new government. Pu Shan became an interpreter for Premier Zhou and Chairman Mao. I, too, felt a powerful urge to return, but my path was set.

It was around this time that I was told by the provost that part of my stipend was being terminated, by government order. The political winds in postwar America were rapidly shifting to the hard right. Zhou Enlai had declared the United States to be China's most dangerous enemy.

I was in the real world now, and my childish sloganeering seemed naïve as I calculated how long I could last with my remaining funds. I took a job washing dishes in the cafeteria to make ends meet, which I managed only with great sacrifice.

In January 1950, Truman announced that the United States would not provide Chiang with any assistance, but the administration also blocked efforts to seat the People's Republic in the United Nations.

Soon afterward, I was surprised to learn from the provost of Harvard that the U.S. government had changed its mind. It would subsidize all Chinese students attending American universities in full—there were more than thirty-five hundred—regardless of political pedigree.

My financial situation began to improve. My four roommates and I pooled our resources to buy a generously dented used car, which we took turns driving to Radcliffe and beyond for our dates. I had finally begun to enjoy the life of a comfortable college student in an Ivy League school.

That all changed one bright moonlit night as I walked through Harvard Yard, reminiscing about my ten years of hard struggle, working up to five hours a day washing dishes and serving fellow students at the school cafeteria, from high school through my freshman year at Harvard.

I had slaved in the hot summer sun on American farms for thirty dollars a month or, on school holidays, moved piles of books back and forth in a bookstore on Fourteenth Street in Manhattan for fifty dollars a month. I had listened with quiet envy as classmates talked about going to Martha's Vineyard or other fine places that I never dreamed I could visit.

I had been rejected for a better-paying job as a waiter in a Harvard Square restaurant, told by the manager that they didn't hire "coloreds." With a classmate from Horace Mann–Lincoln who also ended up at Harvard, I picketed the restaurant for about a month.

I was fully assimilated, my future secure. I spent all my free time studying, both by choice and by necessity. Horace Mann–Lincoln's academic requirements were less rigorous than those of most private high schools, and its graduates often had trouble when they got to college. I, too, had found my courses challenging, but I buckled down, caught up, and earned excellent marks.

The summer between my freshman and sophomore year—1950— I stayed in Cambridge and took summer courses, to give myself a leg up. I was dismayed when the Korean conflict broke out, when the Soviet-backed North—which borders both China and the USSR— invaded the U.S.-backed South and drove deep into South Korean territory. The last thing the People's Republic needed in its first year of existence was a new war, but Stalin had given his blessing and support to the North Koreans. China had already signed a mutual-assistance pact with the Soviets. The Cold War had begun with a bang.

Under the flag of the United Nations, Truman sent American forces to defend South Korea, and also sent the U.S. Seventh Fleet into the Taiwan Strait, just as the PLA, massing on the coast, prepared to cross over and liberate Taiwan. Although he had promised not to support Chiang's regime, Truman's military advisers were worried that if the Communists seized the large island, U.S. forces would find themselves boxed in on three sides: the Communist Chinese mainland to the west, Communist North Korea to the north, and a Communist-controlled Taiwan to the south. On the fourth side was U.S.-occupied Japan.

If the United States could maintain puppet regimes in South Korea and on Taiwan, China would have a wolf sleeping on its stoop. My fellow Chinese reading-group friends and I were outraged by these developments. Taiwan had long been a bone of contention for China, ever since the 1890s, when the Japanese seized it and forced the Qing dynasty to surrender control.

The Japanese had always treated the Chinese as subhumans and now, with China liberated, the final step in uniting the new nation would be to rid Taiwan of all foreign influence. Premier Zhou Enlai threw down the gauntlet, warning President Truman that "the fact that Taiwan is part of China will remain unchanged forever."

American forces managed to push the North Koreans back toward the border along the thirty-eighth parallel. Zhou had promised that China would act if "the imperialists wantonly invade" North Korea. Chinese troops were massing on the Korean border. War seemed inevitable.

This deeply personal crisis preoccupied my every waking moment. I was grateful for the opportunity to study at Harvard, and for the subsidy from the U.S. government. But, as the saying goes, another man's bread is hard to swallow. My unease was exacerbated by growing political hysteria. Joseph McCarthy, an obscure junior senator from Wisconsin, was beginning his campaign to rid the United States of us treacherous Reds.

There was now open talk among my fellow Chinese Communist friends that some of us were being followed by government agents. There were rumors that some of the more accomplished overseas Chinese students, engaged in technical research as part of their doctorates, had been called in for interviews about their politics.

Those of us who were determined to return one day now worried that, if the political climate continued to deteriorate, by the time we completed our studies the United States might decide that we were too valuable to hand over to Red China and refuse to let us leave. I felt particularly vulnerable. My family's loyalties were well known. Chaoding had permanently settled in Beijing with a new wife and was now a high official in the new government's Finance Ministry.

My aspiration for real friendship between my motherland and America, which had harbored, befriended, and educated me, now seemed quaint. What next?

On that moonlit evening in early September 1950, as some friends and I walked back to our dorms from classes, I heard the notes of Beethoven's Piano Concerto no. 5 wafting through an open window. The music seemed to be slowly dying to a conclusion, but, from a whisper, it began to swell and was joined by a chorus of strings, and then an entire orchestra swooped in with a mighty crescendo.

The music seemed to vibrate in my bones. My chest tightened and my brain tingled. I felt a flush race up my neck and over my scalp. "Gotta run!" I shouted, surprising my friends. I sprinted back to my room to pack an overnight bag. Then I caught a bus to the railroad depot, where I bought a ticket on the night train to New York.

CHAPTER 7

Going Home

Mother was sitting in the kitchen, sipping her morning tea, when I burst in and declared, "I want to go home! Now."

All night on the train I sat wide awake, thinking. Here I was, living like a capitalist, enjoying all the luxuries of life, while my countrymen were preparing to go to war and die for China. My decision was made, but I wanted her approval, just as I had when she taught me the "three cleans" of noodle dough, or when I brought home excellent grades from school.

"Wah! So suddenly?" she asked. "You haven't finished your degree. Why would you give up? Aren't you happy in America?"

"Too happy," I said. "There's going to be trouble between America and China. I want to be in China when it comes. I want to go home before I can't. I can always finish my studies there."

We talked for a long time. She urged me to take more time to think it over. She hated the idea of my being so far away, and she needed to remain in the States until Chin graduated from high school. "It is a big decision, Wah," she said. "I hope you will change your mind." I agreed to wait two weeks, but I already knew exactly what I was going to do.

I called on the provost to deliver the news that I intended to complete my education at Tsinghua University in Beijing, where my father and Chaoding lived. I requested a letter of recommendation.

"But, Chaozhu, you have a fine future here in America," she said. "You can always return when you've graduated. Why would you want to return to such a poor country?"

I had no intention of saying what I felt: I wanted to go home, join the People's Army, and fight MacArthur in Korea. "I'm homesick," I said. "I love America, but China is my homeland. It's where I belong."

The provost shook her head. "I'm very sorry to see you go," she said. "I'll write your letter this afternoon. You can pick it up from my secretary. Also, we'll give you some money for your fare. It's part of the scholarship program. Any student who wants to return to China gets free transportation."

I was delighted. My American friends were dismayed. "You don't understand," I tried to explain. "I sound American, but I'm Chinese. I love my country, and it's time for me to go back." I said goodbye to only my closest friends. I didn't want to do anything that might jeopardize my chances of leaving.

Armed with my letter of recommendation, and my booking aboard the SS *President Cleveland* from Los Angeles, I returned to New York and delivered the news to my mother. She nodded her head as her eyes welled with tears. My heart ached and my eyes also overflowed. "I think maybe it's time for me to go back, too," she said, sighing. "I don't like to have my family spread out all over the earth. I miss my mother."

Chaoli was visiting from California, and he offered to help with my baggage. "I'll go with you to the station."

"No, please don't," I said. "The pain of parting will be even worse. Let me go by myself."

I felt a measure of fraternal affection for Chaoli, but we couldn't have been more different. He was not only assimilated but committed to staying in America. He had no interest in China or its future. Chin also felt no connection to home. She'd been a toddler when we left Fenyang, and a kindergartner when we arrived in New York. To her, China existed mainly in the stories she'd heard.

But the real reason I wanted to go to the train station alone was that my Chinese Communist friends were going to see me off and I didn't want my brother to know about them. I was growing distrustful of everyone by that time. I hadn't even told Mother about my Communist connections.

I said goodbye to the wobbly old table and the greasy, pea green walls of our apartment. I kissed Mother and Chin, shook my brother's hand, and lugged my bag down the sidewalk to the West Side, where I caught a bus uptown to Pennsylvania Station. My comrades and I sat on benches in the waiting area and chatted in hushed tones about the latest news: half a million Chinese troops had amassed on the beaches of Fujian Province to cross the Taiwan Strait for a possible confrontation with the U.S. Seventh Fleet; Chinese troops had moved to the border with Korea; and the United States continued to block the People's Republic from taking its rightful seat at the United Nations. Finally, we shook hands and promised to find one another "on the other side."

As the train eased out of the station, I felt a stab of sadness. My two nations were heading toward a confrontation. After all the goodwill that had prevailed for so long, how had this happened?

But when the train picked up speed and shot out of the tunnel darkness westward into New Jersey, my spirits took flight. I was really going home! The adventure that had begun so many years ago when we fled Fenyang was resuming. I was feverish with anticipation.

I spent the daylight hours gazing out the train windows at the America I never got to know: great industrial cities with forests of smoking stacks; rolling hills that gave way to endless fields of dried corn being crisscrossed by giant threshing machines trailing clouds of dust; windswept prairies; snowcapped peaks; and the baking California desert.

In Los Angeles, finally, I made my way to the dock and boarded the *President Cleveland,* a two-stack combination passenger liner and freighter that ran a regular three-week loop starting in San Francisco with principal ports of call in Los Angeles, Hawaii, the Philippines, Tokyo, and Hong Kong. My destination was Hong Kong, where my transit papers gave me permission to pass through on my way to Canton (the Anglicized name of the city known today as Guangzhou).

I saw first one, then another, and then a group of young Chinese, and realized that I was among a couple of dozen overseas Chinese students who were also returning home. I still had my guard up, but seeing them felt like a confirmation of my decision. I wanted to believe that all across the globe the great Chinese diaspora was rooting for the home team.

The deck plates trembled to life as the screws lurched into gear. As the ship eased out of the harbor, I walked over to the stern, where I settled into a canvas chair to enjoy the shrinking scenery. An American in a suit sat next to me and lit a cigar.

"You Chinese?" he asked.

I nodded.

"There sure are a lot of you Chinese on board. Where's everybody going?"

"Home," I said. "We're going back to China." I was wary.

"Red China? Jeez! You're leaving the good old U-S-of-A for that hellhole?" He shook his head. "I wish you luck, sonny. Sounds like a tough place to live."

I just nodded, stood, and walked to the rail, where I could be alone with my thoughts and watch the California coastline melt into the horizon. I had no doubt it would be the last time I laid eyes on the United States.

CHAPTER 8

The East Is Red

"Move along, there! Eyes front! Keep moving!"

Behind me the *Cleveland* eased away from the dock with a thunderous blast of its horn. The low moan rolled across Hong Kong's crowded harbor. My pulse and pace quickened. My scarred leather suitcase was weighted down with chemistry texts. My shoulders ached and my shirt was wet from my straining in the tropical heat, but my rising adrenaline propelled me forward.

As the ship docked, our clutch of two dozen or so returning Chinese gathered. We were escorted off the ship on a separate gangplank. There was no turning back now. I would soon be reunited with my father and Chaoding. I had become the third in a proud line of prodigal sons returning home. A lump formed in my throat.

I trudged along the narrow space between two columns of tall, turbaned Sikh policemen, fidgeting with their mahogany batons and eyeing the scrawny Chinese with disdain. The British didn't want any Commies defecting into Hong Kong, so the Sikhs marched us directly from the ship to a waiting railway car. Our escorts would take us to the border with Shum Chun, the southernmost port city of the People's Republic of China.

It was hard not to stare at the Sikh policemen's dark, blank faces and massive black beards. Their turbans were tall and magnificent, striped and multicolored, their tailored tunics sashed in a tartan pattern. Each man wore a small saber in a tooled leather sheath, as well as

THE MAN ON MAO'S RIGHT · 65

a pistol in a patent-leather holster. And each held a menacing-looking baton.

During the war, I'd seen Sikh policemen in movies with titles like *Passage from Hong Kong* and *Secret Agent of Japan*. The British employed them for local protection in colonies like Shanghai and Hong Kong. While they looked like maharajas—noble, stern, and vigilant—we'd been warned on the ship of their reputation for mistreating Chinese.

I wanted nothing to do with their batons, so I kept my head low as our rumpled band of returning students, carrying in our hands all we owned, helped one another up the steps of the railcar. On the train, more Sikh policemen kept us confined until we reached the border.

It was October 25, 1950—twelve years after my family embarked on the journey from Kunming into French Indo-China. I'd fled China a child, to escape a war. I returned a man, to fight one.

In the two weeks between the *President Cleveland*'s departure from Los Angeles and the debarkation of our ragtag group in Hong Kong, America and China had gone from estranged allies to archenemies. The news reports received in midocean had been ominous.

Radio Peking (Beijing) broadcast:

The American war of intervention in Korea has been a serious menace to the security of China. . . . The Chinese people cannot stand idly by with regard to . . . the invasion of Korea by the United States and its accomplice countries.

I felt both sad and angry.

General Douglas "Brass Hat" MacArthur, the most hawkish, high-ranking, and reckless officer in the American military, had successfully invaded at Inchon in South Korea, chasing the North Koreans back across the famed thirty-eighth parallel—the border area separating the Soviet-backed North from the U.S.-backed South. All this was taking place on a peninsula roughly the size of Florida, at China's front door and the USSR's back door.

Premier Zhou Enlai had issued a dire warning to President Truman:

If you invade North Korea, we will cross the Yalu River and attack your forces in defense of our ally, North Korea. Truman had already shown his treachery by breaking the promise not to interfere with China's planned invasion of Taiwan by sending the Seventh Fleet into the strait. Now American forces—fighting an undeclared, United Nations "police action"—drove deep into North Korea, right to the Yalu, the border with China. With equipment from the Soviet Union, Chinese troops massed along the river's northern banks.

Worse still, since summer there had been talk of using the atom bomb in the Korean conflict. An organization calling itself the International Committee for the Study of European Questions—an anti-Communist group based in Paris—had announced that it advocated use of the bomb "provided it could prevent war or put an end to it." It had been only five years since the United States dropped two atomic bombs on nearby Japan, and with a ruthless and dangerously independent general like MacArthur in charge of the Korean adventure anything seemed possible.

The America I first encountered—with the welcoming green lady holding her torch aloft—was not the America I'd just left. In the intervening years, the country had beaten two powerful enemies on opposite sides of the globe, incinerating more than a hundred thousand Japanese civilians in the process.

The China I left—which had saved, protected, and doctored the brave American aviators who dropped their bombs on Tokyo in 1942—was now viewed by America's conservative politicians as a mob of godless, bloodthirsty fanatics who needed to be taught lessons in democracy. After five millennia of Chinese culture, the warmongers among America's political leaders regarded us as nothing more than ignorant laundrymen.

I'd told the Harvard provost that I wanted to go home to finish my education. That was true, but I also wanted to fight. Mao had it right, I decided: "Political power grows out of the barrel of a gun."

After an hour's ride on the train through Hong Kong's rugged, tropical mountains we arrived at Luo Hu Station, at the juncture of two rivers. We were herded off the train and escorted again, this time to a bridge across the smaller of the two waterways. Our papers were checked one last time, and then the guards pointed to the other side of the bridge and waved us on.

When we reached the halfway point, marked by a white line on the pavement, there arose a great clamor, as if a stadium full of sports fans were cheering. There were drums and gongs and horns. Tinny Chinese music blared from loudspeakers.

"What is it?" I asked a fellow traveler.

" 'The East Is Red.' It's the song written for Mao during the war."

I remembered reading the English lyrics at Harvard:

> The east is red, the sun is rising.
> China has brought forth a Mao Zedong.
> He amasses fortune for the people,
> Hurrah, he is the people's saving star.
> Chairman Mao loves the people,
> He is our guide,
> To build a new China,
> Hurrah, he leads us forward!
> The Communist Party is like the sun,
> Wherever it goes, there is light.
> Wherever there is a Communist Party,
> Hurrah, there the people are liberated!

The noise grew louder as we approached the Chinese side of the bridge. A crowd of smiling, waving young men and women ran toward us, dressed in blue and green uniforms: soft cotton caps with a red star in the peak and rumpled Mao suits.

One young man clapped me on the shoulder, took my bag, hefted it, and said something. I couldn't understand him, but I was overcome with emotion. I followed him to the Chinese side of the bridge, where I knelt down, tears falling, and kissed my native soil.

I was finally home.

CHAPTER 9

Back in the Bosom

The next days were a blur of smells and sounds and foods decidedly not American: rice, garlic, and so on. No more ice cream, cereal swimming in milk, pot roasts, or hamburgers. But because I was on a personal mission I embraced it all with revolutionary zeal. I was prepared to suffer as my countrymen had during the years I'd been away.

The one thing I did mind was the toilets. I was back in the land of the hated squatter, which required better balance than I had. Also, from time to time I was surprised by a nasty splashback. I had a terrible time staying regular, and this new inconvenience worried me. Constipation had contributed to my grandfather's death, although his problem was the opposite of mine: he couldn't use the Western throne.

A warm welcome at the border included two nights in a clean Canton hotel, the Aichun. Here government officials interviewed the returning overseas students to learn our skills, what sorts of jobs we were suited for, and whether we wanted to further our education. With one of my fellow travelers interpreting, I explained that I wanted to join the Chinese People's Volunteers, the name given to the soldiers who were getting ready to defend Korea and our border against MacArthur's offensive. To avoid a direct confrontation, troops in regular Chinese uniforms would not cross the Yalu River. Instead, they would be outfitted as "volunteers" in the "War to Resist U.S. Aggression and Aid Korea."

We were put on a comfortable soft-sleeper train to Beijing, which meant that we got thin mattresses to lie on instead of the usual hard-seater cars with their wooden benches and no sleeping arrangements. We transferred trains in Hankow, on the Yangtze River. This was where my family had lived for a year, and where my poor grandfather died. I had no idea where he was or I would have visited his tomb to clean it and pay my respects. But I did try to find the primary school I had attended, without success. My Chinese was so bad that I could scarcely communicate and, of course, I was unable to read even the simplest signs.

After an exhausting couple of days of travel during which I caught no more than a few catnaps, the train pulled into the rail terminal in the center of Beijing. I found a telephone office and handed the clerk a slip of paper with my father's number. She asked me a question, but I couldn't understand. I felt like a nine-year-old again. She shrugged and dialed the number, said something, then handed the receiver to me.

"*Ba!*" I shouted, using the Chinese word for "Dad." The clerk flinched. I have a loud, booming voice when I'm excited. "It's me, Wah! I'm here, at the train station!"

"Oh, that's good, son! Go outside to the street and wait. I will send someone to fetch you."

"But how will they know which one is me?"

My father chuckled. "Don't worry, Wah. I will tell him to look for the tallest and blackest Chinese man he has ever seen."

Laughing, I handed the receiver back to the clerk. Our family tended toward dark skin, and I realized that I was the tallest person I'd seen so far in China. I'd left my home country a sickly, malnourished waif, but all that milk and red meat had turned me into a gangly, bespectacled, slant-eyed Gulliver.

I emerged onto the street gawking like a tourist at the noisy crowd of vendors and travelers milling about the entrance. Some vendors hawked a dark broth served in paper cups; others sold white squares of bean curd. Peddlers offered trinkets and toys.

The black-and-white dome of the colonial-era station gave it the look of a wedding cake. It stuck out all the more for sitting in a neighborhood of typical Chinese architecture: one-story, tile-roofed, brick-and-timber walls enclosing hidden courtyards.

Crimson flags fluttered from every building and utility pole: the new national banner, with one large, bright yellow star in the upper left, bracketed by an arc of four small yellow stars. The large star represents the leadership of the Communist Party. The small ones originally represented the unification of the classes, defined by Mao as the working class, the peasantry (farmers), the urban petty bourgeoisie, and the national bourgeoisie ("patriotic" capitalists). (Later, the stars were said to represent China and its national minorities.)

All that undulating red and yellow put a broad smile on my face and filled me with revolutionary pride. It was easy to conjure the People's Liberation Army's triumphant arrival in Beijing, under a cloud of red fabric. Red is the traditional color of the Han ethnic group, which makes up about 90 percent of China's population. Red is also the color of happiness, while gold (the flag's stars are a golden yellow) is the color of good fortune.

Finally, there are five stars, each of which has five points. The number five has significance in many cultures, and in China it represents the four cardinal points (east, west, heaven, and earth) and the center. Five is considered harmonious and balanced.

On the wall of the railway station hung the new government seal of the People's Republic, depicting Tiananmen (Heavenly Peace) Gate under the five stars, framed with stalks of wheat and a cogwheel—the peasantry and the working class. At Tiananmen, on May 4, 1919, the first student uprising had broken out against foreign domination and the feudalistic warlords who allowed it to continue. Considered the birthplace of modern China, it is also the spot where, thirty years later, Mao announced the formation of the People's Republic of China.

In a few minutes, a battered prewar Ford pulled up to the curb and out hopped a young man in a blue Mao suit: tunic, pants, and cotton shoes. He took my bag with a silent smile and motioned for me to climb into the vehicle. The driver carefully picked his way down a crowded street, then made a right turn. Through the left window, I got my first view of Tiananmen Gate, the tall, grand entrance to the Forbidden City, also known as the Imperial Palace. Hanging from the top of the enormous wall face, beneath a sprawling pagoda-style building, was a two-story-tall portrait of Chairman Mao, his expression serene as still water. I was awestruck, as if gazing on the face of a god.

The driver turned left and rattled down a long paved street running parallel to the moat surrounding the high stone walls of the palace. I spotted my father from a distance, standing in his long robe in front of one of the houses along the moat. I was so excited that I grabbed the door latch, nearly leaping from the moving car.

Smiling broadly, Father stroked his stringy beard. He had shrunk! I could now see the top of his bald head.

"Wah, you have come back."

We shook hands and held each other's gaze for a long moment.

"Yes, *Ba*. I am back."

The Chinese, especially the older generations, are quite modest about displays of affection, even between husbands and wives. It would have been odd for Father and me to initiate a hug or a kiss, but I didn't need a hug or a kiss to know how glad he was to see me, and vice versa. For both of us, my return was a wish come true.

I had reached the end of a twelve-year, globe-girdling journey. Through my idealistic, Communist-tinted glasses, events had turned out just as Father had predicted: the good guys had won. I had come home to help defend the prize.

Father's Beijing apartment was modest but in a desirable quarter of the city, a few blocks from Beijing University, where he taught law and was the dean of the law school. I had returned to China four and a half years after him.

The apartment had a small courtyard, with a living room and a long corridor that opened into three rooms. At the end was the kitchen. I was delighted to find that there was a private bathroom with a beautiful Western throne.

My father lived on Beichizi. The *bei* in Beichizi means "northern." *Chizi* means "pond." Beijing was laid out in squares, with a big square in the center—the Imperial Palace, where the emperors lived. Father's rooms were on Beichizi Street, the northeastern side of the moat—thus, Northern Pond.

Father and I sat in his cozy living room, sipping green tea and catching up on developments in our family, our new nation, and the world. Our letters to each other after he and Chaoding left New York had been deliberately superficial. Father had warned me: "Put nothing in writing you wouldn't want the FBI to read."

His eyes sparkled when I reported having personally delivered his Chinese translations to Mrs. Roosevelt. He frowned when I told him that Mother was ambivalent about returning to China. "I will write and tell her she must come soon," he said. "The news gets worse every day. There may come a time when it is very difficult to return from America. China is in the war, and who can say where it will end."

I was eager to see Chaoding, but Father said that his work for the new government involved frequent travel. The country was still recovering from the economic chaos of two decades of strife. There were several currencies in use: gold, old KMT dollars, and the new official notes, renminbi ("people's money"). Chaoding was in the middle of it all, trying to sort this out, along with a hundred other economic crises of a giant nation struggling to its feet.

Chaoding was deputy director of the People's Bank of China. He had become indispensable to his friend and mentor, Premier Zhou Enlai, the man responsible for the administration of the People's Republic and for implementing the policies of Mao and the Party. Chaoding was highly sought after on many accounts: he was a currency expert with many overseas connections at a time when China needed to increase foreign trade; he was widely praised abroad for his research and writings on China's economy; he was fully conversant with international banking and economic practices; he spoke and wrote flawless English; and he had been to Moscow and studied Russian. This last skill was especially useful now that Mao had chosen to ally China with Stalin's USSR.

"Your brother has his enemies," Father warned, examining the leaves in the bottom of his cup. "There are still some who mistrust him because they don't believe he was a double agent working for the Communists. They think he is a Kuomintang opportunist, or pro-American. He has the full confidence of Premier Zhou, but never forget that all walls have ears."

I nodded. Intrigue and discretion were a way of life in our family. I told Father that if China needed me I would go to Korea to fight. "The American politicians are becoming more reactionary every day. They think they can solve all the world's problems with atom bombs. China must stand up!" I declared, brimming with revolutionary fervor.

"You would make a poor soldier with those glasses," Father said, chuckling. "And what will happen if you don't understand Chinese and someone shouts 'Duck!'? First you should go to Tsinghua University and enroll. Chaoding left a recommendation letter for you. It will open all doors. You must relearn Chinese as quickly as you can."

About ten miles from the center of Beijing, Tsinghua is in the northwest quadrant. The following morning, after a breakfast of steamed bread prepared by Father's housekeeper, I embarked on my first foray into my new world. With me I brought a map of the city, my documents, and my Harvard texts. Father had obtained a bicycle for me, and I nervously merged into the stream of traffic snaking its way around the Imperial Palace and down the long, wide boulevards to Tsinghua.

My senses were on high alert. I took my time, studying the Chinese characters in the design of roof tiles, and the intricate carvings around the enormous red doors and high sills of courtyard houses. I stopped to watch a vendor making dumplings, and a group of people standing in a park singing what sounded like patriotic songs.

I felt quite conspicuous in my Western suit, making my way through the sea of blue Zhongshan tunics—known in the West as Mao suits. They were named for the man who invented the fashion, Dr. Sun Zhongshan (also known as Sun Yat-sen). Dr. Sun led China's first revolution in 1911, overthrowing the last of the Manchus, the Qing dynasty rulers whose ancestors invaded from Manchuria in the seventeenth century and subjugated the Hans, China's ethnic majority. My family are Hans.

Dr. Sun had wanted to create a garment that would appeal to the pride of the new Republic of China, a country that had just overcome harsh feudal rule. Fashion had been a weapon of the Manchus' oppression: they forced Chinese men to abandon the traditional style of wearing long hair tied up in a bun and to adopt the Manchu practice of shaving the front part of the scalp and plaiting the back hair into a long rattail (called a queue). Dr. Sun wanted a new garment to communicate China's aspirations to be in harmony with the West.

Also known as the People's Suit, the Zhongshan, which has a narrow turned-down collar and four symmetrical outside pockets on the front, was inspired by Japanese cadet and German military tunics. It became known as the Mao suit in the West because it was all Mao ever wore, with its signature soft cap. After liberation, the suit became popular in blue, a symbol of patriotism and solidarity with the working class. The Zhongshan was especially popular in Beijing, the national capital, where so many people were government and Party workers (known as cadres). I would need to get one as soon as I could.

My day's mission was suffused with irony. Tsinghua had been founded in 1911 with American money and staff to prepare students to study abroad in the United States, so they could then return and improve living conditions in China. This was Chaoding's alma mater. Over the years, it had grown into a full-fledged university. After liberation, the curriculum focused more on the sciences. I was replicating Chaoding's journey in reverse—studying at Harvard in preparation for continuing my Chinese education.

Father had urged me to pursue chemistry so that I might help our native province turn its huge reserves of coal into useful products. I had little interest in chemistry, but a new goal formed in my mind: I would help China build its own atom bomb. Now that I was seeing China from within China, I understood that the young People's Republic was as vulnerable as a fish swimming in a pot. If China had the bomb, the United States and the USSR would be forced to think twice about trying to push us around.

I finally reached the columned, arched entry gate at Tsinghua. I couldn't decipher the Chinese characters etched in stone above the arch, but Chaoding had once informed me of his school's motto: "Self-discipline and social commitment."

After much confusion, I found the right office. With great relief, I discovered that many of the faculty and some of the staff spoke English. Best of all, the chemistry texts were in English, published by Harvard! I explained to the provost that I wanted to join the Chinese People's Volunteers, the unofficial military force that was being organized to defend our Korean allies.

"You can apply for consideration," the provost said, "but it would be best for you to first complete your education. You must learn Chinese. In the meantime, you can apply to join the Chinese New Democratic Youth League, the student Communist Party organization. I'm sure your eldest brother will be an excellent reference." I submitted my application to the Youth League.

When I left Harvard, I had just entered my junior year. I continued as a junior at Tsinghua. While concentrating on chemistry, I also studied Chinese.

Within a couple of days, I had moved into a dormitory and, with my smattering of Chinese and their smattering of English, began to make new friends. What a relief to be among my Chinese peers without having to worry if they were Kuomintang spies!

My Harvard friends would have been horrified by my new living conditions. At Harvard, we lived in tastefully decorated suites of private bedrooms, each with a big closet, a large study table, bookshelves, and an easy chair for reading. Each suite of three or so bedrooms shared a large common living room and a large, modern bathroom.

At Tsinghua, I was assigned to a cramped concrete room measuring about nine square meters (about twenty-nine square feet), reminiscent of a cell. It held four bunk beds—sleeping for eight. Each bed had a thin mattress stuffed with straw, one quilt, and one pillow. A long, narrow table crowded the aisle, with four small stools. One squatter toilet served the entire floor of more than a hundred students. To take a bath required traveling some distance across campus to a communal bathhouse.

At Harvard, we were served standard American cafeteria fare: beefsteak, pork chops, chicken, macaroni, fresh vegetables, salads, fruit, desserts, ice cream, and all the milk we could drink. Because the country was in such poor economic straits, Tsinghua couldn't even muster a lowly bowl of rice or a single steamed wheat bun. Our diet consisted of cooked cereals like sorghum, corn millet, and dried sweet-potato flour, with pickled vegetables. On Sundays, we might have bits of meat or cooked vegetables. The barren dining room had high tables without chairs, so we ate standing up. The diet was so poor, and the toilets so uncomfortable, that I was constipated most of the time, except when I had diarrhea.

My new friends often tested my resolve, asking how I was holding up under the spartan conditions. "No problem at all!" I replied cheerfully. I was neither surprised nor troubled. Having been an avid reader in the States, I had known about the poor conditions in China. I even welcomed the sacrifice as part of my education and apprenticeship as a revolutionary.

If I had any misgivings, it was a touch of guilt about the capitalist luxuries I had enjoyed while my countrymen had been scraping by all those years. It would have been unthinkable to complain about my new living conditions, even if I had wanted to.

I found myself overcompensating at times. With my schoolmates' enthusiastic help, I studied Chinese intensively. My comrades would choose a short, simple article from a Chinese newspaper, and then teach me to read and pronounce each character correctly until I could repeat it by heart and write it out. Progress was painstaking. My pronunciation was a challenge, on top of which some students poked fun at my Shanxi accent. Writing was even more difficult.

One day I was studying in the dormitory when I overheard one of my roommates grousing about the awful living conditions and the monotonous meals. He went on at length about the terrible food and how this was no way to treat China's future scientists.

My reading material at that moment was a Party pamphlet extolling the revolution and explaining that true revolutionaries should strive to lead a frugal life, even more frugal than a peasant's. We were to set a good example for others, to show our bond with the poorest of the poor. "Could you help me with this pronunciation?" I asked him. "There is a sentence here that is very difficult."

He took the pamphlet and read aloud, " 'To be a good revolutionary, one must not complain about poor food.' " He glared at me with reddening face, tossed the pamphlet in my lap, and marched out of the room. Now my face blazed with shame. In my clumsy zeal to show how committed I was, I had offended him. I chastised myself for my bad habit of speaking before thinking.

My mother posing with me in the courtyard of our home in Taiyuan, the capital of Shanxi Province, where I was born on July 30, 1929.

Around 1910, in front of the family home in Fenyang County, Shanxi Province. My father (right) with his second wife (left), my grandparents, some aunts, and two half-brothers, including my eldest brother, Chaoding (next to Father), whose mother had died.

My father was a leading lawyer, and law professor, and he served in several official roles in the cabinet of one of the so-called warlord provincial governors.

The ancestral villa, 2006: Our old family estate in Fenyang—where my father was born and where I lived before going to America—still stands, although worse for wear.

The formal entrance of my family's ancestral villa.

From the villa's roof I saw smoke from fires that had been started by Japanese bombs dropped on Fenyang.

Hankow, 1938: (from left) my sister, Chin; Mother; brother Chaoli; Father; and me.

Me at age six in Taiyuan, 1936.

In Chinese tradition, it was common for whole families to sleep in the same bed—especially during the winter, when the only comfortable place was in the raised, clay sleeping kang, warmed from underneath by excess heat from a cooking stove.

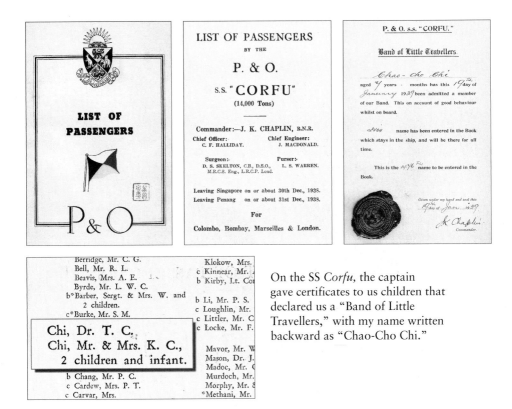

LIST OF
PASSENGERS

LIST OF PASSENGERS
BY THE

P. & O.

S.S. "CORFU"

(14,000 Tons)

Commander:—J. K. CHAPLIN, R.N.R.

Chief Officer:
C. F. HALLIDAY.

Chief Engineer:
J. MACDONALD.

Surgeon:-
D. S. SKELTON, C.B., D.S.O.,
M.R.C.S. Eng., L.R.C.P. Lond.

Purser:-
L. S. WARREN.

Leaving Singapore on or about 30th Dec., 1938.
Leaving Penang on or about 31st Dec., 1938.

For

Colombo, Bombay, Marseilles & London.

P. & O. s.s. "CORFU."

Band of Little Travellers.

Chao - cho Chi

aged 4 years - months has this 19th day of
January 1939 been admitted a member
of our Band. This on account of good behaviour
whilst on board.

460 name has been entered in the Book
which stays in the ship, and will be there for all
time.

This is the 4476 name to be entered in the
Book.

Given under my hand and seal this
19th day of Jan. 1939

JK Chaplin
Commander.

Berridge, Mr. C. G.
Bell, Mr. R. L.
Beavis, Mrs. A. E.
Byrde, Mr. L. W. C.
b*Barber, Sergt. & Mrs. W. and 2 children.
c*Burke, Mr. S. M.

Chi, Dr. T. C.
Chi, Mr. & Mrs. K. C., 2 children and infant.

b Chang, Mr. P. C.
c Cardew, Mrs. P. T.
c Carvar, Mrs.

Klokow, Mrs.
c Kinnear, Mr.
b Kirby, Lt. Co
b Li, Mr. P. S.
c Loughlin, Mr.
c Littler, Mr. C
c Locke, Mr. F.

Mavor, Mr. W
Mason, Dr. J.
Madoc, Mr. (
Murdoch, Mr.
Morphy, Mr. &
*Methani, Mr.

On the SS *Corfu*, the captain gave certificates to us children that declared us a "Band of Little Travellers," with my name written backward as "Chao-Cho Chi."

1939, aboard the SS *Corfu:* Father, Mother, Chin, me, and Chaoli.

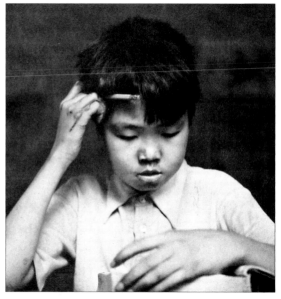

1939, New York, shortly after we arrived, with three family friends. My older brother, Chaoli, and I are on the floor in front of my father and mother.

I started my English-language education at City and Country School in Manhattan, where I was fussed over like a foundling puppy.

With my rogue tooth and some classmates, at City and Country School, New York City, early 1940s.

My father and some associates launched a Chinese-language newspaper, the *China Daily News*, in 1940 in New York's Chinatown, with the clandestine agenda of promoting both the cause of China and the Chinese Communist Party. Once war broke out with Japan, he was recruited by the U.S. Office of War Information (OWI), a predecessor of Voice of America, to translate and disseminate war reports and propaganda in Chinese.
(U.S. Office of War Information, Staff Photo)

Form 1099 TREASURY DEPARTMENT INTERNAL REVENUE SERVICE UNITED STATES **INFORMATION RETURN FOR CALENDAR YEAR 1942** INSTRUCTIONS TO PAYORS Prepare one of these forms for each payee in accordance with the instructions on return Form 1096. Do not include payments to nonresident aliens reported on Form 1042. Forward with return Form 1096 so as to reach the Commissioner of Internal Revenue, Returns Distribution Section, Washington, D. C., on or before February 15, 1943. Copy of this form as filed with the Government should be furnished to the employee whose income is reported in first column to assist him in preparing his income tax return.	To Whom Paid (Full name and house address)	**Kung-Chuan Chi** **233 E. 12 St.** **N.Y.C.** (If employee is a married woman, name of husband should also be furnished)			Employee's social security number, if any ....
		KIND AND AMOUNT OF INCOME PAID			
	SALARIES, WAGES, FEES, COMMISSIONS, BONUSES (If single $800 or more. If married $1,200 or more)	INTEREST ON NOTES, MORTGAGES, ETC. ($800 or more aggregate amount of above items)	RENTS AND ROYALTIES	OTHER FIXED OR DETERMINABLE INCOME	FOREIGN ITEMS ($300 or more)	DIVIDENDS ($100 or more) (Total paid, including amounts claimed nontaxable)
	☐ SINGLE MARRIED ☒	$	$	$	$	$	$ **1323.43**
By Whom Paid (Name and address)	**Office For Emergency Management (OWI)** 79—31996—1 **122 E. 42 St.** **N.Y.C.**				(OVER)

Washington Square Park, 1941: with a cousin (left); Harriet Levine (Chaoding's wife); and their two sons, Emile and Carl.

1945, just before my father returned to China: A half-brother, Chaofu, is on the left, and I am on the right, with Father, Chin, and Mother.

My father with Van Johnson.
(Time Warner)

Thirty Seconds Over Tokyo, 1944: More than halfway through the film, my chubby old dad appears in a doorway in a rural Chinese hospital. He is on screen in many scenes, tending to the injured flyers or standing around looking very wise, kind, and Chinese. *(Time Warner)*

1945–1950, Times Square to Harvard Yard: Graduation Day from City and Country School, in New York's Greenwich Village.

With my closest friends at Horace Mann–Lincoln High School.

One summer I worked on a farm in Connecticut. The other field hands took one look at my dark skin and declared that I was a "nigger."

In high school I drew a caricature of myself as half Western and half Chinese. My heart and mind were Chinese, but I loved my American friends, food, and experiences—including a brief period I spent at Harvard as a co-owner of a battered jalopy a friend and I took turns using on dates.

1950–1952, Harvard Yard to Tiananmen Square to Panmunjom: with a group of Chinese colleagues.

With a comrade, in front of the "office" during the Korean War cease-fire talks.

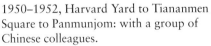

Arriving at the "Truce Tent" under the watchful eyes of U.S. journalists. *(Official U.S. Navy Photograph, National Archives)*

Negotiating-tent compound. *(Official U.S. Navy Photograph, National Archives)*

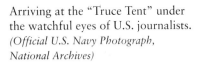

Baize-covered tables where talks took place. *(Official U.S. Navy Photograph, National Archives)*

Arrivals: China's Major General Hsieh Fang and North Korea's Major General Lee Sang Cho. *(Official U.S. Navy Photograph, National Archives)*

For the U.S./U.N. command: Vice Admiral C. Turner Joy and Major General William K. Harrison. *(Official U.S. Navy Photograph, National Archives)*

When a cease-fire violation was claimed, a field investigation was required, and I went along to take notes. Here, a spent American illuminating shell (a giant flare dropped by parachute for night maneuvers) had landed on our side in a demilitarized zone. I am on the far right. *(Official Chinese Photograph)*

The "askance," or dismissive, posture of the American official observing was typical of the way the United States commanders acted in our presence. I am second from right. *(Official Chinese Photograph)*

1954, Beijing: in uniform with medals earned in Korea, with my parents and brother Chaoding. Father holds my official citation for bravery.

Chaoding and my sister, Chin, with Father and me (1958).

Xiangtong and I married on May 25, 1957, in an informal, "revolutionary" ceremony with a few friends and colleagues at Xiangtong's office at the Chinese Red Cross in Beijing.

Our fifth anniversary, in 1962.

With our two sons (Xiao-bin, four, and Xiaotan, six) in 1970, when Xiangtong was away in Jiangxi Province working as a "barefoot doctor" at a May 5 cadre school.

1964: my parents in the courtyard at their home near the Forbidden City, in Beijing, three years before my father died. I am holding my months-old eldest son.

1966: grandmas and grandkids. My mother, left, and Xiangtong's mother, holding our second son, Xiao-bin, at ten months. Xiaotan is two years old.

1980, Beijing: one of the last pictures of my mother, with my sons, Xiao-bin (left) and Xiaotan, at about fourteen and fifteen years old.

1959: Having worked on a farm in Connecticut, I enjoyed some aspects of my required community service at a local peasant commune near Beijing. But conditions were harsh, as a developing famine had everyone on short rations. I was thin to begin with, and when Xiangtong came to visit me, she was horrified to see my ribs poking out.

1976: Seventeen years after the photo above, I found myself back on a farm for the fourth time, this one for foreign military bureaucrats. Here, hearts heavy with loss and stress, my Foreign Ministry comrades and I are ritually marking the tenth anniversary of Chairman Mao's May Seventh Instruction, the order that created these political reeducation schools for government cadres. I am on the right, with a drum.

1976: My Foreign Ministry colleagues and I (at right) are as stressed as we look, at an office meeting (note character posters in background) to show our resistance to a group of ambitious, powerful, and vindictive radicals in the government and the Ministry who were condemning us reformers as "capitalist roaders" and "rightists." The whole nation was on edge about the future. Zhou Enlai had just died, and Mao was failing.

The man on Zhou's right: 1964, in Karachi, with Pakistani president Ayub Khan. In the early 1960s, Zhou launched a campaign to form alliances with "third world" nations, from Ghana to Albania. *(Xinhua News Agency)*

We return on a cold day at Beijing Airport from one of our many extended trips abroad (date unknown). *(Xinhua News Agency)*

June 1965: Zhou exchanges gifts with a Tanzanian official on a tour of African nations. *(Xinhua News Agency)*

1963: with Egyptian president Gamal Abdel Nasser in Cairo. *(Xinhua News Agency)*

1964: escorting Chairman Ibrahim Abboud of Sudan on his visit to China. *(Xinhua News Agency)*

October 1, 1959 (possibly): the tenth anniversary of the founding of the People's Republic, atop Tiananmen Gate. I am in the background just left of Chairman Mao. Below us are reviewing stands for ranking officials and the diplomatic corps and, beyond, a worshipful throng of a million or so people hoping for a glimpse of the chairman. *(Xinhua News Agency)*

1964: interpreting for the chairman in his residence during a meeting with President Ayub Khan of Pakistan. *(Xinhua News Agency)*

February 1971, Tiananmen Gate: The most famous picture of me appeared on the front page of all the Chinese newspapers and in publications around the world. This was the first time anyone other than heads of state and Communist leaders had been shown standing next to Chairman Mao in the most sacred place in China. (*Xinhua News Agency*)

Chairman Mao and Lin Piao with American author Edgar Snow: Looking for an open door

China Policy: Time for a Thaw

Newsweek coverage: Mao was speaking with American Edgar Snow, author of *Red Star Over China*. Snow understood that Chairman Mao was showing an interest in Sino-U.S. relations. Off to the side, looking out of place, was Lin Biao, Mao's chosen successor, who would later be exposed as a traitor and die trying to escape capture.

My reunion with Chaoding was emotional, colored by the bitter-sweet quality of his new life. Harriet and his two boys—whom he dearly loved and who were a part of our family in New York—had tried to live in Shanghai but had given up and returned to New York before liberation. Chaoding had no choice but to let his wife go. He had risked his life to help build a Marxist future for China. It would have been a betrayal of his life's work to selfishly abandon his country for an easy life in America.

Even if Harriet had been willing to stick it out in China, their marriage would have created insurmountable problems for Chaoding and endless grief for her, an American in a nation at odds with her homeland. Chaoding's marriage to Harriet also would have prevented him from playing a leading role in the Party, which took a dim view of fiancés and spouses with "complicated" political biographies.

Zhou Enlai, Chaoding's mentor, always vouched for his patriotism and commitment, and the premier had to do so at times because of lingering suspicion among some in the Party that Chaoding was, at heart, an imperialist. He had lived in America, been trained in American institutions, enjoyed the friendship of officials in the American government, and advocated strong business ties with the West. His enemies said, as they later sometimes said of me, "He drank too much American water." My brother was a Marxist, but he was also an economist, a man who approached his work scientifically, disdaining ideological rhetoric.

He understood the role business played in getting China's economy going again, and was convinced that good relations and active trade with the West would hasten the process. This made sense, but it caused controversy when he hired personnel for the People's Bank who had superior qualifications but "unreliable" political backgrounds—those who had perhaps not been rock-solid Communist activists who diligently followed the Party line, or who had relatives abroad.

Soon after Harriet returned to New York, Chaoding became the third husband of Luo Jingyi. A former classmate of his, she had an eight-year-old son by a previous husband. She worked in a nongovernment organization called the Friendship Association.

Jingyi's first husband had been a noted Communist leader who was assassinated by the Kuomintang during the White Terror in 1927. As a result, when the couple asked the Party to bestow its blessing on their marriage, the decision was easy. They had both made great sacrifices for the revolution, and Chaoding had the full support of the premier.

Chaoding and Jingyi lived with Jingyi's young son not far from my father in Beijing's center. Visiting their apartment was a lesson in Chinese history. It was crammed with antiques, art objects, and ancient books. Chaoding earned a high salary compared with the average cadre. He gave a third of it to Jingyi to run the household and spent the rest on old artifacts.

In his free time he scoured the shops of the city, buying porcelain and jade objects, paintings, bronze trinkets, old books and manuscripts—whatever caught his fancy. He was a scholar of Chinese history. He explained, "Even in a revolution, it is important to preserve our heritage." Early on, he made a few mistakes and bought counterfeit antiquities. In time, he learned to tell the difference, and soon other collectors brought him objects for authentication.

Not long after I started my classes at Tsinghua, Father received word that Mother was returning with Chin. Chaoli, as expected, stayed behind in California. None of us doubted that it would be many years before we saw him again.

My two beloved nations were now at war.

CHAPTER 10

The Atomic Death-Belt Plan

Just before the People's Republic was founded, Chairman Mao announced that China would "lean" toward the Soviet Union in its foreign policy, as opposed to forming a full-scale alliance. Stalin had committed $300 million in aid to China and, by inference, a nuclear umbrella against U.S. aggression. But Stalin was cunning, and Mao cautious. China would strive to be a Communist state, but it would be a homegrown Chinese brand of Communism, not a rubber stamp of the Soviet model. It would be a "people's democratic dictatorship," with land redistribution as the first major initiative.

In the speech he gave in mid-1949 to commemorate the twenty-eighth anniversary of the founding of the Chinese Communist Party, Mao explained that China "must lean either to the side of imperialism or to the side of socialism. Sitting on the fence will not do." In announcing China's arrival on the world stage, Mao warned, "We must not show the slightest timidity before a wild beast. . . . Either kill the tiger or be eaten by him—one or the other."

By the time I returned, that policy was undoing decades of goodwill between my two nations. In schools and on walls in public places, recruiting posters were plastered declaring a policy of "Resisting Americans, Assisting Korea, Protecting Our Homes, Safeguarding Our Nation." One depicted a white dove above a drawing of a graveyard of white crosses, an American GI helmet perched on the top of one cross, and a tattered American flag draped over the crosspiece.

There were rallies every day, some organized by government cadres, some made up of students, some of workers. Even a housewives' union staged a demonstration. America was the tiger intent on eating China, and so it became the imperialist tiger that had to be killed.

Meanwhile, citizens were urged to sacrifice and work hard. Our newspapers carried inspirational stories of workers who had met or exceeded production quotas. If necessary, we were told, "five persons should eat the rice of three." China's long civil war was over, but the struggle continued.

The first serious clashes in North Korea between the Chinese People's Volunteer Army (PVA), led by General Peng Dehuai, and the U.S.-commanded United Nations troops, led by MacArthur, took place just as I was arriving in Asia. Chinese troops had launched a surprise attack on U.N. forces, charging in a massive wave, blowing bugles and whistles, then quickly melting back into the mountains, a classic Mao war strategy.

Although the *People's Daily* carried only sketchy reports of these first skirmishes, even university students far away in the capital city sensed that something big was afoot. Calls for volunteers became more urgent. Fellow students suddenly packed and left without explanation. The rhetoric in the newspapers became more aggressive and vivid: "The imperialist tiger wants to eat human beings. When it does so depends only on its appetite. No concession can stop this tiger."

At the end of November, the *People's Daily* reported that General Peng had launched an all-out offensive that forced the U.S. Eighth Army into the longest retreat of any unit in American military history. The North Korean and Chinese troops had captured thousands of pieces of equipment and wiped out thousands of "puppet soldiers" of Syngman Rhee (South Korea's president, who took his orders from MacArthur), inflicting heavy casualties on large concentrations of American and British troops. Our hastily trained, poorly equipped troops, lacking proper winter gear, had triumphed over a modern army with a nearly unlimited supply of weapons and mastery of the air.

It was a hard-won, stunning victory. There were huge rallies on campuses and elsewhere, with bugles, red banners, and speeches of defiance with raised fists. The tiger had been lured down from the mountain and drawn into the trap.

The North Korean–Chinese People's Volunteers' drive continued into January 1951, ending with the capture of the South Korean capital of Seoul. Young China had proved that it did not need the wealth and resources of the West to assert its right to self-defense. Because of poor equipment, shortage of logistics, and the lack of protection from the air, our victory was won at a very high price. However, we did have the wholehearted support of the people and the wise leadership of Chairman Mao, who had shown his excellence at winning battles against a superior force while under unfavorable conditions.

One of my dorm mates had a shortwave radio and at night we sometimes picked up unjammed English-language broadcasts from the BBC and Voice of America, which I did my clumsy best to translate for my Chinese-speaking classmates. MacArthur was publicly pressing Truman for authorization to attack "the Communist hordes in Manchuria," and Truman hinted that the United States might use the atom bomb if the United Nations branded China an aggressor. "We are fighting in Korea for our own national security and survival," Truman proclaimed.

My friends were astonished by such a ludicrous remark. "How can the Americans imagine that we are a threat to them?" they asked me. "They are the aggressors in a war we did not start. We are surrounded, not them." I could only shrug. It made no sense to me, either.

Truman claimed that the Chinese people, "if they could speak for themselves, would denounce the aggression committed by their Communist masters." It was incredible to me that anyone could look at China's recent history and the state of geopolitics and fail to grasp how threatened the Chinese felt. We were determined, as Mao had vowed, never to be insulted again.

MacArthur was agitating for the use of atomic bombs on targets along the China–North Korea border. He was also pandering to the corrupt Chiang Kai-shek regime on Taiwan—now protected by the U.S. Seventh Fleet. Only a year after we'd chased those troops off the mainland, MacArthur wanted to throw five hundred thousand Kuomintang troops at our People's Volunteers. China was fighting a war it didn't want and could ill afford, provoked by the North Koreans, who had been egged on by the Soviets, who were supposed to be China's ally.

The only benefit was that the war had united the nation and created a common enemy: the United States. My loyalty was to China, but I felt no hatred toward Americans, just sadness at the shattered goodwill. It seemed a generation ago that I'd sat in that Manhattan movie house with tears running down my cheeks, proud of my father's portrayal of the affection the Chinese felt for those downed American fliers. Now we were trying to kill American pilots, and they were trying to kill us.

The fighting in Korea slogged on through the bitter winter of 1950–51. Losses on both sides were staggering. There were reports of wounded Chinese and North Korean prisoners being executed on the battlefield. The CPV treated their POWs with leniency, assuring them sufficient food and drink. American planes relentlessly pounded Korean villages and towns, killing thousands, flattening the landscape, and driving soldiers and civilians alike into underground bunkers.

In April, when Truman fired MacArthur, we were all delighted. (There was never any love lost between us and MacArthur. Under his support and protection after World War II, a defeated Japan again became a world power. I clearly remember my father sinking into a state of deep depression when he learned MacArthur had been appointed commander in chief of the Allied Command. Father said, "This means that China has lost the war." He was right.) But soon afterward an American congressman—Albert Gore, of Tennessee—openly proposed a truly apocalyptic solution. Short of raining atom bombs on our troops, Gore proposed to President Truman that the United States gather up its radioactive waste from processing plutonium and dump it across the Korean peninsula to create an "atomic death belt"—a Great Wall of wasteland:

> After removing all Koreans therefrom, [the United States would] dehumanize a belt across the Korean peninsula by surface radiological contamination. Just before this is accomplished, broadcast the fact to the enemy, with ample and particular notice that entrance into the belt would mean certain death or slow deformity to all foot soldiers; that all vehicles, weapons, food and apparel entering the belt would become poisoned with radioactivity; and, further, that the

belt would be regularly contaminated until such time as a satisfactory solution to the whole Korean problem shall have been reached.

This would differ from the use of the atomic bomb in several ways and would be, I believe, morally justifiable under the circumstances.

I had escaped the States in the nick of time, and was glad Mother had made it back to Beijing with Chin. Father seemed happier now that the family had been reunited. Chin, however, had become an all-American teenager—interested in the latest clothing, music, and boys. In the spartan and socially rigid culture of China, she was miserable. Like our brother Chaoli, who had stayed behind, Chin was no revolutionary prepared to sacrifice for the motherland.

I couldn't imagine what some of my former Chinese classmates at Harvard might be enduring, now that American politicians were demonizing us and lumping us in with the Soviets. I imagined with a smile that my dear old friends from City and Country School and Horace Mann–Lincoln were probably sitting around a bottle of wine feeling sorry for me just as I was having the time of my life, notwithstanding the meager diet and the squatter toilets.

A month after Congressman Gore's death-belt idea came and went, U.S. general Omar Bradley, chairman of the Joint Chiefs of Staff, testified in Congress about the Korean situation, rejecting MacArthur's recommendation that the United States attack China. It was, he said, "the wrong war, at the wrong place, at the wrong time, with the wrong enemy."

But the Korean conflict dragged on into summer, with both sides fighting over a line of control that was roughly along the thirty-eighth parallel, the prewar dividing line between North and South. Commanders of the UNC (United Nations Command) and the North Korean–Chinese People's Volunteers began to argue over a suitable site to begin talks aimed at a truce.

On August 1, all of Beijing and a huge parade of soldiers and equipment gathered in the big square in front of Tiananmen Gate to celebrate People's Liberation Army Day. It was on August 1, 1927, that the Chinese Communists in Nanchang, led by Zhou Enlai, first rose up against the Kuomintang. The event is regarded as the birthday of the PLA.

Schools, government offices, and other groups sent handpicked delegations to march in the parade or assemble near the reviewing stand. I was eager to march and get close enough to see Mao, but I was not selected to be in the group from Tsinghua. So I rode my bicycle the ten miles to stand far back in the crowd and listen, understanding little, as the dots on top of Tiananmen—Mao, Premier Zhou, the great Generals Zhu De and Peng Dehuai, and others—made their speeches to thunderous cheering and tears of pride. It was frustrating to be so far away. I couldn't make out their faces, and I understood only a few words.

As one of the taller people in China, I could see across the heads of the crowd. I was floating in a sea of happy, restless, noisy Chinese— hundreds of thousands—with red flags and banners flying everywhere. I couldn't make out which dot was Mao at the pagoda railing atop the Heavenly Peace Gate, but the energy of his presence seemed to flow out into the crowd and bind us together as one. Mao evoked rapture. In a culture whose spiritualism is expressed through ancestor worship, Mao had become the father of us all. To be in that crowd was to be in the presence of a deity who was sending his blessing out to each and every one of us. I was swept up in the moment, feverish to "serve the people"—Mao's signature exhortation—to contribute to China's bright and proud future.

After the Army Day celebration, I reread some of the chairman's most influential writings, comparing the English with the Chinese. Along with virtually everyone in the country, I attended numerous rallies and "struggle" meetings, where individuals stood and admitted their "incorrect" and counterrevolutionary thoughts, as well as criticized the comments and actions of others. Because my Chinese was still poor, I watched and listened.

Mao wrote: "If we have shortcomings, we are not afraid to have them pointed out and criticized, because we serve the people. Anyone, no matter who, may point out our shortcomings. If he is right, we will correct them. If what he proposes will benefit the people, we will act upon it. . . . If, in the interests of the people, we persist in doing what is right and correct what is wrong, our ranks will surely thrive."

As students, we were insulated from what was happening in the countryside where, we later learned, chaos reigned. In villages, peasants were encouraged to publicly attack the landlords and capitalists, also known as rich peasants. Land was seized and redistributed. In the process, old scores were settled. In some places, people were beaten to death. None of this reached our ears in Beijing.

Although our student struggle meetings were part of our willing indoctrination into the new Chinese order, they also revealed strong emotions and prejudices. Anyone with a complex biography—growing up in America, for instance—was automatically suspect. If you had relatives who lived in Taiwan or who had served in positions of importance in the Kuomintang—as my brother Chaoding had—you faced close scrutiny when applying to become a Communist Party member. Anyone whose family had been capitalists or landlords—like my father—had to demonstrate his loyalty to the Party and his genuine embrace of the socialist agenda.

Joining the Party was an important goal of mine. It was a matter of family pride, to follow in Chaoding's footsteps. And if I hoped to work on a project as important as the atomic bomb, Party membership was essential. I was certain that I would eventually get there, so long as I did everything I could to demonstrate my enthusiasm for and knowledge of Mao's philosophy.

In studying the Chinese language and Mao's works, I focused on three of the chairman's most important essays: "On the People's Democratic Dictatorship," the "lean to one side" speech he delivered in June 1949; and two essays that he wrote in 1937—"On Practice" and "On Contradiction." Along with "The Foolish Old Man Who Removed the Mountains," these four works represented to me all that was noble, proud, and wise in the new "stand-up" China. As a youthful idealist, I was deeply moved by Mao's teachings.

In his June 1949 speech, Mao said, "For the working class, the laboring people, and the Communist Party, the question is not one of being overthrown, but of working hard to create the conditions in which classes, state power, and political parties will die out very naturally and mankind will enter the realm of Great Harmony. . . . That is, unite the working class, the peasantry, the urban petty bourgeoisie and the national bourgeoisie, form a domestic united front under the leadership of the working class, and advance from this to the establishment of a state which is a people's democratic dictatorship under the leadership of the working class and based on the alliance of workers and peasants."

As we were a people who had been subjugated, exploited, invaded, and humiliated by the rest of the world for more than a century, and who had struggled under the thumbs of the ruling classes for millennia, these words plucked at our heartstrings.

"On Practice" was Mao's signal work on Marxism as it related to China. It was written as an argument against the theoretical dogmatism of some Party leaders who wanted to copy the Soviet model. Like many of Mao's writings and speeches, it was interminable. Nevertheless, it was an important essay in articulating the idea that China would have to develop its own brand of socialism, based not in theory but in practice:

> Discover the truth through practice, and again through practice verify and develop the truth. . . . If you want to know the taste of a pear, you must change the pear by eating it yourself. If you want to know the structure and properties of the atom, you must make physical and chemical experiments to change the state of the atom. If you want to know the theory and methods of revolution, you must take part in revolution.

That same summer, he wrote "On Contradiction," an argument for the yin-yang nature of life, politics, and nation-building:

> Opposition and struggle between ideas of different kinds constantly occur within the Party; this is a reflection within the Party of contradictions between classes and between the new and the old in society. If there were no contradictions in the Party and no ideological struggles to resolve them, the Party's life would come to an end.
>
> Thus it is already clear that contradiction exists universally and in all processes, whether in the simple or in the complex forms of motion, whether in objective phenomena or ideological phenomena.

In these four works, one can trace the roots of what lay in store for China under Mao. He believed that conflict and struggle ("On Contradiction") were necessary and constant in the search for harmony—the endless revolution; that China must look inward for clues to what sort of society it wanted to be ("On Practice"); that political power belonged not in the hands of an élite few but with the masses ("On the People's Democratic Dictatorship"); and that building a new China would require great patience and time ("The Foolish Old Man Who Removed the Mountains").

As brilliant as I thought Mao was, he was a windy writer and occasionally produced a sentence that left me feeling as if I'd gotten lost in a house of mirrors. In "On Contradiction," he wrote:

> Since the particular is united with the universal and since the universality as well as the particularity of contradiction is inherent in everything, universality residing in particularity, we should, when studying an object, try to discover both the particular and the universal and their interconnection, to discover both particularity and universality and also their interconnection within the object itself, and to discover the interconnections of this object with the many objects outside it.

Throughout the rest of 1951 and early 1952, I immersed myself in my chemistry studies and in learning Chinese. I had just begun to write my graduation thesis, in April 1952, when I received a notice instructing me to report to the Communist Party secretary for the chemistry department at Tsinghua University.

"Your request to join the Chinese People's Volunteers has been accepted," he said, handing me some paperwork. "You will report to the address listed on your papers. Pack your things and leave immediately. Speak to no one about where you are going."

I was stunned. It had been more than a year since I'd filled out my application. "But . . . I'm almost finished with my studies," I said. "I'm just writing my thesis."

"The order is to report immediately."

I looked at the papers. "Where is this address?" I asked. "Is it an army base?"

He looked at me, chuckled, and shook his head. "No, comrade. It is the Foreign Ministry."

CHAPTER 11

Welcome to Kansas

Once again I found myself standing in a university quadrangle, contemplating an interruption in my education. This time, instead of Beethoven's Fifth it was the imagined sound of battle bugles that accompanied the sudden change in my life's course.

I took a final look at the great hall where I had attended lectures and the occasional play and Chinese opera (which I couldn't bear). The provost had told me to report to the Foreign Ministry headquarters in the city center. I had no idea what to expect. Would I be lined up with other young recruits and barked at by a battle-hardened drill sergeant?

Whatever awaited, I was anxious to get on with it. I would fight for China's future, even if the opposing force came from the nation that had once harbored me.

I hurried off on my bicycle. But instead of a military camp teeming with fresh recruits I found the serene and majestic colonial-era complex that housed China's foreign-policy apparatus. Two dour, crisply uniformed soldiers holding Soviet burp guns guarded the tall iron gate. I showed my paperwork and was ushered inside. A clerk walked me down a dim, echoing hallway to an office.

I now understood that I would not be carrying a rifle. I had been one of the few people fluent in English at Tsinghua, often sought out to translate writing and interpret foreign broadcasts. Talks between the United Nations and the North Koreans about a permanent cease-fire had been going on for months. If I was truly being accepted into the Chinese People's Volunteers, I was certain to be going to Korea. If I wasn't going to be blowing bugles or throwing grenades, the only other thing I could imagine doing was translating.

I was surprised to be taken into an office and warmly greeted by Fang Dihuai. He had once lived in New York and worked at my father's old newspaper, the *China Daily News*. We exchanged pleasantries, then Fang picked up a file folder from his desk, opened it, and scanned it for a moment in silence. "Do you know why you have been summoned?" he said.

I shook my head.

"What I'm about to tell you is of the utmost secrecy. Not to be disclosed to anyone at any time for any reason." He looked at me with a steady gaze for a long moment.

"Yes, of course!" I felt a rush of adrenaline.

"That includes your family. It is a matter of life and death."

I nodded. Fang handed me an envelope.

"Here are your new documents. You and I and some others are being assigned to take notes in English at the negotiations in Panmunjom. You will stay in a Ministry compound near here for the next few days while you're being trained with the others."

My heart began to hammer against my rib cage.

"There are still many Kuomintang spies around who would be glad to tell the enemy the movements of our staff," Fang went on. "The Americans are bombing North Korea every night. If these spies learned of your plans, they would know a convoy will soon be coming through. Everyone could be killed. Tell no one. Don't even discuss it among your co-workers."

"Yes, yes. Thank you." I backed out, fighting an instinct to kowtow—a feudalistic gesture now frowned on in our new, classless society. I pulled the door closed behind me.

I flew home with my sack of belongings, surprising my mother and father in the middle of their afternoon nap. It took Father a long time to come to the door.

"Wah, what is it?"

"Hello, *Ba*. How are you? I just came by to pay a little visit. Then I must go."

Mother went into the kitchen and I heard the teakettle rattle on top of the stove. Father plopped into his reading chair. "Go, Wah? Where are you going?"

What to say? I held his gaze for a long, sober moment. Then he nodded slightly. "I see. It's a pile of eggs," he muttered, using a Chinese expression for a precarious situation. I sighed with relief.

We made small talk while Mother served tea. Chin was growing up fast, Father said, and was still having trouble adapting. Chaoding was always on the move, so my father had seen little of him lately.

I told Father that my studies were going well and I was beginning my thesis. The conversation was surreal, talking about such mundane matters when I would soon be on a train speeding away from Beijing on my way to the shattered, bloodstained landscape of Korea.

Finally, it was time to go. I said goodbye with a bit more emphasis than I intended. My parents showed no emotion, but when I looked back as I walked away they were still standing in the doorway. My heart ached from having to keep such big news from my dear old dad. He would have beamed with pride to know that I was carrying on the family tradition.

I reported to the Ministry compound, where I was shown my lodging, another cell full of bunk beds. I met my new colleagues, a group of a dozen or so English-speaking scholars and professors who would make up the clerical staff of our delegation at the armistice talks. We spent about a week together in the Foreign Ministry being prepped for our journey and our responsibilities after we arrived. We would work in teams of two, taking notes on what was said in the talks in English, to be translated later. Two note-takers were needed for each session to make sure nothing was omitted or misunderstood.

We were also inoculated against a number of diseases such as cholera. Everyone survived the shots with no adverse reactions, except for me. Although my protein- and dairy-rich American diet had boosted my growth and height, my constitution remained fragile. One of the inoculations gave me a high fever and I had to be nursed back to health.

The sudden call-up of English-fluent Chinese was a result of the first real movement in efforts to hammer out a cease-fire. Fighting had recently deteriorated into a kind of trench warfare, with the line of control moving back and forth along the thirty-eighth parallel. Both sides held thousands of prisoners of war. The discussions included a Chinese demand that "neutral" Soviet troops play a peacekeeping role, which, predictably, was unacceptable to the UNC negotiators. Also at issue was whether, during a cease-fire, the North could build new airfields. This the United Nations also rejected, because that would allow us to put our MiG fighters closer to the front lines.

One of my new comrades was Guo Jiading, who was two years younger than I. He had just completed an undergraduate degree at Fudan University in Shanghai, in the foreign-language department. He had been summoned to Beijing to serve as an oral translator for some visiting dignitaries during the May 1 International Labor Day celebration, but he had been diverted to the Foreign Ministry.

Guo and I shared the experience of finding ourselves abruptly thrown into the service of our country. His easygoing nature and mastery of English allowed us to quickly become friends. Soon we were addressing each other by affectionate Chinese diminutives: Little Ji and Little Guo.

Guo shared my teasing sense of humor. "I think maybe you are not really Chinese, Little Ji," he said, shaking a finger. "You are an American pretending to speak Chinese. You speak it like you've got a mouthful of marbles."

For others, it might have been an insult or even a threat to be singled out in this way, but I gave it no thought. I was both politically naïve and emboldened by my brother's reputation and relationship with China's top leaders. Many people knew about Chaoding. Those who didn't soon heard about him through the grapevine. I never mentioned my connections, out of both modesty and discretion.

Furthermore, among intellectuals and cadres (bureaucrats and party workers in any sort of official capacity), it was regarded as quite a sacrifice for me to have given up a Harvard degree, to have surrendered the easy capitalist life for the discomfort and uncertain future of living in the People's Republic. That got me extra points.

Finally, I had something else going for me that would prove unique and valuable throughout my diplomatic career: I understood the American way of life. The United States had plenty of China experts to draw on from the pool of exiled Kuomintang officials they were propping up on Taiwan. But the People's Republic had just a handful of cadres with my pedigree and my all-American childhood. I could think like a Chinese, but I also understood the "barbarian" thought process. I even got their jokes.

The Foreign Ministry owned no recording equipment, so we had to rely on our ability to take accurate notes, and then to quickly transcribe them. After several days of instructions and indoctrination, we were bused to Beijing's main railway station, the one I'd arrived at from Hong Kong eighteen months earlier. We boarded an eastbound soft-seater for the two-day trip to Shenyang, a major industrial city in Manchuria—China's far-northeast territories. Shenyang had been occupied by the Japanese, then by the Soviets, and finally by the Kuomintang as one of their last holdouts before they fled the mainland.

We had packed whatever we could wrap and tie up in a quilt. I had a couple of language books, a few extra articles of clothing, pencils, and a notepad. I had also brought food for the journey—coarse cornbread and salted pickles, which I washed down with hot water provided by vendors on the train. The bread had an unpleasant pasty texture and little flavor. It was difficult to swallow and rough on my digestive system. But it felt right—the tougher the life, the tighter my belt became and the more engaged I was in the great struggle for Chinese sovereignty and proletarian equality.

On the ride to Shenyang, we did our best to chat among ourselves and get to know one another without discussing destination, mission, or any other revealing details that could be overheard. The conversation was stilted and, during lulls, somewhat grim. If any of my travel mates were nervous or frightened, they kept it to themselves.

I sensed that we were all wondering just how horrid the battlefield might be. It was April 1952, six months after U.S. B-29 bombers had carried out simulated atom-bomb attacks on North Korea. The pilots dropped atom-bomb casings with the lethal weaponry removed on North Korea along the Chinese border. It was a form of terror to keep our side guessing. Both the Chinese and the Koreans responded by digging hundreds of miles of tunnels and thousands of miles of trenches, and throwing up thousands of Russian MiG jet fighters painted with People's Republic insignias and flown by Chinese, Korean, and Russian pilots.

We changed trains in Shenyang and found ourselves on a hard-seater serving as a troop transport for the daylong journey to Andong, on the Yalu River border with North Korea. We were among the few dressed in common Mao suits and carrying no weapons.

As the train pulled in to Andong's station, I was surprised to see on the platform Soviet soldiers manning anti-aircraft guns. We had heard the Soviets were helping us, but it was clear that they were defending the city for China while the Chinese People's Volunteers (CPV) were across the river battling the UNC forces.

Every inch of wall space seemed plastered with propaganda posters. One showed a North Korean soldier and a Chinese soldier side by side, holding their rifles high. They pointed accusing fingers at an ashen-faced American general (MacArthur), who was crawling away from the battlefield. The text read, LONG LIVE THE VICTORY OF THE KOREAN PEOPLE'S ARMY AND THE CHINESE PEOPLE'S VOLUNTEERS. Another portrayed a little Korean girl and a little Chinese girl holding hands in a garden of chrysanthemums. THE POWER OF THE PEOPLE OF NORTH KOREA AND CHINA IS GREAT, it said.

Historically, the Chinese had arrogantly regarded the Koreans as barbarians "in need of taming." But here we were, allied in a global fight to the death on a yawning fault line. For this we had our good friend Stalin to thank. He had encouraged the North Korean leader Kim Il Sung to invade South Korea and then, when things went sour, dumped the problem in the lap of the Chinese to clean up, albeit with Soviet support. The turning point came when the Soviet representative to the United Nations boycotted a crucial Security Council meeting at which the United States pressed the Korean issue. Without that crucial Soviet veto in the Security Council, the United States was able to muster all its allies in the United Nations to "provide military . . . forces and other assistance available to a united command under the United States of America." Whether or not Stalin intended it, China found itself maneuvered into a bloody confrontation with its onetime ally, the United

States, at a time when the Young People's Republic was just getting to its feet.

We were herded onto a truck loaded with supplies. It picked its way through streets crowded with traffic, mule-drawn wagons, and Chinese soldiers. More anti-aircraft guns, barrels pointed skyward, were visible on rooftops and in vacant lots. Dandong was a large, busy, even prosperous industrial center. In spite of the military atmosphere, businesses appeared to be running smoothly, pedestrians strolled carefree along the sidewalks, restaurants were full of diners.

At the riverbank, we saw anti-aircraft guns pointed north, manned by Soviet soldiers. Together with Soviet pilots above, they were there to defend the Yalu River Bridge, vital for the CPV for all its supplies. We parked behind a line of other vehicles, wearing our CPV uniforms: quilted tunic-style jackets, heavy boots, fur caps with earflaps, and overcoats. Although it was April, the weather in the far north was still wintry from the seasonal winds blowing down off the Siberian steppes. Also, we would be traveling through a mountainous region where the nights got quite cold. Our uniforms were unmarked, without even the red star on the fur caps.

All around us, Chinese soldiers were removing their People's Liberation Army patches or exchanging their uniforms for the plain yellowish khaki of the volunteers. There were many true volunteers from China in the CPV, but the bulk of the fighting men were either Koreans who had helped us fight the Japanese or regular Chinese People's Liberation Army troops posing as volunteers. In this way, China hoped to avoid a direct confrontation with the United States.

The sun was low in the sky when the convoy finally rumbled onto the bridge. One of the soldiers riding with us explained that the Americans rarely launched low-level attacks during the day because the Yalu River and the routes south were heavily defended by anti-aircraft batteries.

As we approached the far side of the river and rolled off the bridge, the devastation became apparent. The countryside had been flattened and pulverized, pockmarked with bomb craters. Every building, every tree, almost everything aboveground appeared to have been blasted.

Sturdier structures made of mortar or brick were burned-out shells. People and soldiers sat around holes that led to underground bunkers. The Americans had not dropped the atom bomb, but they might as well have from the apocalyptic look of things.

We crept through this dead landscape, passing the occasional road crew filling in bomb craters. As the sun sank beneath the horizon, our convoy picked up the pace. The drivers had to find their way with headlights dimmed. Periodically we heard random rifle fire.

"Warnings of planes," the soldier explained. The North Koreans had a primitive early-warning system along the major supply routes. Every li or so, someone would be posted on a hilltop with a rifle. If he saw or heard aircraft approaching, he would fire his weapon. Then the next person up the line would do the same, and so on until the entire route had been alerted to a possible attack.

We jounced along atop our baggage, which was on top of the supplies on the cargo bed. To keep from being thrown off the lurching truck, we had to hang on to the ropes that tied the cargo down.

Suddenly a rifle shot rang out and everyone started shouting. *"Binji! Binji!"* Planes! Planes! The driver accelerated, but then slammed on the brakes as we approached a sharp right turn. Just as he hit the brakes, we heard the splattering of rounds striking the earth in front of the truck. Bits of earth and stone shards pinged against the truck. We heard the machine guns chattering, followed by the roar of the fighter as it swooped past overhead, a flicker of exhaust flame trailing from the engine cowling.

"Take cover!" We all tumbled off the truck and scrambled to the sides of the dirt road, feeling our way in the dark as we hunkered down in muddy ditches and crouched behind rocks, waiting for another attack. I lay as flat as I could, covered my head with my hands, pressed my nose to the cold, damp earth, and scrunched my eyes closed. I tried to calm myself by counting the years—thirteen—since that day on the banks of the Yangtze River when I was a nine-year-old cowering among burial mounds while a flight of Japanese bombers droned past. As then, I was both terrified and exhilarated. I had survived my second combat experience.

We brushed ourselves off, remounted, and continued on our way. Later that night, we saw flashes of light in the distance. A town was being bombed.

It took that entire night and the next morning to get from the Yalu to Pyongyang, the North Korean capital. There was little to see along the way: here and there piles of rubble with the occasional chimney still standing, fires sending up columns of smoke.

When we dismounted, we helped throw camouflage over the truck and were directed into a hole in the ground. This led to a bunker, certainly the most unusual foreign embassy in the world. The Chinese embassy in Pyongyang was housed in a bunker, with brick walls and heavy timbers holding up the roof.

The shudder of exploding bombs was a constant here. Bits of soil were continually falling from the ceiling. There was no place to sit, so we settled ourselves on the damp earthen floor. There were electric wires with a few bare bulbs, though some of the chambers were lit by candlelight.

Most of the concussions we felt or heard were distant, but occasionally one landed nearby. I buried my face in my knees and covered my head in case the enemy got lucky. If things were this bad in our embassy, I couldn't imagine how awful they were at the front. At this point, well over a million soldiers and civilians had been killed in the North. More than 150,000 Chinese and Korean troops languished in POW camps on the other side. Our enemies' losses were much smaller, but it was bloodshed and misery nonetheless. I was grateful that I hadn't been given a gun instead of a pencil. Father had been right. I would have made a poor soldier.

We spent another night and a day resting and listening to the bombs exploding. Best of all, we enjoyed a hot meal. Compared with what we'd eaten along our journey, this felt like a banquet: cooked rice and canned food. We were waiting for clearance to continue on to Kaesong, the town near the thirty-eighth parallel where the first talks of a possible truce had taken place a year earlier.

When the line of military control shifted south of Kaesong, the UNC balked at meeting so far inside North Korean–controlled territory. The negotiation site was then moved a short distance away, to Panmunjom. Our living quarters and our offices would be in Kaesong.

With all the shelling, strafing, and bombing going on, our side was arranging the best way to get us across that shooting gallery in one piece. Finally, we had orders to move out. We climbed back on the truck, which was totally unprotected. We were "fair game" for the American fighter bombers.

When we traveled from Kaesong to Panmunjom, we had the yellow flag to protect us, but now we had to protect ourselves. The American pilots were notorious for shooting civilians and livestock just for fun, much as the Japanese had during the war. The wife of one of our top officers had been injured in just such an attack caused by a "stray" bomb.

The UNC commanders and their troops were greatly frustrated by our side's persistence in the face of this relentless shelling and bombing. Indeed, we were underequipped, poorly supplied, and underestimated. Early in the war, an American commander told his men, "Don't let a bunch of Chinese laundrymen stop you." Within days, our troops had forced his men in the First Battalion, Thirty-second Infantry, into its long retreat.

Our advantage was that there were many more of us and this fight was taking place on our doorstep, not half a world away. The new China was emerging to take its place on the world stage. The patriotic energy was high. Even the threat of a nuclear holocaust couldn't make our leaders tremble. In the tradition of Lenin, who dismissed imperialism as a "colossus with feet of clay," Mao added his own unique take on American military adventurism, one that still resonates. Asked in 1946 by the American Communist writer Anna Louise Strong, "Suppose the United States uses the atom bomb?" Mao replied:

The atom bomb is a paper tiger which the U.S. reactionaries use to scare people. It looks terrible, but in fact it isn't. Of course, the atom bomb is a weapon of mass slaughter, but the outcome of a war is decided by the people, not by one or two new types of weapon.

The war had cost our side enormous casualties and resources. (Chairman Mao had lost his most favored son, Mao Anying, killed in a bombing raid.) But we were hardly defenseless. Marshal Peng employed a terrifying tactic refined during years of combat against the Kuomintang's Western style of warfare. Our CPV troops went into action at night, sneaking up in large numbers on battalion-size enemy units, surrounding them, and then attacking with bugles blaring from the wrong directions to create panic and chaos. The CPV troops wiped out many UNC battalions this way, then quickly faded into the darkness to find another target. America may have been winning the body count, but the North Koreans and the Chinese had still managed to hold their ground.

As a result, the political wind in the United States was shifting. Americans were growing weary of an unwinnable war that had killed so many—more than fifty thousand war-related deaths, plus another one hundred thousand wounded. The UNC's so-called police action included small contingents from fifteen nations. British, Australian, Canadian, Dutch, and even Turkish troops fought under the U.S. commanders of the UNC forces, but the bulk of the manpower and firepower was American.

Now, after two years and a couple of million military and civilian deaths, the evolving border between North and South Korea was right where it had been at the start: the thirty-eighth parallel. That was a stunning accomplishment for our side.

It was an election year in the United States—1952—and the Korean conflict cost President Truman a second term. He dropped out of the race after the first primaries. The first order of business for whoever won that November would be to find a way to stop the bloodshed. I explained to my colleagues that this was probably why we had been summoned so suddenly: Truman no longer had anything to lose. We'd inflicted enough pain that the Americans were now looking for the least shameful way out of the mess they'd gotten themselves into.

It was a long, nerve-racking, bumpy ride to Kaesong through more shattered landscape. The road followed the rail line, a constant target of American planes. We finally arrived at a heavily guarded checkpoint and were directed into the protected zone. Both sides had agreed that this no-combat area would be set aside for our staff's living quarters. Our truck pulled up to an old Korean house at the foot of the hill.

An officer who had come with us jumped off the back of the truck. "This is it, comrades," he said. "Welcome to Kansas!"

CHAPTER 12

Two Years of Perfidy
and Fleas

Truce talks had been going on for almost a year by the time we arrived at what the Americans called "the Kansas Line"—the undulating, 115-mile-long battlefront bisecting the Korean peninsula from the Yellow Sea on the west to the Sea of Japan on the east. Along that line, the opposing forces faced each other in a grinding stalemate. Neither side could seriously budge the other, and for a while it was almost like the trench warfare of World War I. But eventually, with the superior armament of the UNC forces, our casualties greatly exceeded theirs.

In the distance, we heard the staccato bursts of machine-gun fire, and the muffled *whump* of bomb and shell concussions. These sounds became our constant companion; it was like living next to a busy railroad track or near an airport. Except for a few noisy ravens that scavenged an existence from the debris of battle, our neighborhood was a scorched, lifeless moonscape. But it was a safe zone, a place where the UNC had promised not to drop its bombs. Although we were on the battlefield, we were not in the battle.

The fighting raged in valleys and on mountaintops, each side trying to grasp or hold on to strategically important topography. It was a war of "active defense": neither side would give an inch because, if and when a truce was reached, the border would become permanent. Each side fought over every last clod of earth. And the blood continued to spill.

Our delegation of note-takers, typists, and interpreters had heard charges that the UNC coalition was violating agreements on neutral zones, the torture of POWs, coerced defections, firing on civilians, and the deliberate bombing of civilian targets. In one instance, the UNC air force had destroyed a dam, flooding local villages and drowning the peasants along with their livestock.

Of course, history has established that there were terrible atrocities on both sides. The basest instincts and prejudices of human nature drove the combatants to be equally pitiless in their determination to prevail.

The ferocity of the Korean War reflected the truth that it was really many conflicts rolled into one confined conflagration that leveled Korea and cost nearly four million lives. It began as a civil war pitting Korean against Korean. Without USSR backing, the North Koreans could not win. Without U.S. backing, the South could not defend itself. As a result, the United States was pitted against the USSR here, just as they already were in Europe. Next, the Chinese weighed in, adding two new conflicts: the United States versus China, plus the wider ideological conflict between the Communist and the non-Communist world.

With China involved, the war was extended into mainly a war between China and the U.S. The UNC recruited spies from the Kuomintang on Taiwan to cross over and infiltrate our troops; and the United States threatened to equip a Kuomintang army to throw against us in Korea. Meanwhile, using gunboat diplomacy, the United States blocked our national unification with Taiwan.

In order to combat Socialism in the Soviet Union and China, MacArthur pardoned Hirohito, the number one war criminal, and helped Japan's right-wing militarists. The United States was now the benevolent ally of Japan, China's cruel tormentor for more than a decade.

In all its complexity and cruelty, the Korean War churned in the near-distance, out of our sight as we established a work routine.

The first day, our delegation drove about thirty minutes, yellow diplomatic flag prominently displayed, to an encampment near the city of Panmunjom. A village of tents had been staked on this barren spot, which both sides had managed to agree was exactly on the line of military control.

Little Guo and I, two other interpreters (one Korean-to-Chinese and one Korean-to-English), and the leaders of our delegation patiently stood at the flaps on the north entrance to the negotiating tent, checking watches for the precise second the talks were to commence. At a signal from a guard standing off to the side, we marched in at the same moment that the UNC negotiators entered from the south.

This elaborate, bizarre script was acted out in complete silence, but for the faint thunder of artillery, the wind tugging at the tent flaps, and the scraping of shoes and chair legs on the wooden platform that kept us above the mud. No one said hello, commented on the weather, nodded, or made eye contact. No one uttered so much as a sigh or a burp as the dozen or so attendees took their assigned seats at long tables covered with green baize cloth.

As we took our positions, nothing—not even a pencil shaving or a bit of lint—could cross an imaginary line running down the middle of the main table. In that bubble of relative safety in the center of the battlefield ran a thin, invisible line. Here the world was now dividing itself into two bitterly opposed factions.

Our side was represented by several North Korean generals and Marshal Peng's chief of staff, with an aide. The North Korean general Nam Il held the status of delegation chief, and he usually spoke first for our side. This gave him face, a social concept highly valued among Asian cultures. It is a concept that Westerners—who place a high value on directness—often find maddening.

In this instance, face was given to the North Koreans because it was their fight. It was our social and diplomatic obligation to grant the North Koreans the dignity of speaking for their own country. Of course, their orders came directly from Mao by way of Marshal Peng, but the marshal did not appear at the negotiating table. As he was one of China's top military leaders (akin in stature and visibility to an Eisenhower, a Montgomery, or a Patton), Peng's presence would have overshadowed the North Koreans and given the Americans an excuse to pick a more public fight with China.

On the other side of the table, the United Nations Command (UNC) delegation was led by Lieutenant General William K. Harrison, a highly decorated, middle-aged West Point graduate whose swagger and imperious manner were unmistakably American. The South Korean representative was relegated to a secondary seat. The United States was running the show and clearly wanted us to know it and be intimidated.

Without notice or preamble, General Nam Il pulled out a sheet of paper and began to read a prepared statement in Korean. I listened to the English interpretation: "The Korean People's Army repeats the demands it has already made regarding the illegal occupation of territories belonging to the Democratic People's Republic of Korea, and the barbaric attacks on civilians by UNC aircraft. Furthermore . . ."

I was shocked to see Harrison roll his eyes. It reminded me of another American insult years ago in Yan'an, an incident that had become legendary among Chinese intellectuals and Party leaders. It had even been reported in the U.S. press in 1945. Major General Patrick J. Hurley, a back-slapping ex-cowboy and the U.S. ambassador to China at the time, literally dropped in on Mao's headquarters one day, ordering his plane to fly there and land without warning or invitation. Mao and the Communist leadership rushed out to the airfield, both offended and losing face because they'd been unable to prepare a dignified, ceremonial reception.

General Hurley left his most indelible impression when he came bounding out of his plane with a volley of Choctaw Indian war whoops. It had been an outrageous display of American hubris. This arrogance, along with other incidents, made it difficult for Mao to resist "leaning" toward the Soviet Union and away from the United States.

After the North Korean general delivered his short statement, our Major General Hsieh Fang, Marshal Peng's deputy, read a brief statement supporting General Nam Il's remarks. When he finished, General Harrison looked at his watch, scanned the faces of his delegation, threw up his hands in a gesture of exasperation, stood, and walked out, his entourage hot on his heels.

The entire session had lasted less than three minutes. Except for the date and the names of the participants, my notepad was empty. My first day on the job, and there had been no UNC remarks to record. Little Guo and I exchanged shrugs as we got up to leave. Then our side filed through the northern flap of the tent and climbed into our vehicles as a convoy of U.S. Army jeeps and other vehicles sped away in the opposite direction, throwing up clods of mud and a cloud of blue smoke.

For the next two years, I lived and worked within this narrow world. Two confined plots of land were separated by a long, narrow road, from which none of our delegation ever dared stray for fear of being shot at or stepping on a mine. At the northern end, near Kaesong, was our living compound—a barracks of bunk beds, tables, stools, and a modest kitchen in which to prepare our meals. The outhouse was a good old squatter.

In the open yard around this and the other buildings in our compound—our offices, officers' quarters, communications shack, guard quarters, and so on—was a basketball net on a wooden pole. I had hated basketball as a youngster, but as an adult I was patient enough to be a good spectator.

That first spring and summer, our barracks became infested with voracious fleas. When the fleas were resting, giant mosquitoes took over. They were so determined and their bite so uncomfortable, we called them "American B-29s." We slept under mosquito netting. This kept most of the B-29s out, but was no impediment to the fleas.

I seemed to be the most popular item on the insect menu, because among my barracks mates I woke each morning with the greatest number of welts. I took to sleeping with my shirt and long underwear tightly buttoned, long stockings pulled over my hands and arms, and over my feet and up my legs. On oppressively humid summer nights, it was the lesser of two evils: sweating profusely was preferable to being pricked all over by the ravenous little bloodsuckers. Still, I'd wake in the morning with my neck and face blotchy with bite marks.

The fleas even accompanied us to the negotiating table. One day, as the delegate of the Korean People's Army stood up and began to make a speech, a flea, having completed its feast, crawled out from my jacket onto the cuff of my shirtsleeve. What to do? It would have been unseemly to make a sudden move and slap my wrist in an effort to catch it. But it would be almost as embarrassing—a loss of face—to be seen as a person crawling with vermin.

The flea sat there. I stared at it, trying to avoid drawing attention to myself. The UNC note-taker across the table shifted slightly and I realized that he'd spotted it, too. I avoided eye contact—we underlings always did—but I felt a flicker of a connection, a shared moment of absurdity.

I flinched when, in flagrant violation of the line of control and in breach of international agreements between the combatants, the flea jumped to the other side of the table. The UNC note-taker shied slightly—no fleas for him, thank you! I fought a smile as nearby heads turned to see what was going on, then returned their attention to the speaker.

That night in the barracks, I acquired a nickname: Flea. It was a joke on two levels: I was one of the tallest people in China, and *flea* in Chinese also means "minuscule."

One of the oddest experiences at the conference table was the day I sat down in my usual seat and looked across into the Chinese face of one of my acquaintances from Harvard. I recalled that Richard Liu had been a Nationalist, opposed to the Communist Party, but he had not been especially political. I caught a sideways glimpse of recognition in his eyes, but we both did our inscrutable best to pretend that we'd never met. I took some pride in observing that he wore the insignia of a mere private first class, whereas I was a warrant officer. Not bad for a Harvard dropout!

The UNC side had the latest wire-recording equipment, and offered to have their staff type up the official transcript. We objected and chose instead to create our own transcripts. It was a challenge to keep up, so we sent to Beijing for copies of Gregg's Shorthand guide and spent our spare time learning how to use it. Little Guo and I competed to see who was faster. At my peak, I cranked out 165 words a minute.

Actual face-to-face negotiations rarely lasted more than an hour. There were often recesses of a few days or sometimes weeks. Much of my work time was taken up with typing and editing statements in English, studying Chinese, and helping my colleagues do their work. Even when the principal negotiators were in recess, lower-ranking liaison groups met to discuss details.

The dominant topic in the talks was the handling of prisoners, assuming an armistice was signed. The UNC negotiators claimed that they wanted to give every North Korean POW the option to stay in the South,

and every Chinese POW the choice to go to Taiwan with the Nationalists. Furthermore, they maintained that the majority of those prisoners
did not want to be repatriated.

We knew from spies that there had been protest riots in the POW
camps in the South, which held more than 120,000 Communist
troops. We also knew that the UNC and the United States in particular were coercing defections, conscripting prisoners to wear enemy
uniforms and serve as cannon fodder. They were doing whatever it
took to discourage these men from returning to their home countries.
We insisted on full and, if necessary, forced repatriation of all POWs.

There was merit to the UNC argument that some Chinese and
North Korean soldiers wanted to defect. It was regarded as shameful to
have been captured alive rather than fighting to the death. Many repatriated Chinese soldiers were, in the end, discriminated against. But our
position was that they must all be repatriated. Any defectors would
surely end up helping the Kuomintang.

When there were actual discussions, I'd furiously scribble my shorthand notes, trying to keep up when General Harrison or another English speaker strayed from his script and began to speak very rapidly,
usually in anger. Often, the tenor of the negotiations sank to school-
yard level.

One day General Nam Il delivered this diatribe regarding a UNC
proposal that UNC personnel be allowed to conduct "screening" interviews with each and every POW before they were repatriated:

> As long as your side does not change this peremptory attitude and
> give up your unreasonable proposal, our side will continue to ex-
> pose at these conferences the absurdity of your proposal. Since you
> are insisting upon your absurd proposition, you will not be able to
> escape the inevitable consequences of your such [sic] insistence. The
> so-called screening is totally absurd and impermissible. The so-
> called result of your so-called screening is doubly absurd and wholly
> concocted by your side. The commandant of your prisoner-of-war
> camp has already declared to the whole world the utter bankruptcy
> of your proposition.

We needed to expand our vocabulary of insults. Our crew of language experts sat down with an American dictionary to see if we could unearth some fresh inflammatory words. Both sides were constantly accusing each other of lying about something—a stray bomb, a troop incursion, pressuring POWs to defect. Our side had used *liar* and *lying* so many times that the words had lost their punch.

Finally, we found a word that was fully loaded with righteous outrage. The UNC, we told our negotiators, was guilty of perfidy and perfidious behavior. "It means treachery and faithlessness," we explained. They were delighted.

The constant theme throughout was land: "This mountaintop belongs to us!" "No, it belongs to *us*." These talks involved detailed maps and discussions about such matters as whether the line of control should be drawn on this side of one big pointy rock or on the other.

Meanwhile, the fighting drove the negotiations, and the negotiations drove the fighting. One day, the line was established in one area; the next day, one side or the other argued for moving it on the basis of the previous night's combat results. It was the darkest of farces, remarkably similar to the World War I–style trench warfare of attrition and nerves.

The two sides were equally entrenched at the negotiating table, with each side feinting and dissembling for psychological advantage. Incredibly, there were even occasions when both sides would enter, take their assigned seats, and sit in absolute silence. These sessions might last as long as a half hour, until one side or the other had had enough and rose to leave. Then everyone jumped up and exited simultaneously. All this without a single word being uttered! I couldn't even doodle to pass the time, for fear that it would be misinterpreted as some sort of signal.

One night after the day's work, my colleagues and I were lounging around the office speculating about the next day's discussions. We were betting that, because the line of control had shifted against the UNC, General Harrison would find an excuse to stomp out in a fit of indignation.

"We could have some fun," someone suggested. "If Harrison does walk out, as soon as he leaves we should all laugh as hard and loud as we can. The reporters and other UNC staff outside will hear and assume Harrison has said something very stupid and lost face."

We all agreed and received permission from our superiors to put the plan in action. That night we sat around the barracks practicing a few rounds of the heartiest, most disrespectful laughter we could muster.

Sure enough, the next day the talks had barely begun when Harrison, who had the annoying habit of whistling, sighing loudly, or drumming his fingers while waiting for the interpreters, took great offense over a minor point. He jumped up and stalked out. As the last of his staff disappeared through the door, we all looked at one another with grins and let loose a gale of howling. Like a gang of mischievous schoolboys who'd pulled off a daring prank, we noisily congratulated ourselves all the way back to Kaesong.

When I first arrived in Korea, I had the foolish notion that peace was just around the corner. We had been summoned to the resumption of stalled armistice talks near the end of April 1952. As the summer dragged on, the fighting continued and the bombs ceaselessly rained across North Korea. We were in for a long stay.

After the armistice agreement was signed, a ceasefire came into effect. The two sides agreed to hold a meeting at Panmunjom to discuss convening the political level meeting. On our side were the Korean and Chinese representatives, China represented by Huang Hua.

But the Panmunjom talks soon broke down. At first, Arthur Dean, the American representative, was willing to consider our proposal, but he later backed down, angering our representative. In English, Huang Hua condemned the American side, declaring it "guilty of perfidy." Flying into a rage, Dean demanded that Huang Hua withdraw the word "perfidy." Huang Hua refused and again and again condemned Dean: "You are perfidious." A furious Dean shouted, "You are just a bunch of common criminals!" He stood up and stormed out of the tent. That marked the conclusion of this stage of negotiation at Panmunjom.

Without revealing details of my work, I sent an occasional note to my father, to assure him that I was well. These security precautions were anything but routine. North Korea was swarming with spies. Kidnappings and assassinations were common. From time to time, we were summoned to interpret and take notes at the site of alleged violations of designated safe zones. The entire route from our living compound in Kaesong to the talks in Panmunjom was a noncombat corridor: no bombing or strafing allowed. This afforded our staff, diplomats, and supply trucks safe passage back and forth. According to the agreement, we had to fly a yellow flag and wear a yellow armband.

There was also a demilitarized zone around the Panmunjom negotiating village. One day, one of our guards reported that an American shell had landed inside the zone. We lodged a complaint, the Americans called us liars, we accused the Americans of perfidy, and an on-site inspection was ordered. I tagged along with notepad and pencil.

Six of us tramped across a rubble field and approached the shell hole, its edge mounded with churned earth. "Look at that crater," our officer said. "We don't have any shells that could make such a large hole. And see the direction of the debris? It scattered north, so the shell must have come from the south."

The Americans refused to acknowledge responsibility, insisting that it wasn't theirs. "How do we know you didn't drag that thing over here from somewhere else and dig a hole around it?" they said.

While the two sides were bickering, I leaned over and looked into the hole. The full, undamaged casing was there, pointing skyward. The shell had failed to detonate. The nose was buried in the earth, but there was enough of the casing exposed that I could see some markings in white.

"There's an unexploded shell in there," I declared in my booming voice. The arguing stopped midsentence and every head turned to face me. Then they all took several steps back. "It has some sort of markings on it."

Without a second thought, I jumped into the crater and slid to the bottom. "Little Ji!" my colleagues cried out.

I squinted through my glasses and carefully copied down the serial number and other stenciled markings, which were in English— indisputably American. I clambered back up and presented the page in my notebook to the American officer in charge. He looked at it and scowled. "Well . . . accidents happen!" he said. "Whaddaya expect? This is war, after all. Nobody got hurt."

On the ride back to our compound in Kaesong, I received much back pounding for my bravery. I enjoyed the attention, but it had been nothing more than an instinctive reaction. Perhaps if I had been married and a father, I might have hesitated. Instead, I had felt more outrage at the Americans' denial of the plain truth than I did concern for my own safety.

Jumping into that crater made me stand out, and it made me feel tall—perhaps even a bit too tall. A high-ranking Foreign Ministry official—an aging general near retirement—had joined our little family in the Kaesong compound. He had been sent personally by Chairman Mao to be the hand in the puppet at the negotiating table. Just as we never doubted that General Harrison got his orders through the chain of command from the highest level—President Eisenhower—the North Korean and Chinese delegates never strayed from their script, which was invariably written in Beijing.

One warm day, lounging on the steps of our barracks, I noticed Chairman Mao's man relaxing with one of our high-ranking negotiators. They sat in a pair of folding chairs outside a hut. Overcome by curiosity, I walked right up to them without thinking. Both generals had always treated me cordially. And while in the new China rank mattered, it did not in a formal way, and even less so in the forced intimacy of our cloistered compound.

The senior of the two, Mao's designate, turned at the sound of my footsteps and shot me a dark, glowering look. "Little Ji, take a walk," he snapped.

I wheeled about and slunk away, red-faced, chastising myself for being so presumptuous and indiscreet. I had become too big for my britches. This would not be the last time my American side showed itself—the side that inspired me to picket a restaurant in Boston that refused to hire blacks, and the side that felt completely safe expressing my anti-capitalist rhetoric in a capitalist society. In addition to learning to speak Chinese, I also had to learn to be Chinese.

With the onset of winter, the mosquitoes and fleas were extinguished by a biting, subzero cold sweeping down from the Arctic, across Siberia and Manchuria, and roaring off the rugged slopes of the Korean mountains. Our office had a wood-burning stove, but the barracks were unheated. We crawled into our bedding at night fully dressed, padded cotton hats pulled down over our ears. Still, some men woke up with telltale white spots of frostbite on the tips of their noses. Bathing was out of the question. In winter we ripened, waiting for spring so we'd again be able to wash in the nearby stream.

Far away, back in my America, the political debate over Korea had dominated the 1952 presidential elections. General Eisenhower, the Republican candidate, declared in a Detroit, Michigan, campaign speech that, if elected, "I shall go to Korea. . . . One word shouts denial to those who foolishly pretend that ours is not a nation at war. This fact, this tragedy, this word is: Korea." Eisenhower railed against "godless Communism," which "strikes at the jugular vein of freedom."

We received this news after Eisenhower defeated Adlai Stevenson. But the president-elect's statements promising no appeasement suggested that the Americans were determined to keep fighting. He promised to beef up the South Korean army and to use psychological warfare as "a weapon capable of cracking the Communist front."

"Pure reactionary rhetoric," I assured my colleagues. We knew, better than most, that there was no such thing as a Communist front. The only "front" was the enormous, atom-bomb-equipped U.S. military presence arrayed on more than a dozen bases in a sweeping, three-thousand-mile arc facing our eastern coast.

From its bases in the Philippines, Taiwan, South Korea, and the Japanese Islands, the United States was in a position to interfere with all maritime traffic into and out of China's ports. Its superior air force was no more than an hour or two of flying time from our capital and other potential targets. The United States could easily do to us what it had done to the Japanese at Hiroshima and Nagasaki.

I could not explain to myself, let alone to my comrades, how the Americans could, in good conscience, look at a map and not see that the Chinese were merely defending our borders. We were not possessed by some ideological mission to dominate the world.

The new Eisenhower administration's first attempt at psychological warfare was to encourage speculation in the U.S. press about a naval blockade, bombing our new airfields in Manchuria, rebuilding South

Korea's army, and allowing Kuomintang forces on Taiwan to conduct hit-and-run raids along our coast. Detailed maps explaining all the trouble the United States could cause China appeared in newspapers around the world.

In the end, it was the last option that Eisenhower chose. In his first State of the Union address to the U.S. Congress in February 1953, the new president announced that the American Seventh Fleet, patrolling the Taiwan Strait, would now stand idle if Chiang's troops tried to attack the mainland. The U.S. policy would be to "use" the Kuomintang to harass the People's Republic.

On Radio Peking, the government announced, "Staggering under the deadly blows by the people's forces in Korea, American aggressors now cast their hopes on the miserable mob ousted from the Chinese mainland." The broadcast predicted that U.S. support of the Chiang regime would one day prove to be "a millstone around the neck."

Eisenhower's announcement produced hearty laughter in our barracks. "What can a few thousand corrupt and lazy reactionaries, who ran away after stealing our treasury, do against half a billion Chinese?" Little Guo asked. "Even the mighty American paper tiger couldn't defeat us. Your Americans are either stupid or crazy or both!"

It was true. I never spoke of it, but the dichotomy between my experiences in the States and what I now confronted at the negotiating table in Panmunjom was never far from my mind. It was always incomprehensible. Just a decade earlier, Father had been on the payroll of the U.S. Office of War Information. His 1942 income statement from the U.S. Treasury showed he'd earned $1,323.43 writing and publishing articles encouraging Chinese support for the anti-Japanese cause.

The people of America had paid for my excellent education. I'd sat in the kitchen of a First Lady, eating her cookies. I'd sat in a darkened Manhattan theater full of Americans and felt their love for the China represented on-screen by my father's kindly old face. My childhood was filled with warm memories of Americans from the day the immigration officer pinched my cheek when we arrived in New York aboard the *Aquitania*. Except when someone mistook me for a black man, I'd felt nothing but the embrace of acceptance and protection.

Now I was on the side that was maiming and killing as many Americans as possible.

Fortunately, I had little time to ruminate. My work was simple enough, but the load was heavy. There were no weekends or days off. It was common to work through the night to grind out translations, type up transcripts, and handle other documents incoming from Beijing, or communications back to the capital.

After many setbacks and detours, an armistice agreement was quietly reached. I had become the number-one typist in our group, the fastest and most accurate on our old, manual typewriters, so I was appointed to type up the final English drafts. Everything was being conducted in complete secrecy by both sides. A signing ceremony was set for July 27, 1953. The fighting continued all the while, as each side tried to grab or retain a few more yards.

The agreement was to be prepared in Chinese, Korean, and English, all copies and originals to be signed—no carbons. The documents had to be absolutely perfect, without a single typographical error or eraser mark. When I mistyped a single letter, the entire page was torn up and I started over.

Right up to the last minute, the two sides quarreled over words and punctuation. Every detail had to be translated in such a way that the meaning was the same in all three languages. As I finished typing a draft, I'd get back several revised pages to be retyped. This happened repeatedly. There was a great rush to meet the deadline, to leave no time for some incident or mischief to complicate matters and cause a delay.

The more exhausted I became, the more typos I made. Finally, after three sleepless days and nights, fighting off the mosquitoes while banging away at my desk, having my meals brought to me and getting up only to stretch or go to the toilet, the task was completed on time.

I collapsed on my bunk and fell into a deep sleep. When I woke at lunchtime, instead of the martial music that always played over the camp's loudspeakers at mealtime, the tune was "The Winds of Peace Are Blowing." Outside, there was shouting and clapping. No one needed a clearer signal that the end of the killing was at hand.

July 27, 1953, was a day to remember. We were driven to Panmunjom for the ceremonial signing of the armistice agreement. On the way, we crossed newly built bridges named Bridge of Peace and Bridge of Victory. Signs telling when the bridges had been built were written in both Korean and Chinese. Entering the hall in Panmunjom, I saw the flag of the Democratic People's Republic of Korea and the flag of the United Nations on both sides. At ten o'clock that morning, General Nam Il and General William K. Harrison entered, signed eighteen copies of the Korean War Armistice Agreement (in ten minutes), and withdrew. That same day at other locations, Korea's marshal Kim Il Sung, the great CPV general marshal Peng Dehuai, and American general Mark Clark also signed the agreement.

Marshal Peng declared, "This is a happy day for our people."

General Clark's public statement acknowledged without saying it the folly of the American adventure in Korea: "I cannot find it in me to exult in this hour. Rather, it is time for prayer, that we may succeed in our difficult endeavor to turn this armistice to the advantage of mankind."

What was supposed to be a swift and decisive American military adventure turned into a fruitless bloodbath. By its end, there was little public support for the Korean War in the United States. The State Department got most of the blame, along with being accused by Senator Joseph McCarthy of being infiltrated by Commies who "lost" to China on purpose.

President Eisenhower once again gave us Chinese something to chuckle about. In his statement, he praised the American puppet, South Korea's President Syngman Rhee, who, like Chiang Kai-shek, had proved to be a cruel, incompetent, and corrupt leader. "Inspired by President Syngman Rhee," Eisenhower declared, "[the South Koreans] have given an example of courage and patriotism which again demonstrates that men of the East and men of the West can fight and work and live side by side in pursuit of a just and noble cause."

A month later, Mao issued his proclamation:

The U.S. imperialists are very arrogant; if at all possible, they always refuse to talk reason, and will do so after a fashion only when driven into a tight corner. . . . [A] new imperialist war of aggression against China and a third world war have been put off.

The imperialist aggressors ought to bear this in mind: the Chinese people are now organized, they are not to be trifled with. Once they are provoked to anger, things can get very tough. . . . Are we going to invade others? No, we will invade no one anywhere. But if others invade us, we will fight back and fight to a finish.

CHAPTER 13

Foreign Devils Face Off

The shooting stopped, but the talking continued. I remained at Kaesong as the conflict slowly wound down. Once the excitement surrounding the end of hostilities dissipated, the work became more routine. I kept at my Chinese studies and looked forward to my return home.

The experience had transformed me from a clumsy, Chinese-challenged university student on the science-doctorate track into a member of China's foreign-policy apparatus, a low-level cadre in the Foreign Ministry. I had studied hard and could now actually read the *People's Daily*. I had participated in one of the seminal events in China's new history, and been a witness to the devastation of war.

The high point of my time in Korea, and one of the proudest moments of my career, was when I stood at attention to have a medal for bravery pinned to my tunic. I may have been the only Foreign Ministry cadre to be honored with a combat-related citation. On a sunny winter day in January 1954, in our compound in Kaesong, our entire delegation held a solemn ceremony to decorate those who had made exceptional contributions to the success of the armistice negotiations.

I was awarded the Third Order of Merit from the Chinese People's Volunteers for jumping into that crater with the live shell to expose the Americans' perfidy. As proud as I was of my work at the negotiating table, transforming all that shorthand into flawless official documents and being praised as "the number-one stenographer" of the PRC, nothing could top having tempted fate on the battlefield.

The armistice agreement called for a peace conference in Geneva in 1954 to settle the Korea question once and for all. A commission would then oversee compliance with that agreement. Our discussions now were in preparation for the Geneva talks.

Our nation was rebuilding itself around Mao's concept of a "people's democratic dictatorship," so expressing personal ambition was frowned on. But I was ambitious. When I returned to Beijing, I hoped to finish my degree thesis and apply to graduate school. I wanted someday to work on the atomic bomb. As a dutiful member of the New Democratic Youth League—the student arm of the Communist Party—I was expected to suppress my personal goals and devote myself to serving the people. I was eager to be accepted as a member of the Party, a process that required a formal application, close scrutiny, and connections. Everything I said and did would be examined, so I kept my aspirations to myself.

After nearly two years in Korea—with no time off and never leaving the confines of Kaesong, Panmunjom, and the road in between—I had grown weary and homesick. From time to time, the Foreign Ministry in Beijing would send us a newsreel to watch, and Chinese opera troupes occasionally came through to put on a performance. But there were no trips into town (no town had been left standing), no hikes in the hills, not even a noodle shop where one could go and have a snack. Although the battlefield had fallen silent, snipers and assassins from the South were known to slip across the border to pick off a stray Chinese or North Korean officer. My dreams began to include the rumblings of the train heading home to Beijing.

At about the time Kaesong began to feel like a prison, I heard the words I'd been hoping for: "Pack your things. You're going home." With my meager possessions of books and threadbare clothing—and, no doubt, a few fleas along for the ride—I made the reverse journey. As much destruction as I'd observed on the way down, the trip back revealed that three years of U.S. bombardment had reduced North Korea to a pockmarked rubblescape. The dazed, slow-moving survivors lived in the worst state of poverty. Every inch seemed to have been churned by bombs and shells. The craters had craters.

Crossing the Yalu River into Manchuria and onto Chinese soil, I didn't kiss the earth as I had on arriving in Canton from New York, but I certainly felt like it. After a long, hard-seater train ride from Dandong, I arrived back in Beijing and rejoined some co-workers who'd preceded me home. My new home was in an apartment block where all Foreign Ministry employees lived.

I happily discovered that in my absence Tsinghua had awarded me my undergraduate degree. I was overjoyed to learn that I had been assigned to the Institute of Modern Physics, where the atomic-bomb project was being developed. I immediately went to my Foreign Ministry superiors to request permission to accept my new assignment.

The director of the Ministry's general office smiled at me and said, "Little Ji, why don't you stay with us and do some chemical diplomacy?"

"Chemical diplomacy?"

"Geneva. We are sending you to Geneva for the peace talks."

I would have to put my academic goals on hold again, but I was excited at the prospect of traveling to Switzerland and seeing more of the world.

Soon after I arrived from Korea, my parents returned to Beijing from a trip to visit Taiyuan, the Shanxi Province capital where I had spent most of my childhood. I saw them for the first time in two years at their apartment on Beichizi Street.

"Wah! What happened to you?" Mother cried out. "You are so skinny! Didn't they feed you in Korea? Come and sit down while I make you some noodles." No matter how grown up or how tall, I would always be her sickly little boy. It was a great comfort to be back in the family bosom.

When I showed Father my merit citation, he broke into a proud, nearly toothless grin. We had a good laugh about how I'd earned it. "I said you'd make a poor soldier, Wah. I was right. Brave or foolish, you survived in spite of yourself," he said. "I see you with new eyes," he added, an idiom for respect.

My parents discreetly avoided inquiring about the details of my work, but they were eager to hear about the conditions in Kaesong:

what I ate, where I slept, and so on. I told them how I'd earned my new nickname and warned that some fleas might have come back with me.

My father said the entire city turned out at Tiananmen Gate to celebrate the signing of the armistice. In its first test on the international stage, the People's Republic had proved itself tough and determined. "The price was very high," my father said. "But I do think no one will try to bully us again."

Father said he had removed a few personal belongings from our old homes in Taiyuan and Fenyang and then turned all his properties over to local Party officials to be used as they saw fit. In Fenyang, our ancestral villa was now providing shelter for several families and their livestock, with granaries to store the harvests. He had relinquished ownership of all seven of his houses and all his croplands.

This had been both a noble gesture and a practical matter. In villages across the country, some of the old landlords had been forced to submit to public humiliation in the form of mass struggle meetings at which they were paraded before a mob of angry farmers shouting epithets. Some of these meetings turned violent and landlords were beaten and even killed.

My father happily reported that our family was still held in esteem in Fenyang, where my grandfather's generosity during bad crop years was legendary. During drought years, Grandfather had reduced or waived his crop shares. When there had been nothing left to eat, he opened his granaries to anyone in need.

Mao's first mass movement, the term for a societywide call for action, had been a sweeping land-redistribution program that included setting up rural farm collectives. My father's holdings would eventually have been parceled out anyway. "This way, it was a peaceful revolution in Fenyang," he explained. "I managed to keep my head and our family honor."

Several days later, we Jis gathered for a midday reunion meal, including my sister, my sister-in-law, her adolescent son, and Chaoding, who was now secretary-general of the Council for Promotion of International Trade. Chaoding never spoke about the specifics of his work, but he was vocal about his frustration with the radicals in the Party.

In his writings, Mao had embraced dialectical materialism,* but he respected money and understood the profit motive. After all, the Communist revolution had been financed in part by donations from Chinese capitalists, both at home and abroad.

Mao and the premier were eager to grow China's economy, but the country had insufficient manufacturing and agricultural bases on which to build, and was dependent on handout loans from the USSR. The only way to grow was through foreign trade.

The premier relied on my brother's international reputation and his expertise in finance. But a conflict was brewing in the Party over philosophy. Chaoding stood with his boss, Finance Minister Bo Yibo, who was in favor of allowing some capitalistic activity and giving equal tax treatment to state and private companies. But Mao accused Bo of being seduced by bourgeois ideas. Such thinking, the chairman declared, was "right-opportunist deviation" that would take China down the capitalist road, away from the socialist future he envisioned.

In the same way that Chaoding had straddled the divide between Communist and Kuomintang, he now straddled the divide between radical (and suspicious) Communist Party leaders and the real world of international business. On the one hand, he had to persuade the radicals that the People's Republic must make concessions to the capitalist world in order to achieve economic growth; on the other, he had to persuade potential trading partners that the new China would play by the rules and respect foreign investment. Chaoding courted further controversy by advocating for a vigorous merchant class. He felt that the professionals and petty bourgeoisie shopkeepers were vital to establishing a healthy economy.

Then came the revelation that two high-ranking officials responsible for supplying the Chinese People's Volunteer Army in Korea had embezzled enormous sums of money. One of the chief reasons the Kuo-

---

*Dialectical materialism was the Soviet-Marxist theory that social conflict caused by material need drives historical events (*The Oxford Dictionary of Phrase and Fable*, 2nd ed., 2005). In one of his major works, "On Contradictions," Mao argued that social conflict came from the natural human desire to rise above the masses, and that it was the greatest obstacle to achieving a classless "dictatorship" of the people. Cadres (officials and government workers) were always being challenged to identify, self-criticize, and "correct" our ambitious, reactionary thoughts and deeds.

mintang had failed to win the hearts of the Chinese people was the discovery of rampant corruption among its leadership. The discovery unleashed a mass movement within the Communist Party to purge the guilty. One of my colleagues had been present when a cadre, who had been accused of corruption, jumped to his death from the roof of the Foreign Ministry. Mao encouraged social conflict and struggle—endless vigilance and revolution in the service of equality. But social conflict, Chaoding complained, could not put food on the table.

"The Party wants me to recruit only people who are politically reliable and have no thoughts of their own," Chaoding groused to my father and me after dinner one evening. "I need professionals with business degrees and experience, but they all have complicated biographies from studying abroad, or having relatives on Taiwan, or some other political dirt. No one has clean hands," he said, showing his palms.

"The new China still smells of mother's milk," Father replied. "In time, things will sort themselves out."

After dinner we all walked to a nearby photography studio and posed for a family portrait. I held my Third Order of Merit certificate and proudly wore the medals awarded for my Korean service.

Now that I was approaching my twenty-fifth birthday, a veteran of nearly two years on the front line of diplomacy, it was time I graduated from the Communist Youth League to full Party membership. I visited the Party secretary at the Foreign Ministry and received the application instructions. I was required to write an essay—in Chinese, of course—explaining my interest and my grasp of the Party's philosophy. The essay would be critiqued, and my loyalty and commitment to the cause would be thoroughly investigated.

The process had been described for me by some older colleagues in Korea. "You will be challenged and criticized," I was told. "You will be asked to write a self-criticism as well, because no one is free of shortcomings. You will have to explain why and how you have come from a long stay in a capitalist country, where the guiding philosophy is 'serve one's self,' to embrace the Communist philosophy to 'serve the people.' You will be challenged about your American education and whether it left you with reactionary ideas."

Unlike fleas from Korea, reactionary thoughts had not traveled with me from America. If anything, my life among the imperialists had stoked my revolutionary idealism. I never lost my love for America and its people. But, having lived there, I also understood that the United States had imperialistic instincts, and I was appalled by the anti-Red hysteria used by politicians to demonize our young government.

My "incorrect" thinking was limited to an innate sense of self-importance. I had been the spoiled brat of a wealthy provincial official and no matter how loyal to Mao's philosophy I had become, no matter how devoted to the dictatorship of the people, I retained a feeling of inevitability about my future. I had no doubt that I would be accepted into the Party, and total confidence that I had a bright future. My personal struggle for many years would be these twin urges: to stand out from the crowd, and to succeed through diligence, like my father's proverbial ant. The role demanded by the Party was that of a cog in the great machinery of revolution and nation-building. Ambition was anti-revolutionary.

As a cog, I now enjoyed the spartan privileges of government housing, meals, and clothing. I lived in an apartment building designated for Foreign Ministry employees. My dormitory-style room housed about twenty other single young men, all of whom observed the ancient and repulsive Chinese habit of frequently spitting on the floor. About this practice I was decidedly reactionary. Hawking phlegm and spitting on the ground, inside or out, was common. It disgusted me. But I kept these complaints to myself.

Sleeping arrangements were equally crude. We shared one long wooden platform made of planks laid on stools. There was a stove for warmth, and no fleas or mosquitoes.

The food was a bit better than it had been at Tsinghua. The cafeteria was equipped with such luxuries as tables and chairs, so we could sit and dine in a more leisurely fashion. I had since exchanged my shabby clothing from Korea for a new blue Mao tunic and trousers, and a pair of cloth shoes with padded soles. This was the uniform of China, at least in the cities and certainly for cadres.

But it wouldn't do for our delegation to show up in Geneva looking like a lost patrol from the People's Liberation Army. I was afforded the rare privilege of being sent to a tailor to be fitted for a simple Western-style suit, two white dress shirts, and a pair of leather shoes. The tailor was perturbed when I walked in. "Too tall, too tall," he muttered through needle-clenching teeth as he measured. "Too much cloth. How will I explain using up so much cloth? I have never seen such a tall Chinese man!"

In mid-April 1954, on departure day, I joined my colleagues at the Beijing train station to begin our weeklong, cross-Asia trek to Moscow. Then, on to Prague, Czechoslovakia, where we would catch a plane for the last leg of the trip into Switzerland. Our party included two of my three best friends from Korea, Yang Guanchun and Qiu Yiunjue. Together, the three of us (plus Little Guo) became the Three Musketeers. I was the fourth: D'Artagnan. This time Little Kuo stayed behind. We would serve as note-takers, translators, and typists—the lowest of the low.

With us were the Pu brothers, two Chinese academics I'd met at Harvard—Pu Shan and his older brother, Pu Shouchang. The brothers knew Chaoding well. One had returned to China just ahead of me in 1950, the other a year later. Both brothers were veteran Communist Party members, and both had earned their Ph.D.'s in economics at Harvard. To this day I have the greatest reverence, respect, and love for them and their families, for at Harvard they were the ones who had recruited me into the community of Chinese Communists and Mao Zedong's writings.

In the United States, the Pu brothers had played important roles in whipping up support for the Chinese Communist Party among overseas Chinese. They were also instrumental in convincing American politicians that Chiang's Kuomintang government was so corrupt that it was undeserving of continued U.S. financial and military support. Their lobbying efforts helped undermine Chiang and hastened the exile of the Kuomintang from the mainland.

Like me, the Pu brothers were fluent in English. Unlike me, they were also fluent in Chinese, written and spoken. Dr. Pu Shouchang had been selected as principal English interpreter for Premier Zhou Enlai. He would be the premier's shadow throughout our stay in Switzerland.

The train headed north from Beijing across the border into the USSR, where we connected with a luxury sleeper on the Trans-Siberian Railroad. I expected our Russian pals to greet us with warm Commie embraces and pat us heroic Chinese on the back for our great success in teaching the imperialists a lesson in Korea, but they were gruff and aloof. They barely acknowledged us.

Compared with my two younger co-workers, I was quite the world traveler, having been to Vietnam, France, and the United States. Nevertheless, I was smitten with Prague's fairy-tale architecture and romantic setting, and with the genuine warmth shown us by the Czechs. Some of our compatriots who had never set foot outside China were goggle-eyed tourists, and childlike in their excitement at taking an airplane for the first time.

As exotic as Prague had been, Geneva's luxury was dazzling, especially for those in our group who had never been abroad. They stared slack-jawed at women in tea shops draped in fur-lined coats and sporting feathered hats, at store windows glittering with jeweled watches and chocolate confections wrapped in gold foil on display in velvet-lined boxes.

"But where are the peasants?" one asked.

I laughed at his innocence. We felt like peasants. "There are no peasants here," I said. "This is a land of the capitalists. Everyone is rich."

We were the poorest bunch of ragamuffins in all Geneva. We had been given little more than spare change when we left Beijing. In Geneva, the embassy staff had rented us a sparsely furnished house with a kitchen where we cooked for ourselves. No one could say how long these talks would last, but we expected to be busy. Foreign leaders were coming from the major nations—the United States, the USSR, France, Great Britain—as well as North and South Korea, Vietnam, and other South Asian states, like Laos and Cambodia, that had a stake in the outcome.

I looked forward to the work ahead. Great events were about to unfold before my eyes. And, for the first time, I would see in person Zhou Enlai, Chaoding's mentor and the man who, by sending our family to New York in 1939, had set me on my life's path. It seemed natural for me to serve the premier, even in my small, insignificant role.

On our journey to Geneva, I was able to find the occasional English-language newspaper and read that the United States and China had been exchanging more heated words. The U.S. press made much of the fact that Premier Zhou had "close contacts with the Soviet Union." This was more of the same propaganda that U.S. politicians were spouting to support the notion that a united Communist front threatened the world.

Meanwhile, Radio Peking accused the Americans of interfering in Indochinese affairs and trying to "shackle" its allies Britain and France into helping the United States "set up a bridgehead in the neighborhood of China in order to attack the Chinese People's Republic." Considering the American fiasco in Korea, I knew the United States had no stomach for another war. But the so-called Great Powers did have an interest in keeping China weak, much as they had for the century leading to World War II. Geneva would be the first time the United States and the People's Republic formally met face-to-face, each regarding the other as a nation of foreign devils.

The conference took place in the stately Palais des Nations, which had been the home of the League of Nations after World War I. The first day we arrived, we were overwhelmed by the anxious mob of reporters and cameramen waiting outside the entrance. Accustomed to the habits and propaganda of the Big Four—the United States, the USSR, Britain, and France—the world was eager to see what we foreign devils looked like without daggers in our teeth.

The premier and his top deputies wore simple Mao suits, which confused the reporters and photographers. "Which one's the head honcho?" they said. "You know, what's-his-name?" A reporter pointed at one of our note-takers as we mounted the steps, shouting, "Hey, is that him? Get his picture, just in case!"

The talks were to take place in an enormous, ornate hall at a large semicircular table. Just outside was a spacious lounge where the delegates could relax and have a smoke or something to drink before sessions and during breaks. Here, for the first time, the highest-ranking foreign-policy officials of the largest and most powerful nations in the world stood with their aides, waiting for the doors to open to begin the conference.

Once I'd located my seat in the conference room, set far behind the seats designed for our delegates, I had no business in the lounge. But that did not mean I wasn't curious, so I slipped through the doors and made myself as invisible as possible.

I saw the premier for the first time. He was instantly recognizable by his bushy eyebrows and strong jaw. Intently listening to one of his deputies, Zhou appeared the most relaxed among our delegation, smiling now and then, but maintaining a dignified, straight-backed posture.

Nearby, a clutch of grim, heavyset, dark-suited Russians surrounded the Soviet minister of foreign affairs, Vyacheslav M. Molotov, a short and stocky man who appeared more affable than the members of his beefy entourage. And far across the large room was the tall, dapper, mustachioed British foreign secretary, Anthony Eden, who was famous for his homburg hats. Close to the Brits were the French, represented by Pierre Mendès France, the foreign-affairs minister.

The Americans were the last to arrive that day, led by a tight-lipped, hawk-nosed John Foster Dulles, the secretary of state. A true American patrician, Dulles, sixty-six, was a Princeton man who took his law degree at George Washington University. He had gone on to become a partner at a prestigious Wall Street firm, Sullivan & Cromwell. Dulles's grandfather and an uncle had both been secretaries of state, and his younger brother was Eisenhower's director of Central Intelligence.

Dulles was the reactionary's reactionary, with a reputation for dealing with Communists as if he were killing snakes. He made the rounds, shaking hands with Eden, Mendès France, and Molotov. As Dulles turned to leave the Soviet delegation, the premier pivoted to face him, smiled, and brought up his hand. But Dulles darted back across the room, aides in tow.

The Chinese delegation watched this little drama with indignant stares. But the premier just shrugged slightly and calmly turned back to the group. He gestured with his hand, as if to say, "It's nothing, forget about it." It was not the first time he had come face-to-face with American bad manners. He had been at the airstrip in Yan'an the day General Hurley dropped in on Mao and uttered his infamous Choctaw war whoops.

A few days later, we learned that Dulles had issued instructions to his staff that no one, under any circumstances, was to shake hands with any of us "goddamned Chinese Reds." Like General Harrison in Panmunjom—with his whistling and impatient finger-tapping—Dulles played a tough guy.

Although Premier Zhou shrugged it off, this insult resonated in a way that no other could. The *People's Daily* featured the incident prominently in its coverage of the conference, declaring it a clear sign that the Americans meant to do China harm. The episode of the unshaken hand would become a legend in our foreign affairs, poisoning our relations with the United States for nearly two decades.

The stage was set for the next three months. The Chinese and the Russians were still wary allies, in spite of Stalin's recent death and the ascendancy of the more moderate Nikita Khrushchev. The two Communist powers fought to play a leading role in the settlement of conflicts in Korea, and in leftover colonial interests in Laos, Cambodia, and Vietnam, where the French were bogged down fighting a Communist insurgency led by Ho Chi Minh. The United States and its allies wanted the United Nations, which in effect it controlled, to play the role of peacekeeper in all these disputes.

What a difference from Korea, I thought as I took my seat against the wall and got out my pad and pencil. Instead of a tent, we were in a castle. Instead of shell concussions, we heard the pop of flashbulbs. Instead of a barren wasteland beyond the perimeter, we were surrounded by the elegant, manicured streets of peaceful Geneva.

My chair was some fifteen or so feet behind where the Chinese delegation sat at the table, a fly-on-the-wall seat. It was a heady experience to see so many important people in one room.

As in Korea, my primary job was to record verbatim everything that was said. At Panmunjom, I was required to take down only the statements of a single representative of the United Nations Command. At Geneva, I had to take down all the statements of more than a dozen countries, often without breaks. As soon as one delegate sat down, another popped up. There were several Chinese interpreters and stenographers to help out, but the workload was staggering and mentally taxing.

I was exhausted at the end of the first day. One of the other Chinese stenographers showed me a better system for organizing my shorthand notes. He explained that one should not write from left to right but from top down: First write down in shorthand on the left side the subject phrase of the sentence. Then start a new line, slightly indented, and write down the verb. Then on a third line, indented from the second, write down the object phrase.

The sentence completed, he told me to draw a line across the page to indicate the end of the sentence, and then start with the next. When the speaker finished a paragraph and paused for the interpreter to translate, I was to draw a double line to indicate the start of the next paragraph's first sentence. This way, when I transcribed the entire statement later that night, I could see at a glance how many paragraphs there were and how many sentences each contained.

This system allowed my two colleagues and me to record everything that was said. But the pace was relentless. The talks began at about nine o'clock and continued off and on all day, sometimes late into the evenings. Eating an entire sit-down meal became a rare treat. Bathroom breaks were infrequent, and always on someone else's schedule. It was twice as hard to concentrate on what was being said when I had a full bladder. I learned to limit my fluid intake during the working day.

As soon as the last session ended, I raced to the embassy to type up the statements for duplication and distribution that night. Then I had to prepare for the following day. All this left just a few hours for sleep before it was time to get up and do it again. As the days passed, I began to feel weak and run-down.

Nevertheless, I jumped at the chance to do some oral interpretation when one of our senior officials asked me if I'd be interested in facilitating a discussion he was scheduled to have with his counterpart on the British delegation.

"Little Ji, do you think you are politically agile enough to walk down a zigzag road?" he said.

"Yes, comrade." I told him that Dr. Pushan, had given me a few lessons in oral interpretation in Korea and found I had a knack for it. Pu had introduced me to the art of saying yes while meaning no.

But, just as we were about to leave the embassy for the Palais des Nations, my vision blurred and my legs buckled. My colleagues caught me and carried me off to a bed in the staff living quarters, where I fell into semiconscious delirium with a high fever.

The doctor who was summoned turned out to be the premier's personal physician, sent on his orders. Using a combination of herbal remedies and antibiotics, he soon had me on the mend. A few days later, I was up and able to get back to work. But the doctor ordered me to get more rest and to eat more often.

"You can't make rice grow faster by pulling on it," he said. "If you try to do too much, you may end up unable to do anything, and will be no good to anyone." In time, I learned to regulate my habits to make sure that I could do my best at all times.

Although it wasn't a combat zone, my world in Geneva was almost as limited and routine as it had been in Korea. From the house we lived in, cars took us to work at the Palais des Nations, then back again at day's end. My schedule left me no free time to explore the city, which, in any case, was discouraged. Even Premier Zhou did not make sightseeing side trips, and traveled only with a convoy of bodyguards.

Ever present was the fear of assassination. Having fully allied itself with Chiang Kai-shek, the United States had repeatedly blocked efforts to seat the People's Republic in the United Nations. The Kuomintang would have been delighted to see Premier Zhou dispatched. There was even fear that lowly members of our staff might be kidnapped, and concerns that a rogue in our group might be recruited as a spy or defect at an embarrassing moment. The press hounded the Chinese delegates everywhere we went. We had plenty of good reasons to stick together and avoid all the dangers and temptations.

After the first few weeks of talks, some of the diplomatic big guns departed, leaving the negotiations in the hands of trusted assistants. Dulles's second was Undersecretary of State Walter Bedell Smith, a top general and an aide to Eisenhower during the war years, a former CIA director, and a past ambassador to the Soviet Union. General Smith was no more sympathetic to our position than Dulles, but he was a notch above in manners. One of the first things he did after Dulles left was approach Premier Zhou in the lounge one day, reach out his hand, and grasp the premier's wrist. General Smith had avoided violating Dulles's orders while managing to establish human contact. The premier smiled, clearly enjoying both the absurdity and the chivalry.

The Geneva conference introduced the premier to the world. Many articles were written about Zhou's charm, poise, and steely diplomatic skills. *The New York Times* published a long feature headlined BEHIND THE BAMBOO CURTAIN AT GENEVA and sub-headlined CLANNISH AND CLOSE-MOUTHED, RED CHINA'S DELEGATES . . . PLAY FROM STRENGTH AND DEMAND BIG POWER STATUS.

The author wrote, "Tough, ruthless, strong-minded, wily, intelligent, here is the Communist who weathered the three grim decades before victory and managed to stay on top through all the mutations of Communist policy—[Zhou Enlai], one of the leaders of the small circle of men who today dictate the destiny of China."

Zhou distinguished himself with his skills and his bearing. He was the kind of person who, if he stepped into a room and you didn't know him, you would feel compelled to stand up. But he also put everyone at ease. I had long admired him from afar. Now I worshipped him.

In the end, the Geneva talks produced pitiful results. Early on during the conference, the French suffered a humiliating military defeat by a revolutionary insurgency at Dien Bien Phu, in Vietnam. As part of the Geneva Accords—as the final documents came to be known—France ultimately agreed to withdraw from its Indochinese colonies. Now the Vietnamese ended up with a parallel of their own—the seventeenth—that split their country in two, setting the stage for a new war involving the United States five years later.

But the issue of Korea was never resolved, nor has it been as of this writing, more than a half century later.

I will say that Geneva was a big victory for me. I was publicly acknowledged by our delegation leaders as an exemplary member of the Chinese Communist Youth League because of my hard work and accurate note-taking. I was proud, and glad to have this new commendation to add to my Communist Party application.

After the conference ended, I flew back to Prague. From there, I took the train through Moscow and across the Siberian summer, with its long days and short nights. I spent many hours in my berth toiling away at my Party application essay.

Back in Beijing, I went directly to the Party secretary at the Ministry and submitted my application. I fully expected that my stellar family history, my Third Order of Merit, and my trusted position in Korea and Geneva would result in immediate acceptance.

Over the following weeks I was called in for a number of interviews, the first to articulate why I wanted to join. Next, I was summoned to write about my failings, my "incorrect" thinking, and how I might amend my ways.

I had a hard time coming up with things about myself that needed reforming. However, in spite of my zeal, I found that I could convince myself that I needed to cleanse my mind of residual reactionary thinking left over from my years in the States. In another interview, I was directed to write yet another confession, trying a little harder to struggle against myself to become a better Communist.

I was then summoned before a Party committee, again to articulate why I wanted to join, and then to parry challenges from Party officials. Didn't I have a brother who had remained in the United States? What was my opinion about a sibling who had cast his lot with the enemy? Hadn't I been cozy with my imperialist schoolmates at Harvard? Didn't I secretly miss the life of privilege I had enjoyed in America? Didn't I secretly think myself better than others?

Although much of it seems absurd in retrospect, at the time I believed that struggle and self-criticism were truly part of becoming a committed member of the Party. The committee zeroed in on my Achilles' heel, telling me that I needed to rein in my arrogance and haughtiness. I was not surprised by the criticism. I'd grown up feeling privileged, and I did sometimes come across as cocky and sure of myself. I pledged to work hard to tame my high self-opinion and dedicate my life to the Party and to serving the people.

Weeks went by, then months. I had no doubt that I would eventually prevail, but it was clear that I had yet to pass muster.

With my Geneva experience, I had again honored my father. Once again, he knew better than to ask probing questions. Upon my return, he was happy just to see me. And I swelled with pride when he bragged to his friends, "That's my son. He works for Premier Zhou."

CHAPTER 14

The Premier and I
Cheat Death

Geneva effectively extinguished my scientific career, and I returned to the filthy, spit-slick floor of my Foreign Ministry dormitory, hung up my Western-style suit, donned my tunic, trousers, and cotton shoes, and settled into the life of a bureaucratic cadre.

I had evolved into an accomplished shorthand note-taker in English—as fast and accurate as anyone in the Ministry. I had also established a reputation as the fastest, most accurate transcriber-typist. While such work might have seemed mundane and clerical in any other setting, it had been crucial in both Panmunjom and Geneva. I had learned that when terms and language of international agreements were accepted by both sides after months of negotiation there was an extreme sense of urgency to get them signed—especially where life and property were at stake. The Korean armistice brought an end to mass deaths. The Geneva Accords of 1954 defused tensions that could have led to more bloodshed.

These documents had to be letter-perfect and smudge-free, and both sides wanted them executed within hours, before events on the ground could change or seeds of doubt could sprout in the mind of some diplomat or his distant government.

A single misplaced comma can change the meaning of a sentence, contradict the purpose of a treaty, unintentionally communicate treachery, trigger a demand to reopen a negotiation, or form the basis of a future claim that could lead to political or military confrontation and catastrophe. I welcomed the challenge of this work, but it was stressful to have our senior diplomats standing over me or pacing the floor, fidgeting and chain-smoking while I pecked away, with lives and history hanging in the balance.

I became increasingly adept at translating written Chinese into English, and was growing comfortable interpreting spoken English into Chinese. But my bilingualism remained a work-in-progress, so I spent most of my time studying my native language. I joined a gregarious, hardworking group of language experts, many with overseas backgrounds similar to mine. But they were fluent in Chinese, and many toiled away translating foreign newspapers in various languages for high-ranking Ministry officials and Party leaders.

In addition to struggling with Chinese, I struggled against my haughty nature—the principal criticism that seemed to be delaying my acceptance into the Party. Chairman Mao might have been exhorting China toward a classless society, but I continued to harbor pride in my family connections, my intellect, my superior education, the excellence of my work, along with a sense of my exceptional commitment to the revolutionary cause.

I was quick to point out the casual "reactionary" comments of my colleagues. They in turn delighted in pointing out and teasing me about my self-righteousness. "Little Ji, you must go and drink some more from the Chinese well," I was told. I had no choice but to grin and bear their taunts, because they were right. A good Communist should avoid placing himself above the common man. I found that I was constantly checking my responses to those around me in an effort to correct my "individualist" thinking and lack of modesty.

The autumn of 1954 found our Foreign Ministry humming. Chiang Kai-shek's ragtag navy of surplus U.S. World War II vessels had been intercepting shipping into and out of our ports. Our small naval forces had been launching retaliatory raids to test whether the U.S. Seventh Fleet would interfere. These minor engagements were important symbolically, rekindling mainland hopes for unification with the historically Chinese string of islands just off our coast.

The United States signed a security agreement with the Kuomintang administration, and talk among American politicians centered on the possible use of small, tactical atomic weapons to protect its new ally. Premier Zhou's public response was quick and biting. He called America "the most arrogant aggressor ever known in history, the most ferocious enemy of world peace and the main prop of all the forces of reaction in the world."

Against this tense backdrop, that fall Nikita Khrushchev became the first Soviet leader to visit Beijing. He left behind a faint glow of improved relations with the Russians, which included promises of industrial and financial aid. But Khrushchev also sowed the seeds of a political dilemma for Mao and the hard-core Marxists in our government. A moderate, Khrushchev was beginning to distance his regime from that of his predecessor, Joseph Stalin. Although Stalin had been treacherous, he had also been the godfather of China's Communist movement.

Ultimately, Khrushchev declared Stalin a murderous despot obsessed with maintaining a personality cult. Mao, a much greater personality to the Chinese than Stalin ever was to the Russians, read this denunciation as something of an insult. Mao and his hard-line followers saw Khrushchev's revisionism as pandering to the capitalists, a betrayal of the Marxist cause. Wary at the best of times, relations between the USSR and China began a long, gradual deterioration.

China also received a state visit from Jawaharlal Nehru, India's first prime minister. India and China had a long-standing dispute regarding our common border—yet another nineteenth-century "gift" of the Great Powers of Europe. This line had been capriciously drawn on a map in London by a British diplomat, moving areas of China into India and thus into the British sphere of influence. The People's Republic had established a new line of control to correct this injustice, and now the Indians were squawking.

Nehru's visit was publicly billed as bridge-building. The premier proposed that the two nations agree to a policy of "Five Principles of Co-Existence" for all Asian and African countries: respect for territorial integrity, nonaggression, noninterference in internal affairs, equality and mutual benefit, and peaceful coexistence.

Secretary of State Dulles, ever hawkish, continued the attempts to isolate China, this time by pressuring the United Nations to create the Southeast Asia Treaty Organization (SEATO). The Americans wanted their allies to form an anti-Communist front in Asia, much as the formation of NATO countered Soviet designs on Europe.

In the United Nations and elsewhere, the United States portrayed Red China as a hungry Communist tiger with a growing appetite for its Southeast Asian neighbors. With pressure mounting, Premier Zhou eagerly accepted an invitation to attend a regional conference of thirty Asian and African nations.

In spite of our protestations to the contrary, China was viewed with suspicion by our neighbors, and even by African nations such as Egypt. Our assertion of authority along our borders—in Korea, with India, and over our coastal islands—was being framed as Soviet-inspired imperialism.

The conference was to take place in Indonesia, on the island of Java, a former Dutch colony. Its main issue would be how the region's former colonies—many of them victims of recent Japanese aggression—could ally themselves as nations to remain independent. Under discussion would be strategies to keep *all* the hungry tigers of the world at bay, including the United States and the USSR. The conference was billed as the "first intercontinental meeting of colored peoples in the history of mankind."

I hoped to be among those attending and was overjoyed when, in early April 1955, I was told to pack my bags for the long train ride from Beijing to Canton. There, I would enter Hong Kong, this time with a diplomatic passport, and no Sikh policeman could threaten me with a mahogany baton. I was to link up with Premier Zhou's senior staff and a small contingent of journalists for the flight to Java. I was excited to learn that I would be traveling on the same plane as the premier, a Lockheed Constellation chartered from Air India. The plane was known as the *Kashmir Princess*.

Where Geneva had been the People's Republic's diplomatic début on the world stage, Bandung was to be our chance to present the case for our peaceful aims without being seen as water carriers for the Soviets or being shouted down by the United States. Instead, the premier would be speaking before a roomful of our neighbors and other nonaligned, second-tier nations that were, like China, striking out on their own.

A week or so before I was scheduled to leave for Hong Kong, I was told that the *Kashmir Princess* was too small to take everyone who had been assigned. As the team's junior person, I got bumped from the flight. Passage was booked for me on a ship from Hong Kong to Jakarta. I had to leave at once in order for my arrival to coincide with the rest of our delegation's air arrival. This was a minor disappointment. I would miss the excitement of traveling with the premier, but my consolation was a few relaxing days of living in relative luxury—no spit on the floor, a soft mattress, and a few protein-rich meals.

During the voyage, I practiced my shorthand skills to keep myself battle-ready. Steaming due south through the South China Sea, we sailed through waters I had cruised as a child when my family left Vietnam for Marseille on the *Corfu*. Here I was, a young man in my twenties, having seen so much of the world. The way things were shaping up, I would be seeing a lot more. I had no regrets about terminating my academic career. This was the life I might have dreamed of, had I dared.

A short cab ride with an embassy aide from the Jakarta docks and I found myself settling in to a compound full of diplomats. Officials of every rank and role were here, enjoying the tropical weather and the exotic fresh fruits we never saw at home. After preparing for the conference, I had stowed my bag, freshened up, and was sitting with some other cadres in the courtyard when shouting erupted from the open office windows.

Our ambassador, Huang Zhen, burst through the door onto the porch, his face twisted with panic. "A great tragedy!" he cried as all heads swung his way. "It's horrible! The *Kashmir Princess* has crashed into the sea! It was just announced on the radio."

My scalp prickled and my heart lurched into high gear. A cacophony of voices echoed off the walls of the compound as senior officials raced inside barking orders for our military attaché to be sent to the crash site. A hushed silence descended over the embassy. Tears flooded my eyes. Could it be true that the premier was dead? What would happen now?

We waited in glum silence for further news. An hour or so later, Ambassador Huang appeared on the porch and called us near. "Comrades, do not be alarmed," he said. "It is true that the *Kashmir Princess* has crashed into the South China Sea. All the passengers were killed. But the premier was not aboard." A murmur rippled through the crowd, then applause. My eyes flooded again, this time with relief.

"Premier Zhou was delayed by an attack of appendicitis, and he made a side trip to Rangoon to meet with Burmese officials and Prime Minister Nehru. So he did not travel on the *Kashmir Princess* as planned. The premier will soon arrive."

Then it hit me that I, too, had been spared. Instead of ending up at the bottom of the South China Sea, I had placidly sailed across its surface. Once again, fate had stepped between me and the claws of death. Then I had a second, numbing realization. I knew a number of the people on the plane. Some were journalists from China and Eastern European Communist newspapers whom I'd met in Geneva. There were a handful of fellow Foreign Ministry cadres as well.

The speculation began at once. Information was sparse at the time, but the weather had been reported as clear. The gossip raging through the embassy staff was that this could only have been an assassination attempt. The possibility that the plane the premier was to fly on had suffered a malfunction was just too coincidental to be believed. Who would want to kill the second most important person in China, and who had the resources? The United States and its Kuomintang stooges on Taiwan. Hong Kong, where the plane took off, was infested with Kuomintang spies.

Could the Americans have been so bold as to have shot it down? Almost a year earlier, just a week after the Geneva Accords were signed, our nervous and overeager air force had shot down a British civilian airliner near Hong Kong, thinking it was a spy plane. There were survivors, but several Americans had been among the dead. Our MiGs had also challenged a French airliner, but no shots were fired. These incidents had been peacefully resolved, but tensions remained.

In November 1954, the People's Republic claimed that more than two hundred Kuomintang spies and counterrevolutionary organizers had been surreptitiously airlifted into China. Our Security Ministry reported that more than a hundred were killed, along with five American crew members of spy planes that had been shot down.

Our anxiety next turned to the premier's safety. If he had flown to Rangoon instead of directly to Jakarta, he was overdue there. The Burmese government had sent a delegation to the Rangoon airport to greet the premier's plane, but it never arrived. An air of mystery began to envelop the conference. None of us could relax until we knew that Zhou Enlai was safe and well. Everything depended on him.

"This is why Chairman Mao never travels by plane," a senior delegation member told us. "He only travels by armored train. It's too easy to sabotage or shoot down a plane."

The rest of the day was consumed with exchanging and parsing fragments of news and speculation. All passengers and crew aboard the plane had been killed, the ambassador had said. But we learned that some of the crew had survived and been rescued.

Later, we learned the premier had known of the danger. He had informed the Hong Kong authorities and Air India and asked them to take every precautionary measure. They assured the Chinese government that they would do everything possible to protect our people. Unfortunately, despite all precautions, the assassination plot was carried out.

Objective historians agree that the attempted assassination of Premier Zhou Enlai was financed and equipped with American funds and expertise, and carried out by a Kuomintang agent. Both the United States and Chiang Kai-shek had a huge stake in disrupting the Bandung talks. They wanted to weaken China's ability to form any regional coalitions that might compete with SEATO, Dulles's proposed alliance of U.S. puppet regimes.

An American code clerk and part-time CIA gofer stationed at the U.S. embassy in New Delhi later revealed that he had delivered to a Kuomintang contact in Hong Kong a package containing two time bombs. The plane crashed in shallow waters, and three of the crew lived to give eyewitness accounts. An American-made clockwork mechanism was found in the wreckage, and the Hong Kong police declared it a case of "carefully planned mass murder."

By all accounts, the bomb that brought the plane down was put on it by a Chinese Nationalist working as a ground crewman at the airport where the *Kashmir Princess* was being fueled for the flight to Jakarta. He hid it in the right wheel well, and it exploded about an hour short of Jakarta, at eighteen thousand feet.

The crew had enough time to hand out life jackets and open the doors for quick escape. But the Constellation broke up upon impact and the main fuselage sank so fast that the passengers drowned, along with all but three crewmen.

The saboteur was later unmasked and managed to flee Hong Kong for Taiwan aboard a CIA-owned aircraft. He was reportedly paid a fortune for his role.

We lower-order cadres knew few of these facts in April 1955, but none of us doubted that there was foul play involved, and that our entire nation had been spared a catastrophic loss. Geneva had launched the premier's reputation as a gracious, earnest, worldly intellectual, who had lived in Paris and Moscow as a young man and who could straddle the divide between China and the world community. Zhou's death would have had far-reaching effects, and in the near-term would have rendered Bandung a diplomatic disaster.

Instead, the conference was a resounding success. In his prepared speech at the start of the conference, Zhou talked about the things that bound all Asian nations together: colonialism and racism. "The population of Asia will never forget that the first atom bomb exploded on Asian soil," he said.

Zhou listened politely for days as representatives of many of the other twenty-eight nations expressed disapproval of China's actions, as well as their dark suspicions of our goals. Finally, the premier rose, shocking us note-takers into motion by setting aside his prepared remarks. I got out my pad and began scribbling an impassioned and powerful speech that directly addressed the issues raised:

> The Chinese Delegation has come here to seek unity and not to quar-
> rel, to seek common ground and not to create divergences. There ex-
> ists common ground among the Asian and African countries. . . .
> Their peoples . . . are still suffering from the calamities of colonial-
> ism . . . whether [they] are led by the communists or nationalists.

As for the America he had publicly denounced as the greatest threat
to world peace, in this private session the premier conceded (at his own
political peril among the hard-liners back home):

> I respect the political and economic systems of America, and China
> has no intention of going to war with the United States. . . . Al-
> though the present situation is tense, let us not lose the peace.

The delegates clapped at some of the premier's remarks, and even
though my eyes were glued to my scribbling pencil and my mind was
focused on the premier's every syllable and sigh, I felt a definite change
in the room's atmosphere. The applause grew more frequent, and when
Zhou finished and sat down the entire crowd gave him a standing ova-
tion. It was a moment of great rhetorical and diplomatic triumph that
became known as the "Bandung spirit," and it was another reason for
me to love him.

During an interlude in the talks, we all went back to the embassy
compound in nearby Jakarta. It was a hot, humid night, and the dormitory fans did little to dispel the stifling heat. Unable to sleep, I sat in
a chair under the awning on the porch, watching from afar as the premier conferred with his aides. His group broke up. He stood and
turned, locking onto my gaze, his bushy eyebrows knit together. Then
he took brisk strides across the broad courtyard. He seemed to be holding his left arm stiffly. I sat up straight.

As he approached, I stood at attention. He wore a faint, mischievous smile. "Who are you?" he asked softly.

"Premier, I am Ji Chaozhu, Ji Chaoding's youngest brother."

He nodded, smiled, and said, simply, "Fine." Then he walked away.

I was startled, puzzled, and honored all at once. I revered Chairman
Mao in a godlike way: as a remote, inaccessible, iconic figure, an olive-

drab speck at the center of the reviewing rail atop the Heavenly Gate. But Zhou was one of China's contradictions—warm and human. I felt as if I already knew him. And, for the first time, Zhou had actually spoken to me. I felt myself being drawn into the inner circle, joining my brother and my father as a witness to history.

CHAPTER 15

The Other China

The contradiction in personality between the chairman and the premier reflected profound contradictions emerging in China's new culture. Much of the conflict took place out of sight and earshot of central government cadres like myself, and was rarely reported in the Party-controlled press. It was both political and practical.

I would learn much later that the land-reform movement had been a violent business costing the lives of a million or more landlords and their families. If they weren't killed outright in revenge for past exploitation, they were hounded to death or chose suicide. The landlord class had dominated rural society for nearly two millennia. In the first three years of the new nation's existence, it was wiped out, and all arable land was redistributed to the peasants. This campaign was the first of many manifestations of Mao's style. "What boundless pleasure it is to struggle against other human beings," he'd written.

The one land-reform incident I witnessed fortunately ended without bloodshed. During my Tsinghua University days, in 1951, I asked for and received permission to attend a struggle meeting in the countryside. I wanted to witness what was happening with my own eyes. I thought it might enhance my understanding of Chinese Communism and improve my chances of being accepted for Party membership.

I biked to a village just outside the city, quickly finding the meeting by following a group of peasants in wide straw hats all walking in the same direction down dusty alleys. Turning a corner, I found a mob of

THE MAN ON MAO'S RIGHT · 143

people in simple, drab garments and sandals milling about the front gate of the landlord's walled courtyard villa. This home was much like the one my landlord father and grandfather had owned and occupied in their rural village in Shanxi Province.

The perimeter of the block-size villa was surrounded by a high wall with no openings or windows, capped by a swooping, pagoda-style roof of yellow tile. The front gate was framed by a tall ornamental archway built of thick wooden beams with intricate carved patterns, decorated with red and gold paint. Standing wide open were heavy red doors decorated with patterns of fish, flowers, and birds. Above the entryway, an old, Confucian saying had been painted in gold characters. I couldn't read it, but all houses seemed to have one—a simple exhortation such as YOU WILL BE REWARDED IF YOU ARE MODEST.

Beyond the traditional high wooden threshold (the higher the threshold, the higher the rank of the owner), I saw a stone wall with a decorative frieze. This was also traditional, providing privacy from prying eyes, and, for the superstitious, it was thought to ward off evil spirits.

I parked my bike and strode to the back of the crowd, where, from my height, I saw the landlord standing at the front, head bowed as a woman screamed at him. The crowd egged her on. One after another, the peasants took turns, some weeping bitterly as they recounted the indignities and misfortunes they had suffered at the landlord's hands. With all the screaming, it was hard to make out more than a few words here and there. The landlord did not move or flinch, just stared at his feet in submissive humiliation.

He was not beaten or physically molested in any way and did not, as was often the case, have a crude placard around his neck listing his crimes against the peasants. Perhaps he had been a beneficent landlord like my grandfather.

After an eternity of this abuse, the poor man was permitted to return to his villa, which had been confiscated by the local officials. He and his family were allowed to keep just one room, while the peasants joyously went to the fields to divide the land equally among all the villagers. The rest of the landlord's villa was assigned to peasant families.

This ritual was acted out all across China, a purge participated in by hundreds of millions of rural people. Organized by Party cadres, this was an eager response to Chairman Mao's call to "all the people and cadres of the country . . . to . . . cleanse our society of all the filth and poison left over from the old!" The poison was millennia of dynastic feudalism that had allowed the few to exploit the many. Now the many were having their revenge.

I came away from the experience both grateful that my old father had been spared such an indignity and convinced that the land-reform movement was liberating the Chinese peasantry, literally and figuratively. For centuries, China's tenant farmers had cultivated the land of others in exchange for a share of the harvest. They had lived on the margins of existence, always knowing want and deprivation, exposed to all the calamities of nature and man. When Mao and Zhou first declared the founding of the People's Republic of China (PRC), the average life span in the nation was only thirty-two.

Mao united our nation. The key to his victorious philosophy was the leadership of the Chinese Communist Party. Mao united all those who could be united, only resorting to armed force when there was no alternative. Land redistribution won the leadership enormous support from the peasantry, who were then more than 80 percent of the population. His intuition and understanding of peasant culture were what propelled him to the top of the Party. He well understood the power of untapped rage.

In the early days of the civil war with the Kuomintang, Zhou Enlai had been first among equals in the Party leadership. He had lived abroad, in Paris, had been a Communist organizer, and had a cosmopolitan sensibility. He had advocated organizing the intelligentsia, bureaucrats, and factory workers in the cities as a way to build the Party and defeat Chiang's Nationalists. But Zhou's approach triggered the retaliatory massacres of the White Terror.

As a librarian at Peking University, Mao had been drawn to Chinese history and philosophy, reading ancient writers from Confucius to Sun Tzu, the author of *The Art of War*. A voracious reader, Mao became interested in the plight of China's vast army of impoverished farmers. As the Communist Party evolved, Mao's military tactics—borrowed from the ancients—proved effective against the Kuomintang. And his focus on organizing the peasants in the countryside had proved more successful than Zhou's efforts to marshal the urban factory workers.

Thus Mao's vision, and his ambition, earned him the leadership of the Party and of the revolution. He got there by means both noble and ignoble. He knew that in order to win the support of the peasants the Communist soldiers must treat them with dignity—sleeping in the streets, helping the men, respecting the women. But he also gave orders that resulted in bloody purges within the Party, leading to the torture and execution of the innocent with the guilty.

As early as 1927, Mao defended the violence of the Communist movement by writing, famously, that "a revolution is not a dinner party. . . . It is necessary to create terror for a while . . . otherwise it would be impossible to suppress the activities of the counterrevolutionaries in the countryside or overthrow the authority of the gentry. Proper limits have to be exceeded in order to right a wrong, or else the wrong cannot be righted."

Events proved Zhou wrong in his strategy of first trying to win over the cities. But Zhou remained ever loyal to Mao, and when the dust settled he accepted a secondary role as Mao's chief administrator. Mao had won China's soul, and this would always give him the last word. It had been that way since the successful conclusion of the Long March.

In 1949, Mao the revolutionary leader was transformed into Mao the leader of a nation. The goals changed, but his methods did not. The mass movements that he had exploited so successfully before liberation had bound the Chinese people together. But soon they began to be a hindrance to progress and, ultimately, a destructive force.

Following the embezzlement revelation during the Korean War, Mao launched the first of what became a series of campaigns. Just before I left for Korea, he had announced the Three Antis: anticorruption, antiwaste, and antibureaucraticism. The purpose was to prevent "the corrosion of the cadres by the bourgeoisie."

This was quickly followed by the Five Antis: antibribery, anti–tax evasion, antifraud, antiembezzlement, antidisclosure of state secrets. Laborers were encouraged to criticize their bosses and expose their crimes and their "right-opportunist thinking." Cadres turned against other cadres. Another man at the Foreign Ministry jumped to his death after a crowd demanded that he confess to a petty corruption charge. No one ever learned whether he was guilty. The shame of accusation was enough.

Children were urged to turn in their parents, wives to expose husbands. The accused were dragged before mass struggle meetings, forced to wear humiliating signs and tall paper dunce caps. Some were summarily executed.

Later, Mao called for the mass extermination of rats, sparrows, flies, and mosquitoes—a campaign he called the Four Withouts. No one could argue against eliminating flies, mosquitoes, or even rats. But when it was over Beijing's dawns were silent and the crops—which the sparrows had been blamed for eating up—were now devoured by insects the sparrows used to eat.

The few Party leaders who dared to challenge Mao, or to even think of disagreeing with him, were summarily purged and sent to live with the peasants for "reeducation." During the period of the worst political upheaval, it was my paradoxical good fortune to be far away in a war zone, scratching flea bites and jumping into craters to examine unexploded shells. People with biographies similar to mine—trained in the West—had been singled out during the "Anti-"crusades, especially during a related Thought Rectification Campaign. Criticism and struggle meetings were encouraged against bureaucrats and intellectuals who needed to be reeducated—to cleanse our thoughts of bourgeois and capitalist ideas.

I returned to this environment from Korea with my Third Order of Merit medal, having established my credentials as a battlefield hero. I had played my silent but crucial role in the negotiations to end the fighting in China's first great military success. Then, in short order, I was off to Geneva, followed by Bandung. I was therefore somewhat isolated from the worst of the chaos. At the height of the upheaval caused by these mass movements, I heard the rumors and felt the mood of anxiety in the government. But I was preoccupied with my work and with developing my Chinese-language skills.

Following the Bandung Conference, in the late spring of 1955, my Chinese had improved enough that the Foreign Ministry began assigning me to interpret for the working staffs of visiting dignitaries. The Bandung spirit had stimulated visits between China and a number of other nations, many of whose diplomats came from former British colonies and continued to speak English in their foreign dealings. India and Pakistan—two nations only recently liberated from British rule—Egypt, and Nepal all spoke English in their dealings with the PRC.

My assignments began with light-duty situations, shopping or interpreting Chinese movies that were shown at the diplomatic guesthouses while the principal dignitaries were off meeting with the premier or other high-ranking officials. My Harvard mentor, Dr. Pu Shouchang, had been the premier's principal English interpreter almost since liberation. He was over forty years old and had told me once during a conversation that he would soon be retiring. "I'm getting to an age when my old brain cannot keep up the way it used to," he said. "Soon it will be time for a younger mind to take over. That could be you."

I was astonished, too humbled to dare speak. I had no doubt that I could do it, but I kept that arrogant little thought to myself. I vowed to redouble my language studies so that I would be ready and worthy should such a day arrive.

Toward the end of September 1956, the premier of Nepal, Tanka Prasad, made a state visit during which I was assigned to guide and interpret for his bodyguard and his personal servants. This included sitting with them at the most distant table at the welcoming state banquet that first night. Tucked away in the corner of the room, invisible but always at the ready, we mere spear carriers could relax, share our thoughts on what was happening in the world, swap cultural anecdotes and curiosities, and speculate on how our leaders were getting along.

But during the tour with my little flock of fellow servants a Foreign Ministry official pulled me aside and whispered, "You're to interpret for the premiers at dinner. Make sure you get back to the office in time to receive your instructions."

I floated through the rest of the day. I had not seen Premier Zhou up close since Bandung. Now I would be sitting just inches away, interpreting a conversation between these two world leaders. I was confident and eager.

Late that afternoon, after washing up, buffing my shoes, and don-ning my one good Mao suit, I presented myself at the front door of the Beijing Hotel, where the banquet was to take place. I waited to the side as an honor guard in full regalia assembled to greet Premier Prasad's car.

When it arrived, I took my position to Prasad's right, and slightly behind, trying my best to be as invisible as possible. To his left was our protocol officer, Han Xu (later the Chinese ambassador to the United States). After some small pleasantries, Han escorted Prasad to the head table, where Premier Zhou Enlai greeted him with his signature warm but dignified smile.

What was said is lost to me now, but I recall that those first words of greeting were a piece of cake, and I was proud of myself. Once Prasad was seated, Zhou Enlai stood and delivered his welcoming remarks, reading from a prepared statement in Chinese. I had a copy in English.

Premier Zhou read the first paragraph in Chinese. Standing to his right and slightly behind the premier, just between the two dignitaries, I then repeated the paragraph in English. My loud, clear voice filled the room as I carefully enunciated every syllable, pleased to show off my impeccable command of this exotic language. The premier then read the second paragraph in Chinese, and I repeated it in English.

It was so easy, I allowed myself to become distracted by the majesty of the moment. I waited for the premier to finish his Chinese while gazing out on the huge round principal banquet table—a table set for kings—and the many large round tables beyond. Every chair was occupied by a vice premier, minister, ambassador, or other high official—the cream of our Foreign Ministry and the foreign diplomatic corps. Their eyes were riveted on the premiers, and on me. They were utterly rapt, hanging on every word that came out of my mouth. I was again a flower intoxicated by its own scent.

So intoxicated that I failed to notice when the premier strayed from the script. The statement had neglected to make any reference to the chairman of the ruling Nepalese party, Prasad's boss. Zhou extemporaneously added a few words of praise for his leadership.

He said this as I was off floating on my pink cloud. I mechanically read the prepared paragraph in English, and triumphantly folded my hands in front of me. The premier turned and gave me a direct look that made my heart skip a beat.

"No! No! Little Ji," he said, his voice piercing the decorum like cannon fire. "You interpreted wrongly! You are too excitable!" He waved with disgust to an aide. "Get me another interpreter."

My body glowing with a furnace of humid shame, I handed my English translation to the replacement interpreter and slouched around the edge of the room until I reached the last table in the corner, where Prasad's underlings diplomatically stared into their soup bowls.

Compared with our daily fare at the Foreign Ministry, the meal was truly a banquet, featuring luxuries such as fish and duck. But I had little appetite. My stomach churned and I wallowed in a pit of silent self-criticism. I had made a hash of the greatest opportunity of my life. Of all people, I had shamed the premier! In front of everyone who was anyone! I slept miserably that night, and woke wishing it had all been a dream.

But at breakfast Han Xu told me the premier wanted me to interpret for him at another official welcoming ceremony, this time hosted by the mayor and other Beijing city officials. I received a stern lecture: "Listen to everything the premier says. Concentrate on the two leaders and don't bother about anything else."

"Yes, yes, comrade! I will not fail this time."

I rigidly followed his instructions, paying no attention to anything said by anyone other than the two premiers. As the ceremony began, the mayor of Beijing delivered his ceremonial greeting, describing a gift he was presenting to Premier Prasad, and a banner of welcome.

Premier Zhou turned to me, this time with a wry smile. "Little Ji, why don't you interpret for our guest what the mayor just said?"

I was startled. The mayor had his own interpreter. My heart pounded. Hawk-eyed on the body language of the two principal officials, I had only been half listening in order to be prepared to accurately repeat anything that Zhou or Prasad might utter.

What had the mayor said? I racked my brain. Something about gifts! I turned to Premier Prasad and said, "The mayor will now present some gifts to Your Excellency."

Premier Zhou turned and looked directly at me again, but this time his smile was thin and cold, and an eyebrow was arched. "What about the presentation of the banner of welcome?"

My heart sank. My second chance and I'd failed again! But at that moment the interpreter for the mayor stepped forward and, reading from his prepared English text, delivered the correct translation.

I had been saved! Desperate to redeem myself, I whispered to the premier, "That part has been interpreted." I was a fool. I had not yet discovered that the premier had studied English. He understood it quite well, but was shy about speaking it.

He glared at me for an eternal-feeling moment and then, leaning toward me, said in a low voice, "Little Ji, you did not tell the truth." But he said nothing more about the incident and continued cheerfully chatting with the Nepalese prime minister. I continued to interpret without further incident or embarrassment.

In spite of this clumsy beginning, Dr. Pu began to relinquish his role as Zhou Enlai's principal English interpreter and I learned to stay on my toes at all times. Several months passed, and after many more interpretation sessions with the premier went well my new role became permanent.

The premier had a studied openheartedness in dealing with foreign guests. He spent hours with them discussing differences and similarities in cultures and politics. He often asked visitors for observations or criticisms of what they had seen or experienced in China. He once asked an Australian doctor this question, to which the doctor enthusiastically replied, "Oh, everything is just fine!"

Zhou smiled and replied wryly, "You haven't been here long enough." This self-deprecating humor is not so unusual for us Chinese. As implacable as we may appear, we take great pleasure among ourselves in poking fun at our cultural idiosyncrasies, like our parsimoniousness, or in teasing one another about our peccadilloes.

I was surprised and delighted to find such openness in a man of Zhou's position and dignity, now the third most important person in the largest nation on earth, after Mao and Liu Shaoqi, chairman of the state. His dignity was unstudied, charismatic. He put everyone at ease, endearing himself to just about anyone who met him, and especially those who worked directly with him.

He wore the same five-button, military-style tunic as the rest of us. I noticed on more than one occasion that the edges of Zhou's shirt collars were frayed in spots, with a lone thread sticking out here or there. It took all my will to restrain the urge to pull them off.

He took keen interest in the lives of official visitors, but he also took an interest in those who served him. As an interpreter, it was common for me to miss meals. Often, during official talks, I interpreted for hours at a time. I'd accompany the premier and his guest to a lounge, where they might have tea, then perhaps a walk in a garden. I then went with them to the banquet hall, where my job was to sit behind and between the premier and his guest while they exchanged toasts and commented on the food. I was not expected to take so much as a drink of water, let alone eat.

Premier Zhou often expressed concern that we functionaries were not being fed. In the years ahead, I observed that he often went out of his way to ensure lower-ranking officials or aides were made comfortable. He often put food on my plate while I was busy repeating his words in English.

I became the Foreign Ministry's principal English interpreter, attending events with Marshal Chen Yi, the vice premier, who was also about to become foreign minister. Zhou was shedding some of his diplomatic workload to focus on the business of being premier. Around this time, he visited the Ministry to give his annual pep talk to the staff. He delivered an inspirational speech that elicited repeated and enthusiastic applause. He was revered by the staff, many of whom had also spent time abroad and shared his intellectual curiosity. In a Communist cadre system that strongly discouraged initiative or straying from the Party line, the premier insisted that the Foreign Ministry—as the public face of China—work hard to win our new nation allies.

"Make as many friends as possible, talk frankly about our opinions, talk about weaknesses as well as about good points," he told us. We were to be discreet—remain polite while disagreeing—but not to be too inscrutable. We were to deal with provocative situations in a calm, thoughtful fashion. "Establish goodwill, understand the situation, propagandize, influence one's opponent, win hearts." This controlled openness was possible only in the Foreign Ministry, and only because of the premier's great stature. China needed friends abroad.

Domestically, Chairman Mao was intent on cleansing the Party of "right deviationist thinking" and the "filth and poisons of the past." This manifested itself in purges and mass movements: the chaos of our ongoing revolution. The Foreign Ministry was evolving as an island of accommodation in a sea of political zeal.

But of all the things the premier said that day in his annual pep talk, the one that lodged in my consciousness was to "tell the truth at all times. Otherwise, you will not only harm yourself but, worse, you could harm the state."

As someone who had fibbed to him in my first fumbling attempts at interpretation, I was stung by his remarks. I vowed never to let him down again.

CHAPTER 16

Calm Between the Storms

The Communist Party held a national congress, when major political and policy shifts took place. Little of what actually happened at these closed sessions found its way into print or on the radio. And there was no television yet. What was reported was understood by all to be the official Party line. Every phrase was read and parsed by academics, intellectuals, and the cadres.

The Eighth Party Congress in 1956 produced a major policy shift. Early that year, Mao had made expanding the economy a top priority. The War to Resist U.S. Aggression and Aid Korea was over. The Communist Party was unchallenged. Mao's pronouncements had called for decentralizing the government. "We need a little liberalism to facilitate getting things done," he said.

But there was a shortage of trained experts. Had my life taken a different path, I would have been one of those precious chemical engineers that China needed to develop its industrial base. Invitations were extended to skilled Chinese living overseas to return and help build up the country.

Even the anti-Western cultural bias eased somewhat. In the parks, one could see young women openly wearing colorful blouses. In good weather, there was often live music and dancing in public spaces. In addition to traditional Chinese opera, an occasional waltz might now be heard, or even the works of American composers such as George Gershwin.

At the Eighth Party Congress that fall, Mao described the nation's first economic blueprint—the Five-Year Plan—as being more "bones" than "flesh." The new contradiction for Mao was that the bureaucracy had so much control that it was stifling innovation:

> We must build the country through diligence and thrift, combat extravagance and waste, and encourage hard work and plain living and sharing weal and woe with the masses. Some comrades have suggested that factory directors and heads of schools and colleges might live in sheds, and this, I think, is a good idea, especially in hard times. There were no houses whatsoever when we crossed the marshlands on the Long March, we just slept where we could. . . . We all came through. Our troops had no food and ate the bark and leaves of trees. To share happiness and suffering with the people— we did this in the past, why can't we do it now? As long as we keep on doing so, we shall not alienate ourselves from the masses.

Mao's reference to the Long March by his People's Army—the darkest hours of the Communist revolution—touched on a significant fault line in Chinese politics. The leadership of the country and many senior officials and cadres had been in the fight for national autonomy from the start. They were known as base-area veterans—*laobalu*. For decades they had fought and suffered for independence, and some were staunch followers of Mao.

And then there were others, like Chaoding and myself, who had been overseas or sequestered in academic institutions, or out of the fight for any number of perfectly good reasons. Invoking the hardships of the People's Army veterans was Mao's way of reminding us that they regarded themselves as occupying the higher moral ground.

The Chinese leadership, including my brother Chaoding, were eager for the country to start catching up to the industrial world. But not everyone agreed with Chairman Mao's enthusiastic call to economic arms. In its public statements, the Party Congress pointed out that China was still a backward agricultural nation. The postwar years had spawned a population boom that threatened to outstrip our ability to support it. From an estimated 530 million people in 1949, there were

583 million of us according to the 1953 census, and roughly 600 million by the time of the Eighth Party Congress. The hand-wringing over this was becoming apparent. On a visit to a country school with a foreign visitor, I saw the premier shake his head and mutter to himself, "What are we going to do with all these children when they grow up?"

The new Party line was that violent class struggle must now take a back seat to organizing our social system and industrializing our economy. Mao's call led to a program that involved sending bureaucrats, cadres, and even military officers to spend time working on farms and in factories in an effort to spur production. Workers should be allowed to strike and students should be allowed to demonstrate, Mao said: "The world is full of contradictions."

After all the purges and killings and social upheaval, the relaxation of the political atmosphere was a great relief. So many of us had biographies that could be cast as suspicious, mine perhaps most of all. Still, just about everyone had something in his background that could be exploited or twisted under the right (or wrong) circumstances.

Attention was also drawn away from the threat of internal strife by events on the far borders of the Soviet Union. Anti-Communist uprisings had broken out in Hungary and Poland. The USSR sent tanks into the streets of Budapest, threatening the Poles with equally harsh treatment.

To those who expressed concern about a global reaction against Communism, Chairman Mao declared that the uprisings were evidence that these Eastern European Communist regimes had failed to complete their class struggle, leaving too many counterrevolutionaries around to stir up trouble. This was not the problem in China, he declared. The problem in China was that "the Communist Party must learn its lesson. . . . We must be vigilant, and must not allow a bureaucratic workstyle to develop. We must not form an aristocracy divorced from the people."

In February 1957, Mao raised the stakes. In a major speech to a large audience that included scientists, writers, and even representatives of small opposition groups, he declared, "Let a hundred flowers blossom, let a hundred schools of thought contend." It would be a few months before the speech was published, but recordings were sent around the country to be played at gatherings of the intelligentsia and Party cadres.

We were all encouraged to criticize our superiors and even the Party. This new line gave many hope that the repressive methods used in gaining control of the country might now give way to a more open, expressive society.

But not everyone was convinced. In particular, intellectuals well remembered the mistreatment they suffered in the early days of the republic. They were in no hurry to stick out their necks only to have their heads chopped off. Now that government officials had to contend with open criticism, a new form of chaos broke out. This provided me with yet another opportunity to make a fool of myself.

The most visible manifestations of this "rectification" effort were the many big character posters that began to appear on walls. They were written in large letters on big sheets of newsprint, and allowed anyone, including me, to announce a particular criticism of some leader or of the Party itself.

Eager always to be the good soldier, I racked my brain trying to think of something or someone to criticize. I still needed to prove my worthiness for full Communist Party membership. I had completed a year of probationary membership, but my Party chief at the Foreign Ministry informed me that I remained guilty of self-pride and lack of modesty. My probationary period had been extended another six months. I was angry and frustrated. My loyalty to the Party was unquestionable, and my self-pride was simply the confidence of a good Party worker. But I kept these grumblings to myself.

After one of my interpretation sessions at a state banquet for Premier Zhou, I noticed that whenever he participated in a toast he held his little glass of maotai—a clear, sorghum-based liquor traditionally served at special occasions—slightly below the upraised glass of the honored guest.

But when Marshal Chen Yi, now the foreign minister, toasted, he always held his glass slightly above the honored guest's. Aha! I thought. The premier, being a humble man—unashamed to wear threadbare shirts—was showing his modesty by allowing his guest to dominate the toast.

I set to work describing on my character poster how I thought the marshal should emulate the premier's modesty during state dinners and receptions. When I was finished, I felt great pride in having found a way to participate in the Hundred Flowers Campaign without criticizing the Party and having a chance to publicly praise my hero, the premier. I confidently tacked my character poster on the wall at the Foreign Ministry, next to dozens of others.

The marshal visited the Foreign Ministry offices a few days later, to read the posters and then address the assembled staff. He praised us for our helpful criticisms and suggestions, but then he said something that hit me like a punch in the head.

"I would like to correct the impression given by one of these posters, which shows a lack of knowledge of protocol matters," he said. "It is traditional during an official toast for the host to hold his glass higher than the guest's. This is a sign of respect.

"It is true that Comrade Zhou does not do this. But the reason has nothing to do with his modesty. His right arm was badly injured in an accident many years ago when we were headquartered in Yan'an. You may notice that he holds his right arm somewhat stiffly at times. The injury limits his movement so that he is unable to hold a glass up high."

A titter swept the room. Only a few close friends dared glance my way, but the whole roomful of co-workers might as well have been pointing and laughing at me. I was mortified.

After delivering his talk, the marshal came down from the stage to mingle with the crowd. I kept my eye on him to make sure to stay as far away as possible, but he searched me out and made me sit down next to him. "So! You are the Little Ji who wrote that big character poster about me," he said. I bowed my head and stared at my shoes. He patted my shoulder and said warmly, "Don't worry. I welcome all criticisms. I just felt I should point out the correct protocol so none of our staff get the wrong idea."

Like the premier, Marshal Chen Yi had a warm, engaging manner. He asked where I came from, what I had studied in school, and what had been my aspirations. I explained that I started out studying chemistry and had once hoped to work on the building of our first atomic bomb.

He laughed and said, "No matter. You are welcome here in the Foreign Ministry. But you could keep up your chemistry interests in your spare time."

From then on, I became the marshal's principal English interpreter when my services were not needed by the premier. Like the premier, I came to love Marshal Chen Yi, regarding both men as father figures.

Chairman Mao spent a great deal of time trying to convince nervous Party cadres around the country that the Hundred Flowers Movement was a "drizzle," not "torrential rains." He toured the provinces by train for several weeks, explaining to local officials that the class struggle against the landlords and the bourgeoisie was complete. As the rectification movement grew, newspapers published articles written by prominent intellectuals and others criticizing the Party and the bureaucracy.

For the first time, dissidents openly spoke of Party members and cadres acting as if they were better than the masses, complaining that the élites enjoyed the luxuries of privilege while treating the peasants like slaves, a reversion to feudalistic instincts. On probation for Party membership, I was disinclined—especially after mistakenly criticizing the marshal's toasting habits—to express any serious doubts I had about the Party leadership. Besides, I had few.

China was being led by the true heroes of the revolution, men who had sacrificed much to free the Chinese people. The chairman, the premier, the marshal, and other ranking members of the Party all bore scars from being injured or wounded. They had lost family members, lived like true revolutionaries in the caves at Yan'an, and overcome everything the Japanese, the Nationalists, and the Americans could throw at them. Although he didn't take part in the Long March, or live in the caves, my brother Chaoding had sacrificed his American family and career to return and do his part. The sense of purpose was pervasive, and I felt it as keenly as anyone.

Some of the writing that appeared in the press made me furious, especially an article by Luo Longji, a ministerial official and the leader of a small coalition party called the Democratic League. Luo chastised the Party, declaring, "The Marxist-Leninist small intellectuals [are] trying to lead the petit-bourgeois big intellectuals, the greenhorns trying to lead the professionals!"

The Party seemed unusually tolerant of such insults, and I worried that this blooming and contending business might grow into a Hungarian-style revolt that could undermine the progress China had made.

While the Hundred Flowers Campaign was blooming, so did my personal life. Approaching the age of twenty-seven, I was growing anxious to settle down. I wanted a companion for life, and a chance to provide Mother and Father with a baby or two to bounce on their knees. But, as outspoken as I could sometimes be when it came to political matters, I was shy around girls, an insecurity left over from my days in the States.

I had a pronounced snaggletooth that jutted outward at an angle, which in the past I had used to get a laugh out of my schoolmates. That had pegged me as something of a class clown. While I was growing up, haircuts were rare and always done at home, perfunctory and frugal. My clothing was occasionally shabby and, as I shot up, ill-fitting. My largely middle- and upper-class American schoolmates showed up after summer and winter vacations decked out in stylish new outfits. In that pond, I was a scrawny catch.

But there was more to it. In the States I had been a foreign oddity, focused on doing my best in school and thinking incessantly of the day that I would return to China. I couldn't see myself marrying an American girl and being distracted from my goals. I had also been trained to avoid all other Chinese, including girls.

Returning to China, I discovered that I was still a foreign oddity, in spite of my authentic Chinese roots and my service in Korea. Even the premier sometimes referred to me affectionately as his "foreign doll."

Women seemed to regard me as a quaint weirdo, a "foreign devil" who had grown up abroad and returned speaking clumsy Chinese, a man essentially clueless about how to be a real Chinese. Unwilling to risk the shame of rejection or ridicule, I made no effort to engage the women I encountered. Besides, I was always busy, and I had no money.

The change came when I enrolled in a part-time French class offered at the Foreign Ministry. The class was also open to non-Ministry people working in other organizations and government offices. What better language for finding love than French? One of my classmates was an English translator at the Red Cross Society of China, a semi-official organization under the Ministry of Health. Wang Xiangtong worked in the International Liaison Department and wanted to broaden her language skills in the hope that she would be chosen to go abroad on special missions, like others in her group.

At first, she was just another Chinese girl with short black hair, dressed as we all were: in a rumpled blue cloth jacket, pants, and black leather shoes. But she caught my eye now and then, and I found myself blushing. There was a sparkle in her gaze, a glint of fire and intelligence. Looking at her face made me feel like smiling.

The ice finally broke one snowy day early in 1957. I had arrived at class ahead of time, but had then been summoned back to the office by my boss. As I left the building, I paused on the doorstep to admire the blanket of fresh snow that had turned the otherwise gray city into a sparkling jewel. I spotted Xiangtong hurrying up the sidewalk. Just as she neared the door, she slipped and landed smack on her bottom. Before I had a chance to rush forward to help her, she'd jumped up on her own and brushed herself off. I smiled nervously, and she returned a warm grin. My heart melted on the spot.

This momentary exchange evolved into small talk between lessons. To my delight, I discovered that she was not only learning French but had studied English in Shanghai and was quite good. So now I had something to offer her as well. After a few days without a rebuff, I mustered the courage to ask her for a date, to see an American movie at the International Club. She accepted without hesitation. A decisive woman! Another good sign.

During the period of liberalism that Mao had declared, for the first time American magazines, books, and the occasional film became available. Before then, any Western literature or movies were banned. Even showing an interest in such "cultural pollution" was enough to cast doubt on one's patriotism.

So being able to watch an American film in China was a guilty new treat, let alone seeing it with someone who could understand most of the dialogue. I had grown up going to movies, and had missed the experience. The date allowed me to interpret what she didn't understand, and explain some of the idioms and the cultural background of the story. We shared an intense curiosity about language and culture.

I don't recall which film we saw, but it probably was an old black-and-white film, in English, and made in Hollywood. Such films were screened mainly for members of the foreign embassies and high government officials. I could get tickets from my brother Chaoding.

Next, I invited Xiangtong to lunch. When the check came, we both reached into our pockets and produced money to pay. I insisted and she relented. At our second lunch date, she insisted on paying, but I noticed that the bank note she pulled out was creased in exactly the same place as the one she produced the first time: it was the same bill. I let her save face by allowing her to pay, although she was clearly even poorer than I. Hopelessly smitten, I vowed I would win her heart, and then do everything in my power to guarantee that she had enough food for the rest of her life.

Our bond rapidly grew. One fine spring evening we were quietly chatting on a park bench when her ready smile suddenly faded and she fell silent. She stared down at her folded hands. Finally she said, soberly, "Chaozhu, I have something important to tell you. Something that may be a problem." She took a deep breath and announced, "My father and three brothers live in Taiwan."

The stricken look in her eyes, a look of pain mingled with fear, tore at my heart. "That doesn't matter to me!" I blurted. But it mattered plenty in politics, and she knew that as well as I.

As complex as my biography was, I had the support of the premier and a vital role in the Ministry. People with family members or relatives living in Taiwan were several rungs down the ladder—automatically suspect, with no hope of ever joining the Communist Party, and thus barred from the best assignments.

Just seven years had passed since Chiang's Nationalists fled the mainland, and it was widely understood that there were Kuomintang spies and sympathizers everywhere. Having relatives in Taiwan was a stubborn stain on one's reputation, even in Xiangtong's case, where her Taiwan connection was the result of several cruel twists of fate, not of disloyalty.

Xiangtong explained that her father came from an educated family in Jiangxi Province, south of the Yangtze River. At the age of fifteen, his family sent him to Paris, where he studied for fifteen years before returning to China. Her mother came from a big family with twenty children, and her maternal grandfather had been a wealthy magistrate serving the Qing court, China's last dynasty.

Xiangtong's father and mother met and married in Beijing while her father was teaching French and working as an architect. She had grown up in a big, comfortable courtyard house with two gardens and servants. But her peaceful childhood ended with the Japanese invasion of Beijing in 1937, when she was seven. It was around that same time that my own family's peaceful life was upended and we began our long journey that ended in New York.

The puppet regime set up by the Japanese tried to recruit her father, but he refused their repeated enticements until he realized that, unless he collaborated, he would be in mortal danger. He fled to the French zone in Shanghai, and the family followed a year later. They struggled to survive on his savings as the war raged around them.

After the Japanese were defeated and the civil war resumed, the entire family moved back to Beijing. When she was sixteen, Xiangtong's parents shipped her off to New Zealand to live with a childless uncle who was the Chinese counsel general in Wellington. Her aunt and uncle tried to persuade her to marry the son of a local Chinese family, a man ten years her senior. She refused and, missing her family, returned to Shanghai in the summer of 1947 to study language and literature at Fudan University.

Soon after the war, China recovered Taiwan from Japan. To build up its economy, the Chinese government called on citizens to move to Taiwan. With the Japanese departure, many important posts were left vacant. Since Xiangtong's father knew Wei Daoming, then governor of Taiwan, in 1946 he landed a job there as general manager in the Provincial Taiwan Ceramics Company. Xiangtong's three brothers followed, leaving mother and daughter behind.

When the People's Liberation Army defeated the Nationalists and sent them fleeing to Taiwan, Xiangtong's father and brothers were marooned, unable to travel back to the mainland. Xiangtong and her mother, likewise, were stuck in Beijing.

Worse still for her father, the Kuomintang forced him out of his good job. He returned to teaching, but only after being required to join the Nationalist Party.

The Korean War and the U.S. decision to side with the Kuomintang sealed her father's fate, a fate that settled like a curse on Xiangtong's head. She was one of the best English interpreters in her office, often called on to escort English-speaking guests. But her bosses always sent along someone else who knew enough English to be able to report anything she might say or do that seemed suspicious. The Red Cross sent delegations abroad every year to international meetings, but Xiangtong was never invited along. They feared that she would try to defect, to be reunited with her father and her brothers. Knowing English was for Xiangtong both an asset and a liability.

Without my saying a thing, she knew that marriage was on my mind. We already acted like a couple who'd been together for a long time. I was not surprised when she finished her sad story and she said, "I thought I should let you know about my situation before deciding to go on with our friendship."

"Well, I don't care!" I repeated, taking her hand in mine. "We all have complicated backgrounds. Look at me!" I chuckled. "Educated by the foreign devils at Harvard, and my older brother Chaoli staying behind in America. But it hasn't kept me from working for the premier. Besides, attitudes are changing. A hundred flowers are blooming, and you are the most beautiful of them all."

Xiangtong blushed and looked away. I felt a wave of such tenderness that I had to stifle a sob. The story of her separation from her father and her brothers, and the political discrimination she had experienced in her work, was heartbreaking. But the swell of emotion also flowed from my joy: I had met someone intelligent, thoughtful, openhearted, and beautiful, all in the same package. How much we shared, I thought. We were both strangers within our own culture. We understood each other.

Not wanting her to think that I was acting out of pity, I waited a couple of weeks before I popped the question. I had brought her a gift of a French dictionary, and after we looked up a few words I took her hands in mine and said, simply, "We have synergy. Let's help each other. I am begging for your hand in marriage."

"Why so soon?" she said shyly.

"Oh, you agree. . . ." I answered, and threw my arms around her, kissing her on her lips. When we had finally calmed down, we discussed when we would do it.

"Maybe we should wait until you finish your probationary Party membership," she suggested. "That way, in case there is any question about my father . . ." Her reasoning made sense, so we agreed to wait.

I rushed back to my dormitory that night and immediately wrote to my parents, who were away in Taiyuan, where my father was serving as vice chairman of the People's Political Consultative Conference for Shanxi Province. "I have met the girl of my dreams," I wrote. "And we intend to marry. I am asking for your blessing and good wishes."

The next evening after work, I visited Chaoding and Jingyi, to announce my great news. I was distressed to find my beloved eldest brother looking puffy and pale. He suffered from diabetes, as well as the stress of his work. He had been in and out of the hospital a couple of times over a short period.

As I explained Xiangtong's family history, my brother's smile faded. Jingyi shook her head with a look of disapproval. She worked at the nongovernmental organization the Friendship Association. Like Chaoding, Jingyi could trace her political roots to the beginnings of the Communist Party. She counted among her closest allies Kang Sheng, the head of the secret police when Mao and Zhou were ensconced in Yan'an in the early days. Kang, in turn, was a close ally of Mao's wife, Jiang Qing, the former actress, who, thus far, had played the role of offstage wife to the emperor—rarely seen, and never heard. But she was Mao's wife all the same. Given all the people they knew between them, my brother and sister-in-law were privy to the thinking at the top. "This is a very bad idea," she said flatly. "You will have nothing but trouble marrying a girl with such a background."

I looked at Chaoding, hoping that he would say something a bit more optimistic, or even congratulatory. He only nodded and gazed with somber expression into his teacup.

"I don't care what anyone thinks about her background," I said. "I'm in love with her and she's the only one for me! Besides, things are changing. Soon no one will care about the past."

My sister-in-law uttered a loud, peevish sigh. "You are young and blinded by love, Little Ji," she said. "Look at your elder brother here, who sacrificed so much for the revolution. Yet he is still attacked by the old Eighth Route Army veterans in the Party as if he had been in bed with Chiang Kai-shek instead of risking his life for the Communist Party! Things are changing, yes. And they will change again, Little Ji. Maybe sooner than you think! A flower cannot bloom forever."

Chaoding was less strident, but he still tried to talk me out of marrying Xiangtong. "You have an important position in the government now," he told me. "You must think about every decision you make, especially while you're only a probationary Party member."

I left their home disappointed, but just as determined to marry Xiangtong. In the weeks that followed, Chaoding and Jingyi campaigned to change my mind. They tried to fix me up with girl who was studying English, supposedly sweet and beautiful, the daughter of a revolutionary cadre and herself a Party member. I refused to see this other woman, making it clear that I wanted to hear no more about her, or even to learn her name.

Happily, my parents were more liberal. Upon receiving my letter, my father immediately set out for Beijing to greet his future daughter-in-law. We met for a warm family chat, Father smiling and stroking his stringy beard throughout. It gave me a glow to see him sharing this big moment in my life, and no doubt anticipating the prospect of grandkids to spoil. He had loved having Chaoding's two little boys around when we lived in New York. The next day he made it official. We had his full support.

Soon after, Xiangtong and I met Jingyi for lunch. Walking her home afterward, we passed the stall of an elderly fortune-teller. Instead of reading palms or studying tea leaves, he had a little bird in a tiny cage to perform the magic. The fortune-teller shuffled a stack of paper slips, each with an answer to a common question, then enticed the bird to pick one out with its beak, after which the bird got a reward of a grain of rice.

Jingyi decided to have her fortune told. The bird did its duty, and the fortune-teller handed her the chosen slip of paper. She read it, blushed, then handed it to me. Xiangtong and I read it together: "Do not interfere in the marriage of others!"

That was the end of the lobbying. In time, Chaoding admitted that Xiangtong and I had much in common, which explained why we got along so well. Like me, Xiangtong had made a conscious choice to be where she was. She had returned to China from New Zealand, just as I had returned from the States. To our surprise, we also discovered that we had both served in Korea. She had been a translator in the General Political Department of the People's Liberation Army until she was mustered out in 1954, when the fighting ended.

It was the rule at the time that Communist Party members, even those on probation, must obtain permission before making major decisions like marriage. I presented myself to the Foreign Ministry's Party representative in charge of such matters and formally asked for permission to marry Xiangtong. A gentle middle-aged woman, she looked through Xiangtong's files and smiled at me. "I see no problem here, and I congratulate you two!"

She signed the documents. We were now approved to become husband and wife. Xiangtong and I decided that since we had permission, we might as well strike while the iron was hot, and begin our lives together.

We needed a place to live. Without one, the marriage would have to wait. But we had the good fortune to find one right away. A young Foreign Ministry couple who were being transferred abroad left us a small, flimsy lean-to. It had a brick wall at the back, a tin roof above, and cardboard panels separating it from other family lean-tos in a row of lean-tos. This shabby urban jungle backed up against one of the outside walls of a large government compound of brick and colonial-era buildings. There was a small park in the middle.

Our neighbors included some noted writers and intellectuals, as well as the Tang family. Tang Mingzhao had been Father's colleague in the newspaper business in New York. The older of his two daughters, Nancy, had been like a member of our extended family. Now they lived in one of the permanent buildings in the compound in what was, by our standards, a luxury flat. Though Tang Mingzhao played an important role in the new government, we never talked shop.

Our lean-to was just nine square meters (about nine by eleven feet), barely big enough for a simple bed, a dresser, a small table, and one chair. Our water source was a communal spigot, the toilet a squatter with a mud floor. You could hear the neighbors' every sigh and belch through the paper walls. It was very nearly camping out. But to us it was a castle—our first home. No more dormitories!

We marked the start of our lives together with a small ceremony in Xiangtong's office. Nothing was required, and no one had money for elaborate weddings. Even if there had been some religious or other tradition, Xiangtong and I were ardent revolutionaries who disdained such feudalistic practices. As poor as we were, I did manage to buy her a gift of a colorful blouse, like the sort young women dared to wear during the blooming and contending. It cost a third of my monthly salary.

On the evening of May 25, 1957, we officially signed our marriage vows in a small conference hall at the Chinese Red Cross Society. Xiangtong's mother had bought enough red silk to make her gown. I wore my good gray Mao suit. We were greeted by a small crowd of friends, co-workers, and family. They all signed their names on a piece of pink silk to bear witness to our marriage.

My boss, the director of the General Office of the Foreign Ministry, and Xiangtong's boss, the president of the Chinese Red Cross Society, took turns saying a few kind words, followed by family members. My third brother, Chaofu, said a few words, then Xiangtong's mother added a few more. Unfortunately my parents were in Taiyuan.

We spent almost half a month's salary to buy candies for our guests, and we danced to some traditional Chinese music. My mother gave Xiangtong a gift of a new bicycle, about as big a luxury for us as getting a car.

The honeymoon suite consisted of a thin cotton mattress laid atop some boards lashed together on a rough frame. In addition to our single table, I indulged myself with the purchase of a bookshelf for my growing library. Our lean-to came with a spittoon for those who had that disgusting habit. Neither of us did, but it was there to let visitors know not to use the floor.

After the party at the Red Cross Society, we were driven to the lean-to. Xiangtong made up the bed while I put my precious books on my new bookshelf. Then we each set out our family photos and other keepsakes, like my medal from Korea. Finally, we paused with our backs to the courtyard, my arm around Comrade Xiangtong's waist, and surveyed our vast estate.

It felt good to be home.

CHAPTER 17

Contradictions at the Top

Xiangtong and I married in the middle of a monthlong period when the Hundred Flowers Campaign reached a feverish, nerve-racking pitch. The Party leadership seemed to have declared open season on itself, allowing unfettered publication in the government-controlled press of letters and articles by intellectuals, officials, and others attacking the Party, sometimes in the most provocative and inflammatory language. The charges were cronyism, hypocrisy, corruption, repression, and mismanagement.

There were elements of truth in much of the criticism, but some of the writers made outrageous statements, in one case even suggesting that the Communist Party withdraw from government offices and schools. Demonstrations challenging the Party broke out on college campuses, and in some places there were reports of violent clashes with the police. Students held mass debates about capitalism versus socialism. They demanded democratic reforms. The first Democracy Wall appeared at Peking University, layered with hundreds of handmade signs and posters. This emboldened some professors and other intellectuals to publicly endorse the growing rebellion.

The rhetoric seemed to reach an incendiary level in an article written by a science professor at the China People's University in Beijing. It appeared in the *People's Daily* near the end of May, right after our wedding. The article practically called for a Hungarian-style insurrection:

Who are those whose standard of living actually has been raised? It is those party members and cadres who used to wear torn shoes but are now riding in sedan cars. China belongs to its 600 million people, including the counterrevolutionaries. It does not belong to the Communist Party. . . . The masses will beat you down, kill you, overthrow you.

Just a week or so later, Chairman Mao answered the growing unrest and escalating rhetoric. He did it in the *People's Daily*, writing a blistering critique of a short story by a noted hydraulics engineer and university professor, Huang Wanli. The newspaper published Huang's story next to an essay by Mao, though unattributed, headlined, WHY IS THIS?

Huang had previously made himself unpopular with the Party in an official capacity by challenging an ambitious plan backed by the Soviet Union to dam the Yellow River, declaring the proposed project environmentally unsound. History proved Huang correct, but at the time he was regarded by Party leaders as a troublemaker interfering in China's industrial progress and its relations with the USSR.

Huang had also criticized the Party for ignoring the warnings of a fellow academic, Ma Yinchu, the president of Peking University. Ma had criticized government inaction to slow China's population boom, arguing that unless birth-control measures were adopted the nation's future development would continue to lag behind the rest of the world's.

Like many educated Chinese, including Chairman Mao, Huang wrote essays and poetry. And, like many Chinese writers over the millennia, his stories were infused with symbolism. Huang's allegorical story "The Road Turns Over," was a thinly veiled criticism of individual Party officials and of Communism itself. Now the founder of the People's Republic had made him a target of official disapproval in the most public way possible.

You could hear a pin drop in the Foreign Ministry that morning, as we sat at our desks poring over our newspapers, reading the lines, then trying to read between them. It was clear that while we had slept the night before, a hard political frost had blown in, killing off the Hundred Flowers.

Like me, both Huang and Ma had been educated abroad, making them easy targets. They were intellectuals with overseas connections and bourgeois pasts. But, unlike them, I had confined my blooming and contending—aside from my blunder about the foreign minister's toasting habits—to pointing out bureaucratic inefficiencies, not attacking the Party or calling for anyone's overthrow. In my character posters, comments, and the letters I wrote to newspapers, I had been a vociferous critic of the radicals advocating rebellion. I was a Communist's Communist!

Xiangtong and I, along with colleagues in our offices, digested the chairman's words with varying responses but uniform shock. After encouraging dissent, Mao had suddenly and viciously turned on the dissenters. The Hundred Flowers Campaign, as Mao would later put it, "let poisonous weeds sprout and grow in profusion, so that the people, now shocked to find these ugly things still existing in the world, would take action to wipe them out."

My initial reaction was one of enthusiasm. I had viewed the unanswered torrent of dissent as a threat to our hard-won independence. How could China, struggling just to keep our people fed and our borders secure, move ahead in the world if we had to fight yet another civil war? Hadn't the Chinese people suffered enough?

Mao had again proved himself a brilliant tactician, I thought. He had employed his signature strategy, borrowed from the ancients: retreat first and lull the enemy into thinking he's winning, then launch your attack when it's least expected. But during the following weeks Mao's writings and speeches turned ominous: "Bourgeois Rightists, who summon the storm and churn the waves, plot in secret and incite discontent among the masses. . . . There are Rightists in every city and they want to topple us. We are now closing in on them. We have lured the snake from its lair."

Some ardent critics who had been encouraged to speak their minds now rushed to recant. Zhang Bojun, the minister of communications, who weeks earlier had written an article advocating a multiparty system of government, now wrote a letter, prominently published in the *People's Daily,* in which he declared, "I have failed to live up to the expectations of the Communist party and Chairman Mao, who has guided me and trusted me these past years. I committed a serious mistake ideologically."

It was too late. The storm had broken. What would come to be known as the Anti-Rightist Campaign, a massive and disruptive political purge, now began in earnest. My sister-in-law's words came back to haunt me: "A flower cannot bloom forever." But the little fortune-telling bird may have brought us good luck. Had Xiangtong and I procrastinated for just a couple of weeks, the Party official whose approval we needed would not have been smiling and would not have given her blessing to our union. Living in our modest little shack, we felt very fortunate to have each other.

Over the coming months, well-known intellectuals who had been making constructive criticisms were now denounced as bourgeois rightists and ousted from their jobs. They were forced to submit to mass struggle meetings during which they had to stand before an enormous, hostile crowd angrily shouting criticisms, and then admit their impure thoughts. Prominent literary figures were condemned for opposing the Party's ban on works that glorified individualism and hero worship. Among them was a writer known by her pen name, Ding Ling. She had been a Party member since the 1920s, and her boyfriend had been assassinated during the White Terror. It was astonishing that even someone with such an impeccable political biography was unsafe.

The walls and halls of Peking University became plastered with posters denouncing Professor Ma Yinchu, even though I had heard Zhou express similar concerns over China's burgeoning birthrate. In launching the Hundred Flowers Campaign, Mao had said that it was supposed to elicit criticism that would help the Party govern better. Now that he'd spoken out, Ma was condemned for propagating the reactionary theories of bourgeois Malthusianism.

Huang and Ma were not wild-eyed radicals advocating another civil war. It was not they who had been calling Chairman Mao's rule "arbitrary and reckless," or accusing the Party of Fascist tactics. Nor were they heartless landlords and capitalists who had been exploiting the peasants.

But the newly condemned were demoted or lost their jobs. They became social and political pariahs among colleagues and friends. In many cases, they were sent into internal exile, forced to work on rural farms while contemplating their "wrong" thinking and being reeducated to be good Communists. As during the land-redistribution upheaval, there were reports of people being beaten, and more than a few could not cope with the loss of face and committed suicide.

Xiangtong came home from her office at the Red Cross Society one day to report that a colleague's husband who had been branded a rightist had disappeared without notice or explanation. The poor woman assumed the worst and, as many spouses were encouraged to do, officially divorced him to save herself and their children from sharing his disgrace. Her mother-in-law was so distraught that she hanged herself.

As the summer and fall of 1957 unfolded, the nation's intelligentsia—estimated at five million people in government and education—was on edge. I had criticized some of the more flagrant attacks on the Party before Mao's critique appeared, so my credentials as a loyalist were unchallenged. I was praised by others for my commitment.

In addition, I still felt protected by my professional and family connections to the premier, and by the fact that Zhou Enlai was my brother's mentor and my brother was one of Zhou's trusted subordinates. I was the premier's foreign doll, his Little Ji. Our relationship was professional but warm. He often asked after the health of Xiangtong and my parents, especially my father.

Spending as much time as I did with the premier, I soon learned to read his body language. He understood spoken English and listened closely to everything I said. I could tell when he disagreed with the way I had interpreted a word or a phrase by the way he shifted in his chair. He held himself in a dignified pose at all times, but he had inconspicuous mannerisms—a look in his eye or a twitch at the corner of his mouth—that I could read as surprise or disdain at some remark by a guest whom he found provocative or ignorant.

And he read me as well. He knew that banquets were especially exhausting work. With no bathroom or tea breaks, they entailed several hours of nonstop thinking in two languages, translating and repeating to a visiting king or premier or president Zhou's every word, and vice versa. Meanwhile, there was the constant cross-chatter to be expected at a large round ceremonial banquet table full of political leaders all vying for center stage, while flocks of waiters swooped in to serve and clear. How many times must I have explained to a foreign visitor what maotai was, and how it was drunk in traditional Chinese toasts!

I grew very tired at times, and the premier always seemed to notice when I was getting droopy and encouraged me to eat.

I also felt safe because I had by this time established myself at the Foreign Ministry as the best at my trade. I was served well by my mastery of English, the care I took with tricky interpretations, my familiarity with Western culture and idioms, my patriotism, and my fearlessness. Though always respectful, I was neither intimidated nor tongue-tied in the presence of power.

But for the first time since I had returned from the United States, I had a growing sense of disbelief at what seemed to be happening in my beloved country, especially when the Party condemned Dr. Pu Shan, one of my principal and most beloved mentors. He was the Pu brother who had introduced me to the Chinese Communist Reading Society at Harvard. He had taken me under his wing in Korea and helped launch me on my interpretation career. His brother had been the premier's interpreter and had groomed me as his successor.

Pu Shan was someone I knew personally and whom I knew to be a loyal Communist. He became one of the first ranking officials in the Foreign Ministry to be openly branded a bourgeois rightist. He was made to stand and endure verbal abuses during struggle meetings organized by his former colleagues, although few had their hearts in it. He was well liked and respected.

This injustice I could not bear. Violating the convention of the time to avoid guilt by association, I visited Pu Shan and his wife, who had also been branded a rightist. Arriving at their modest one-room apartment in the Ministry housing compound, I was so wound up that I burst into tears when he opened the door. I sat on the edge of their sofa, pouring out my despair and pledging my loyalty in the language we'd shared at Harvard.

"I will never believe you are bourgeois rightists!" I said. "I have and will always think of you with gratitude as true comrades who taught me what the Chinese Communist Party was all about and led me to devote my whole life to the Chinese revolution. I will always regard you as model Communists!"

Pu Shan smiled and patted me on the knee.

"Do not worry about us, Little Ji," he said. "A good Communist must always be ready to accept criticism from his comrades and superiors." He and his wife put on courageous faces, but when I left it felt like a death in the family.

My heart ached as I walked back to the office, struggling to hide my grief and discouragement. It was all so senseless and socially violent. I knew I would be the only one who dared brave a political rebuke for fraternizing with a condemned rightist. But my affection and gratitude for Dr. Pu had trumped all other considerations. In the end, no one noticed or complained.

Pu Shan and his wife were soon officially fired from their posts at the Foreign Ministry and expelled from the Party. Pu was then sent to a collective farm for reeducation. It would be years before I saw them again and their Party credentials were restored. To this day, I cannot think of that time without a lump in my throat.

The mass movement against bourgeois rightists gained momentum. Quotas were issued. Some departments were ordered to purge 5 percent of their staffs as "rightist." How that number was arrived at was unexplained, but Mao had speculated in a speech that between 2 and 10 percent of the population were probably bourgeois rightists. Mao said and wrote many provocative things, and, often enough, a casual comment like that set off a chain of knee-jerk bureaucratic responses that ended in the adoption of policies that were divorced from reality.

The usual suspects at the top of the list of purge candidates were those with overseas connections. Many of the Chinese comrades I had met while in the States were branded as rightists or, worse, as counter-revolutionaries. A student who returned on the same ship I did killed himself. His wife went insane. One by one, the unfortunates disappeared into the political and social desert. In a culture that places the highest value on having and keeping face, losing it was catastrophic, unbearable.

By the time it had spent itself, some five hundred thousand people had been "weeded out" during the Anti-Rightist Campaign. Many were the best and the brightest, the most educated and the most potentially valuable to China's future. Although quite a number were later exonerated, those who weren't driven to premature deaths in some cases spent as many as twenty years living in private purgatories.

Chairman Mao was unapologetic. In a 1958 speech, he boasted that the Anti-Rightist Campaign had surpassed a famous purge that took place around 200 B.C., when the first Qin emperor ordered that all books be burned and intellectuals who opposed him killed.

It is often difficult for those who haven't experienced it to comprehend how so many people could tolerate such intolerable conditions. At the very least, I am often asked, "Why didn't you try to escape or defect?"

First, I had no desire to leave. I had enjoyed my life in the lap of American luxury but now had a higher purpose. I would have loved to have had the chance to sit down to a greasy hamburger with french fries and a chocolate milkshake. But I have always prided myself as a Chinese, and I embraced the gruel and pickles when that was all there was to eat. Our little lean-to was just as good as a palace. To me, the deprivation was the crucible in which I was being molded into a good Communist.

Of course, it is understandable that many Westerners would find it next to impossible to understand my state of mind at that point, or the state of mind of others like me. And while I indeed began to have some doubts about Mao himself, I never doubted the Party as a whole, and was confident that it would successfully pull through.

Some of my colleagues may have thought me naïve, as did my sister-in-law. I saw myself as an idealist in the service of China's future greatness. An optimist, I wanted things to work out for China, and I accepted that it would take time and be difficult. Whenever my resolve faltered, I conjured the image of Father's proverbial ant, never giving up in its single-minded quest to ascend the stairway.

For those who may have considered leaving the country, there were few safe exits. The borders were sealed. Exit visas were reserved for official business only. And the outside world was quite hostile. The British in Hong Kong wanted nothing to do with us Reds. Anyone caught sneaking across the border was immediately returned to suffer the most grievous consequences.

Meanwhile, China was squabbling with most of its neighbors over ancient, simmering boundary disputes that had reignited in the vacuum left by the end of foreign domination. Our troops were on alert on our borders with Korea, the Soviet Union, India, and Pakistan, among others.

A battery of our long-range guns were dug in on the coast, their barrels pointed at the small nearby islands occupied by U.S.-backed remnants of the Kuomintang. Our side launched occasional artillery barrages on Quemoy and Matsu, just to let the other guys know that we were still serious about uniting the Chinese islands with the mainland. We couldn't fight the mighty U.S. Seventh Fleet, but we could make a nuisance of ourselves in other ways.

Perhaps the biggest reason people suffered in silence through the bad times was to protect their families. Anyone who was labeled a "rightist" and was punished left behind family members who would then also be condemned. In addition to losing face, they would be ostracized. Hounded to the margins of society, some were forced into remote villages, where they lived in unheated, unsanitary quarters, subsisting on meager diets, robbed of their health. This happened to a number of high-ranking officials after they were purged from the Party. Some of China's greatest thinkers and leaders died alone and in squalor.

In this poisonous atmosphere, millions of us kept our doubts to ourselves, even among family and friends. There was no benefit from complaining, and no one to complain to. We were all in the same boat, and did our best to grin and bear it. I was one of the lucky ones. I had a true coconspirator in life—Xiangtong—and too much work to spend time feeling sorry for myself, or for others.

In addition to my usual chores and my continued language studies, the premier had encouraged me to begin reading ancient Chinese history. "Soon enough you will be asked to interpret for the chairman," he said. "He likes to reference the ancients, and it will be easier for you to give the correct interpretation if you know the context." The book he recommended—a classic entitled *Mirror of Government*—was extraordinarily difficult and frustrating for me to read. But the premier wouldn't have suggested it if it wasn't important, so I doggedly kept at it.

Although I had yet to be summoned to interpret for Mao, it was becoming clear that, of the two men, Mao was the flame and Zhou was the keeper of the flame. Zhou always consulted Mao before making major policy decisions. There was never a suggestion that he coveted Mao's role, nor did he speak of Mao obsequiously. But the premier had his own way of showing that he disagreed with the chairman's methods.

While the cadre class and the intellectuals hunkered down during the Anti-Rightist Campaign, there had been friction at the highest levels of the Party, though almost always behind closed doors. Cadres working directly with our leaders were never privy to outright arguments, but the tension between the two principal factions was felt within each ministry.

Sometimes called democratic personages, rationalists like my brother agreed with Professor Ma about overpopulation and saw the political exile of smart, committed cadres as a waste of talent. The premier was, likewise, a realist and a humanist. I would later learn just how many times he and others like him went to bat for one accused person or another, in some cases actually saving their lives. But in all public ways the premier was very loyal to Mao.

The radical faction were fanatical believers in the Chinese brand of Marxism the chairman espoused. They read his writings and heard his speeches as though receiving the word of God. This group also included the politically ambitious, many of whom plotted to destroy any other leaders who disagreed with or criticized Mao.

There were fundamental differences between the two camps. Jiang Qing, her accomplice Kang Sheng, and their clique were evil and ambitious. On the other side were true revolutionaries like Premier Zhou En-lai, Marshal Chen Yi, and others. The chairman knew how to get his way by siccing Jiang Qing, Kang Sheng, and their faction on Premier Zhou and people who supported Zhou.

The contradiction between the styles of China's two leaders became starkly apparent to me in the middle of the Anti-Rightist purge that took place in 1957. Since liberation in 1949, Mao had essentially been holed up in his quarters in Zhongnanhai, a sprawling, walled, heavily guarded park district next to the Forbidden City, in the center of Beijing. The huge compound—on the scale of New York's Central Park—included two lakes and manicured grounds, and had been created by an ancient emperor. Inside this compound lived Mao, the premier, and certain high-ranking Politburo members. Serving them was an enormous office and security staff. It was also home to high-level government and Party offices.

In his courtyard house, surrounded by his enormous library and his aides, behind three layers of security, Mao wrote his essays and speeches railing against American imperialists, and later he aimed at the Soviet revisionists.

Meanwhile, in another part of Beijing, at a hotel reserved for foreigners, I accompanied the premier as he hosted a delegation of international youths including a group of eager young American students on their way home from a World Youth Festival in Moscow. Zhou was jovial and gracious, posing for pictures with the awe-inspired American students and their chaperones, assuring them that the gates of China were open to Americans. "But it must be on an equal and mutual basis," he told them. "The people don't want to be kept from making contact. The Chinese people are willing to be friends with the American people."

One of the visitors, a young writer from New York, asked the premier if Taiwan could be reunited with China by peaceful means. Without a hint of rancor, Zhou replied, "If the United States will evacuate its troops."

The premier sought accommodation. These were sentiments Mao would have couched in more bellicose language, and often did. Several years later, during a difficult negotiation between Premier Zhou and Prime Minister Jawaharlal Nehru over a serious border dispute, I was helping to put the final touches on an important communiqué from our side, a reply to an uncompromising letter from Nehru. The draft of the premier's answer was firm but cordial, his usual style. He always tried to leave doors ajar.

My colleagues and I had finished translating the letter into English. It had been approved for release when we received urgent instructions to stand by: there was one more sentence coming. When we retrieved it, we were startled at how crude it was: "Mr. Nehru, if you think that we Chinese people can allow you to shit and piss on our heads, then you are badly mistaken." It was like nothing I had ever heard the premier say or write. There was no doubt in our minds that this came straight from Mao.

The letter was sent with the offensive last sentence, and that was the end of the negotiations. India attacked China and we fought a short border clash.

Mao's invisible hand was everywhere in China. His placid, all-knowing eyes gazed down on hundreds of millions of us every day. Millions of copies of poster-size portraits of the chairman had been distributed throughout the country and dutifully hung in every office in every official building and in the living quarters of every patriotic home.

There was no such cult around the premier. He usually traveled with just one bodyguard and a secretary. On domestic trips into the countryside with a visiting dignitary, he'd sometimes order his driver to pull over so that he could hop out and chat with a farmer. More than once, the farmer had no idea who he was at first. When his identity was revealed, the premier always attracted a lot of attention, although he was never mobbed or threatened in any way. That would have been most un-Chinese behavior, in any case.

Zhou was sharply attentive to everything around him. On a trip to Shanghai, the foreign dignitary he accompanied was treated to a concert by a choir of young boys. When it ended, the premier asked to speak with the host and sternly rebuked him for making one of the boys sing his solo so long at a high pitch. "He has a beautiful voice, but it will be ruined if you damage his vocal cords with so much strain," Zhou said.

The premier's interest in the comfort of others was not limited to foreign dolls and small children. Marshal Chen Yi, the foreign minister and vice premier, was a stout old warrior who was noticeably less robust than the premier. Zhou took a particular interest in his well-being. We were in Burma once, in extremely hot, humid weather, attending a horse race with the Burmese leader, when the premier noticed the back of Chen's thick neck glistening with sweat. Zhou handed me his own fan and told me to go and sit beside the marshal and fan him. Chen smiled appreciatively.

While the premier flew here and there trying to build bridges and resolve disputes, Mao rarely left his compound. Important guests were usually brought to see him in his study. This was as much a function of safety as it was protocol. The chairman had once gotten the urge to go out to a restaurant for lunch and was spotted by someone in the street. It took his security detail hours to clear the streets of the thousands of people who showed up hoping to catch a glimpse of him.

The rare times he traveled, Mao used a special armored train staffed with a private army of security agents and secretaries. His security people even ordered the stations along the route cleaned up, shut down, and guarded until his train had passed.

As the Anti-Rightist Campaign wound down in 1958, a new form of mass chaos was brewing: the Great Leap Forward. Mao had ordered the collectivization of all agriculture. Land that had been redistributed to the peasants was now taken back and made communal property in huge cooperatives. The peasants were left with small plots of their own, for subsistence farming only. All other activity was for the communal good, to be shared equally.

Cadres were to join the peasants in the fields, factories, and construction sites. Even Mao made an appearance at a dam-building project to have his picture taken with a shovel in hand. The premier spent a number of days laboring at a new reservoir being built at the Ming Tombs outside Beijing.

Eager for China to catch up to the rest of the industrialized world, Mao came up with schemes that were supposed to increase productivity but had the opposite effect. Collectivization, which Mao thought would infuse the population with a sense of group purpose, instead removed the people's incentive to work the fields. Productivity fell, but bureaucrats responsible for meeting quotas falsely reported an upsurge in output and enthusiasm on the part of the people.

Isolated, the chairman believed these reports, which included a famous photo, widely published, of a child appearing to be perched atop a standing field of wheat. The caption claimed that by planting wheat close together farmers had been able to produce unheard-of yields. The photo had been staged. The child was actually sitting on a bunch of very closely transplanted wheat grown especially for this purpose. But no one dared tell that to the chairman. Actually, the 1957 harvest had been a good one, though not as good as what was reported.

Another of Mao's goals was to speedily catch up with the United States and Britain in the output of steel. Instead of large, efficient steel plants, production was to be a cottage industry—a mass movement of the people. Everyone in the country was ordered to build backyard furnaces to make steel.

Millions of crude brick-and-mortar fireboxes were slapped together out of available materials. Precious trees were felled, and where there were no trees people took down heavy wooden doors and collected furniture to use for fuel. Into these roaring fireboxes went every spare scrap of metal that could be stripped or collected: iron gates, pots and pans, utensils, furniture, tools, everything. Provinces, cities, counties, and villages vied with one another to produce the greatest amount of steel. At night the entire countryside throughout China was speckled with the glowing dots of these homemade furnaces melting useful objects into lumps of gray metal.

The result was not steel, of course, but thousands of tons of useless melted scrap. The scheme was a fiasco, a waste of resources that destroyed millions of useful tools and objects. But the reports to the chairman and in the press touted the program's great success, much like the exaggerated claims of wheat production.

In the spring of 1958, almost a year after Mao's "Why Is This?" critique in the *People's Daily*, an essay by the chairman appeared in the début issue of a new Party magazine called *Red Flag*. In his essay, the chairman praised the humble virtue of the Chinese people:

> The outstanding thing about China's 600 million people is that they are "poor and blank." This may seem a bad thing, but in reality it is a good thing. Poverty gives rise to the desire for change, the desire for action and the desire for revolution. On a blank sheet of paper

free from any mark, the freshest and most beautiful characters can be written, the freshest and most beautiful pictures can be painted.

By the end of the Great Leap Forward three years later, fiascoes and paying back the huge "debts" the Soviet Union forced us to pay for accepting their weapons during the Korean War had produced a famine of historic proportions. There would be some thirty million fewer of those poor, blank Chinese.

Nearly a decade after liberation, China seemed to be trapped in a permanent state of revolution and poverty.

CHAPTER 18

Beating a Drowning Dog

In spite of the dour outlook, Xiangtong and I looked forward to becoming parents. In Chinese culture, lineage and legacy are matters of great pride. In the old days, naming protocols for offspring of generations yet unborn were carefully recorded on long scrolls. These were consulted when a new boy child came into the world. My name had been prescribed before my great-great-grandfather was even a gleam in anyone's eye. But the months passed without a pregnancy.

Meanwhile, we rode out the storms in our modest lean-to. We had enjoyed almost a year of camping in the middle of our lovely compound, which felt very much like a village hidden within the bustle of a great world capital. We had no privacy. The walls were just straw paper, and when anyone had a young child we all stayed awake at night listening to it squall. This community was a family of sorts, and it was comforting for us to be among people we trusted.

In one of the permanent buildings lived Tang Mingzhao, my father's old crony and New York newspaper associate. Soon after we had moved in, Tang invited Xiangtong and me to his house to refill our thermoflask with hot boiled water. This ancient Chinese habit of having hot water on hand is still prevalent today. Everyone owns a tall thermoflask that can hold as much as a half gallon or so of scalding hot water and keep it that way for hours. Water was boiled for safety and to make the staple green tea that was and remains ubiquitous in our diet and social customs.

Nancy helped to refill our thermos with water. Xiangtong and I were always exhausted at the end of our workdays' long shifts and six-day weeks. We commuted by bicycle in all weather.

Tang began to send Nancy to fetch our thermos and return it refilled and steaming hot. Nancy was born when the Tangs and my family lived in New York. Our fathers were so close that my father gave Tang's daughter her Chinese name: Wensheng. She was born while her father was traveling, and the name my father proposed for the little girl means, roughly, "hearing of birth." The name stuck.

Like many foreigners with names Americans have trouble pronouncing, the Tangs decided that life would be easier if their daughter had a Western name, too. They settled on Nancy, and that's how I addressed her.

Nancy arrived in China for the first time in 1950, at the age of nine. She went to school in Beijing and her English was very good. At the Foreign Language Institute, her English was well above the others. When my father had been the editor in chief at *Overseas Chinese Daily* in New York, her father had been the representative of the Chinese Communist Party. Tang was both a good friend to my father and my eldest brother, Chaoding.

We took all our meals, six days a week, in our office canteens. Sundays we were on our own. Because we worked so hard the rest of the week, I suggested to Xiangtong that instead of going to the trouble of cooking on our day off we should just have some biscuits washed down with hot tea. "That way, we can enjoy more of our free time," I said.

"No way!" she declared. "It isn't much, but this is home and I won't have us eating like beggars at home!" So we bought a small coal stove, setting it up in a corner of the yard. Then we scrounged up a couple of pots and pans and basic utensils. We stood looking at all this stuff and realized that neither of us had ever really cooked before. Xiangtong had grown up with servants and a mother who cooked. I, too, had had the benefit of servants for part of my childhood, and my mother had always cooked. In New York, I was always eating at the homes of friends or in school cafeterias. I washed dishes at Harvard, but I'd never cooked what was served on them.

The first time I put on a pot of water to boil, I asked Xiangtong how

I would know when it was ready. She laughed at me. "And you wanted to be a chemist and help build an atom bomb?" she said. "A lucky thing for China you didn't!"

We muddled along until the big test came. I had invited a colleague to join us for a special meal of noodles with a sauce containing a great and rare luxury in those lean times: ground pork. Xiangtong washed the vegetables and began to cut them up. Wanting to be helpful, I volunteered to prepare the sauce. I placed the empty frying pan on the hot stove and realized that I didn't know what to do next. "Xiangtong, should I put the meat in first or pour in some oil?"

She looked at me squint-eyed, deciding whether I was pulling her leg. I really didn't know. She shook her head woefully. "First pour in some cooking oil," she said. I did, and then I asked, "How about the sauce? Should I put in the chopped meat or the sauce first?"

She set her knife down on the table where she was preparing the vegetables. "Finish cutting up these pickles. I'll cook the sauce."

As ignorant as I was about the science of food, I was worse when it came to housekeeping. I was known among colleagues who had lived or traveled with me for leaving chaos and disorder in every room I occupied. One day, shortly after our marriage, Xiangtong was out when I was suddenly summoned to the Ministry for some urgent business. When Xiangtong returned, she thought we had been robbed (although there was nothing to steal). One drawer of our little dresser was half open, with a sock dangling over the edge. My dirty trousers, jacket, shirt, handkerchief, and socks lay in a pile on the bed. I was a grown-up on the outside, but inside there was still that spoiled little brat who had his own personal servant and doting mother to take care of everything.

I also still had in me some of the Chinese kid in New York who had been oblivious to ill-fitting clothes and unruly hair. I once complained to a colleague on the way to a diplomatic event that the tailor had made my new suit so badly that it actually hurt my shoulders. He checked the back and burst out laughing. I'd left in the hanger! Another time I was walking with some of my pals and kept tripping on the sidewalk. "This stupid sidewalk is so uneven," I complained. "I could kill myself stumbling." My friends looked down and guffawed. I was wearing two different types of shoes!

In spite of the oppressive political atmosphere, I was finally accepted as a full-fledged Party member. While I was certainly proud of this accomplishment, my worldview remained unchanged. It had been wrong for the Party to condemn my dear friends Dr. Pu and his wife. And I could see as well as anyone that mistakes were being made on a grand scale at home, and that China was getting nowhere with its principal diplomatic goal: U.N. membership.

In the summer of 1959, I was distressed to read in the foreign press that the U.S. Congress had adopted a resolution to ask the United Nations to continue denying the People's Republic its seat at the international table. The vote was 368 to 2. The United Nations was dominated by the Americans, so a quarter of the earth's population would remain voiceless. Meanwhile, the corrupt Taiwan regime was allowed to represent the Chinese people at the United Nations. Chiang Kai-shek's "bandits," as we called them, were now officially pretending to speak for six hundred million of the world's most disenfranchised citizens.

In summing up the poisonous atmosphere, one congressman declared the People's Republic "a deadly enemy of the United States." I understood that internal politics drove this harsh rhetoric on both sides, but it saddened me, because I also knew that the Chinese and the American people had been—and could again be—great friends. And, on a personal level, at times I yearned for the company of my old school chums back in the States. If they could only see me now!

Following the examples of Mao and Zhou, young cadres in government ministries were volunteering to go to the countryside to work side by side with the poorest farmers and peasants in the communes. For China to make its Great Leap, it needed great efforts by all. Everyone was encouraged to pitch in, and bureaucratic cadres in particular were encouraged to go to the country and learn from the peasants.

I volunteered, and was assigned to work at a commune in the far-southwestern suburbs of Beijing. I would be leaving Xiangtong behind for many months—from planting to harvest season. I hoped that I would return to find her belly swollen with my family's next generation.

I was eager to do my part, especially when I learned that the commune I'd been assigned to was close to the cave where the infamous and controversial skull of Peking (now Beijing) man was discovered in the 1920s. The skull of *Homo erectus* dated back more than 250,000 years. A treasured Chinese artifact, *Homo erectus pekinensis* had disappeared from a Beijing museum in the chaos of war. The account most often repeated is that a small contingent of American marines stationed in Beijing, fleeing the Japanese invasion in 1937, took the skull to save it. The marines were never heard from again, and the skull went missing. There had been rumors, including one that their ship was torpedoed and sunk. But suspicion lingered that Peking man had ended up in a private collection. All that remained in China was a few bone fragments.

A casting had been made before the skull disappeared, and it was displayed at the 1939 New York World's Fair, where as a fresh-off-the-boat nine-year-old fascinated by paleontology, I had paid my last nickel to see it. Now I would have the chance to visit the caves where the skull had been discovered. Scientists believed at the time that it was an ancient ancestor of the Chinese people. Much later, DNA testing challenged that theory, concluding that we Chinese, like all other *Homo sapiens,* got our start in Africa.

When I arrived at the commune village, I was assigned to live with a poor peasant family in their hut. I was surprised to find that I would be sharing the experience with Xu Ming, a senior Communist cadre who had been branded a bourgeois rightist. Xu had been exiled to the countryside. A veteran Communist Party member who had spent many years in the United States, he had also been involved in the newspaper Father started in New York.

I also knew Xu from Korea, where he had been on the Panmunjom armistice negotiating team. He had been a good friend of the Pu brothers. Here was another case of someone I knew personally who could not possibly be an anti-Party bourgeois rightist. But it would have attracted the wrong kind of attention to make too much of my association with him, or my sympathy. He understood that as well. We avoided appearing chummy by always conducting ourselves professionally. When we did speak, it was with blank faces and low solemn tones.

The peasant hut we were assigned to had two rooms, each with an earthen sleeping kang. The first morning, the farmer's wife asked me what I wanted to eat.

"I would love a fried pancake," I said, eager to sample the local cuisine. On the farms where I had worked as a youngster in Connecticut, the farmers' wives always put up a hearty breakfast to fuel us for a day of hard work.

But this farmer's wife paused in the doorway and shot me a narrow-eyed look. Then she muttered, "Sure," and walked out of the room.

Xu Ming, sitting next to me on the edge of the nice, warm kang, leaned over and whispered in my ear, "These people have no oil. It's hard to find, and expensive."

Feeling stupid, my face aglow with embarrassment, I rushed out to the courtyard where our hostess was stoking a fire. "I really prefer to eat exactly what you eat!" I declared, my voice booming a little louder than usual. I was relieved when she smiled. We had steamed cornbread and pickles.

The Great Leap Forward and the People's Commune Movement—the formation of huge agricultural and industrial collectives—was well under way when I got to the village. In this commune, a kitchen and a dining hall had been set up where everyone could eat for free. For the first few months, the meals were almost always the same: steamed wheat or cornbread and pickles. A few times a month, there was a big pot of cabbage soup and occasionally we found a few slivers of pork in the broth.

When I arrived, there was no limit on how much we could eat. But the quality and quantity of the food declined as spring turned to summer. Before long, there was only stale cornbread and a small ration of pickles. If we arrived late, it became increasingly common to find nothing left.

Everyone lost weight, but none of us cadres dared utter a word of complaint. I was as hungry as the next person, but I felt noble suffering alongside the poorest of our people. I embraced the idea of labor reform as a way of keeping us bureaucrats from becoming too self-satisfied.

We were slowly starving to death, but our workload never abated.

We were even sent back to work after supper. One evening we were assigned to work with a large road-repair crew. By the time everyone had gathered at the job site, it was nine o'clock, almost sunset.

There were hundreds of laborers, including a half dozen or so of us Foreign Ministry cadres, two of whom were full-fledged ambassadors who had been sent to the countryside for labor reform. The Ministry cadres tended to stick together, and as the work went on and on—we were digging up and moving earth and rocks—it looked as if there would be no rest period and we might be made to work through the night.

The two ambassadors called us aside and said that we should just stop working and get some rest. "It makes no sense to ruin our health this way," said one. "No one will care if we just walk away." We did, and no one paid us any mind.

Occasionally, we made up games and competitions to pass the time. One day a demobilized soldier and another friendly young chap challenged me to a match, to see who in ten minutes could trundle the most wheelbarrow loads of earth up a mound we were building. I accepted and started loading my wheelbarrow, huffing and puffing up and down the mound of earth.

Observing us was a friend from the Ministry, Xie Heng. She was the wife of another close friend who would one day be the Chinese ambassador to the United Kingdom. Xie strode over, wagging her finger and scolding me. "Little Ji, how can you compete with such strong young fellows?" she said. "You'll hurt yourself, and that would not be good for the revolution!" I took advantage of her intervention to tell the young men I was exhausted and would concede defeat. I was turning thirty that summer, but I was still—thanks to our meager diet and hard work—quite thin for my height. I was hardly built for heavy labor.

The team leader agreed, and I found myself reassigned to tasks such as seeding the fields. The soil had already been plowed, which made the job even easier. I also led the plow donkey out to the fields. The donkey wanted to work about as much as we did. One day I found the beast lounging in its own waste. I pulled at its reins, but it refused to budge.

An elderly peasant yelled, "Hey, stupid! Pull him up by the tail!"

The donkey's tail lay in a fetid puddle of manure and urine, under a cloud of flies.

Like everyone else, I'd read Chairman Mao's essay in which he related that, as a young man, he found peasants smelly and dirty and intellectuals clean. When he joined the revolution, however, he realized that the peasants were pure and the intellectuals, before they became true revolutionaries, were the truly unclean ones.

I sighed. Between the chairman's story and the old peasant's taunt, I had no choice. I plunged my hands into the filthy soup, fished out the donkey's soggy tail, and gave it a light yank. The donkey immediately stood up and docilely followed me to the fields, donkey waste drying on my hands. If my Harvard pals could see me now!

One of my muscular young colleagues from the Foreign Ministry took the chairman's message quite literally and enthusiastically. He often volunteered to carry two buckets filled to the brim with night soil. With the human waste dangling from each end of a shoulder pole, he took it to fertilize the fields. As he walked along, he sang and the buckets swung back and forth. He splashed feces and urine on himself until the peasants yelled, "Hey, stupid! The dirtier the work, the cleaner you must try to be!" After that, he became more careful.

I had always wanted to try to grow a beard like my father's, but ever since Korea I was obligated to keep myself properly groomed at all times, especially while I was on call twenty-four hours a day to interpret for our leaders. When I got to the commune, I knew that I had about six months before I would return to the civilized world. I quit shaving. Like many Chinese, including my father, my facial hair was sparse and the result was less distinguished than I'd hoped. One day a middle-aged peasant greeted me from behind as "old gentleman!"

I laughed. "How old do you think I am?" He held up six fingers—he thought I was at least sixty!

Just as spring was in full bloom, Xiangtong paid an unannounced visit. She found me in a field, and when she got a good look at her husband her jaw dropped. "Chaozhu! You look worse than the peasants," she cried. "Your ribs are showing! And what is this growing off your face?" She was both horrified and annoyed that I'd let myself go.

She'd brought a camera and I begged her to take my picture with the beard, but she refused. So I shaved and washed and had someone take our picture working together seeding the fields. She played the role of the mule pulling the seeding device. We had a couple of days together, during which she and I visited the cave where Peking man was discovered. Xiangtong was bored, but I was fascinated by the history and the archaeology.

She was still not pregnant. We were beginning to worry that one of us was infertile. When we could manage it, we would find a doctor to check us both out.

On evenings at the commune when there was no night work, we were sometimes required to attend struggle meetings to criticize and correct the bourgeois rightists among us. These were principally group recitations of Chairman Mao's directives on class struggle—the need to be merciless to class enemies, to "beat the drowning dog," a Chinese expression meaning to crush a defeated enemy. I kept my reservations about all this anti-rightist business to myself. Sitting in a corner of the room, exhausted by the day's hard labor, I recited a few Mao quotations by rote and struggled to keep my eyes open.

Other meetings were held to discuss how to increase crop yields by hauling more manure to the fields. It was mostly the younger people who spoke, full of revolutionary idealism, while the older peasants squatted on the floor puffing on their pipes, spitting on the earthen floor, looking glum, and saying nothing.

Some of us Foreign Ministry cadres quietly chatted among ourselves about how there could possibly be a harvest as large as had been reported for 1958 when most of the manure we now saw being carried out to the fields was plain yellow dirt. Something wasn't adding up, but maybe we were just ignorant about farming. Using the same leap-forward methods of 1958, 1959 should again yield a huge harvest.

But as the food situation at the commune grew worse, rumors circulated that industrial and agricultural production was plummeting everywhere. Starvation, which had essentially been eliminated after liberation, was now spreading rapidly. Mao's big plan for China to "walk on two legs"—to grow rapidly in agriculture and industry at the same time—was failing.

In July, far away in the southeastern part of China, worried Party leaders met at the mountain resort of Lushan to discuss the progress of the one-year-old Great Leap Forward and the People's Commune movements. Marshal Peng Dehuai, one of the principal heroes of the Chinese revolution, the general who successfully commanded the Korean War, the head of the People's Liberation Army, and one of Mao's closest associates, had learned from other high-ranking officials that the reportedly big 1958 harvest had been a fraud. Our grain-output figure had been "cooked up" by local cadres to satisfy their superiors.

The country was bedeviled, the marshal would later write, by "a communist wind"—the tendency to exaggerate production figures and a compulsion among lower-level cadres to take Mao's broad comments as specific orders. "They blindly collectivized great quantities of means of production and livelihood," he noted. "Many peasant households sold out their family property at low prices out of fear it would be 'communized.' In some areas, people were beaten if they did not fulfill their quotas or said some displeasing words."

The marshal sat down and wrote a personal letter to Chairman Mao, to warn him that things were not as they appeared, telling him that "petty-bourgeois fanaticism" was undermining progress. He went on, "The exaggeration trend has become so common . . . that reports of unbelievable miracles have appeared in newspapers and magazines to bring a great loss of prestige to the Party. Though we were poor we lived as if we were rich. We divorced ourselves from reality and lost the support of the masses."

But instead of keeping the letter private, Mao had it reproduced and circulated to the other Party leaders. This was an ominous sign, confirmed two weeks later when, at a high-level Party meeting, Mao openly attacked his old friend of thirty years. Mao accused Peng and his deputies of being part of a "right opportunist anti-Party clique," a "military club" with designs on seizing power. He did this in language that the casual reader today would regard as conciliatory, even self-deprecating. But the combination of releasing the private letter and quoting from it in his criticism made it clear to all that Mao was embarrassed, insulted, and distrustful. He intended to make the marshal a whipping boy for a growing chorus of critics.

Offered the opportunity to write a letter, make a speech to defend himself, or to make a "confession," the marshal stubbornly refused. "Take me out and shoot me!" he defiantly shouted.

Mao was infuriated that Peng had trivialized his great socialist vision as mere "petty-bourgeois fanaticism." But the old soldier would not back down.

Shortly after that, Chairman Mao changed the theme of the Lushan conference from reassessing the mass movements of the Great Leap Forward and the People's Commune to mass exposure and repudiation of "Right opportunism," as represented by Marshal Peng and several other senior Communist officials. Instead of acknowledging and correcting the mistakes of the Great Leap Forward and the People's Commune mass movement, Marshal Peng was officially disgraced, stripped of his duties, and sent home to house arrest and physical labor.

In spite of his rage at the marshal, Mao told the assembled Party leadership, "The chaos caused was on a grand scale and I take responsibility. Comrades, you must all analyze your own responsibility. If you have to shit, shit! If you have to fart, fart! You will feel much better for it."

Mao could be crude at times. But there was nothing crude about his tactics. The message the Party leaders took away from Lushan was clear: at all costs, avoid associating with or becoming a drowning dog.

CHAPTER 19

The Man on Mao's Right

My tour of duty getting "clean" down on the farm ended abruptly one crisp fall morning. I was sitting atop a pile of straw on a horse-drawn cart, trundling down a dirt road on the way to the fields. My commune brigade leader, a middle-aged peasant, came running up behind the cart and breathlessly said, "Come right away. You're to report back to the Foreign Ministry immediately. There's a car waiting. Hurry!"

After grabbing my grubby extra clothes and a picture of Xiangtong and me, I was whisked away at high speed, dust billowing behind us, rolling over the fields where the peasants were bent at work. I asked the driver nothing and he said nothing. For good reason, the rules were strict. My movements could be used by an assassin to determine the movements of Premier Zhou. I never discussed my work affairs with anyone outside work, even keeping most of it from Xiangtong. What she didn't know couldn't get her in trouble.

I could only guess that my sudden summoning had to do with the big celebration being held that day, October 1. A huge parade was to mark the tenth anniversary of the founding of the People's Republic. In any case, I couldn't show up at work looking as if I'd just climbed down off a hay wagon.

The driver sped to the compound, where I raced into the lean-to, tore off my farm clothes, and dug out my good tunic, pants, shoes, and shirt. Xiangtong was at work. Using thermos water, I did my best to wash my face and hands, then scraped the stubble from my face, combed my hair, and double-checked to ensure that I had remembered to take the hanger out of my jacket. My shoes even matched!

The driver raced through the city, taking a long route around to get to the Foreign Ministry and avoid the crowds and the traffic blockades for the parade. I was given a quick set of instructions, and soon found myself standing right where I had seen Mao all those years ago from a great distance. I was atop Tiananmen Gate, overlooking Tiananmen Square. The square had been transformed into a rippling sea of about a million people, with just as many red flags. There were thousands of marching soldiers, and military rolling stock of every description. The roar of the crowd was deafening.

Gathered here were dignitaries from all the socialist countries: Khrushchev of the Soviet Union, Kim Il Sung of North Korea, as well as representatives of the Warsaw Pact nations of Eastern Europe. They mingled with the top leaders of China on the front porch of a pagoda-style, double-roofed hall, which itself was perched atop the high wall surrounding the Forbidden City.

Tiananmen Gate was and remains the emotional center of modern China. Here, in 1919, the Chinese Communist Party had its roots, followed by a bloody, miserable thirty-year struggle to expel all foreign influences and exploitation.

Heavenly Peace Gate was also where Mao Zedong had stood on October 1, 1949, to declare the founding of the People's Republic. I had been at Harvard when I read his speech, my eyes overflowing with tears of joy. "Ours will no longer be a nation subject to insult and humiliation," he had said. "We have stood up."

And then, in the flesh, Mao arrived in a grayish blue Zhongshan suit. He stood at the rail, waving his hand in a calm and relaxed way to a sea of humanity stretching as far as the eye could see. Premier Zhou was there, as were Foreign Minister Marshal Chen Yi; Liu Shaoqi, Mao's heir apparent as head of state; Deng Xiaoping, general secretary of the Communist Party; and a number of other veterans of the early revolutionary battles, men who had risen into leadership roles.

These were the founding fathers of modern China. I would have been in awe except that I am not given to feeling awestruck in the presence of important people. Seeing the skull of Peking man would probably leave me speechless, but not a living human. Still, I was nervous. Time to go to work. Or, as Mao would say, time to serve the people.

My job, along with several colleagues, was to assist all these leaders in their conversations with English-speaking heads and delegates of other nations. I was to make myself as inconspicuous as possible, and at all costs prevent any misunderstandings or incidents. I was there to work, not gawk. I transformed myself into my usual talking foreign doll, standing at attention to the right of the Chinese officials, between them and their guest. This is a Chinese tradition. At a banquet, for example, the guest always sits on the right of the host.

And then there I was, the man on Mao's right. I was a little taller than Mao—who was himself both tall and bulky—and self-consciously bowed my head to appear less visible. I had no idea with whom he was speaking, and what was said was trivial, long forgotten now. But when I leaned toward the chairman's right ear and repeated the visiting dignitary's first phrase, Mao flinched and gave me a dark backward glance. "You're very loud!" he declared.

In my effort to be clear and distinct, I had turned up the volume on a voice I'd been told was quite loud to begin with. I gulped, then adjusted myself without further incident. Not then, or in the next dozen or so years that I frequently interpreted for him, did Mao acknowledge me as anything other than a talking machine. He was not cruel, but he was as oblivious to my presence as Zhou had been attentive.

"Serene" was the word many people used to describe Mao in person. He was a chain-smoker, but not in a nervous way. He moved slowly, regally, and I noticed how our other leaders seemed to imitate him. His eyes, often half closed, made him seem mentally far away, at peace. His enormous forehead suggested intelligence, and his skin was, for a man nearing seventy years of age, very smooth, except for the famous mole to the left of his chin. He seemed, as one foreign writer would later observe, "molded of different stuff from those surrounding him, impervious to human passions."

That day's hosts and guests occasionally retreated to a lounge inside the pagoda, out of sight, to smoke, for something to drink, to sit and rest. I had a few moments here and there to steal glances at the spectacle to end all spectacles, the most magnificent parade imaginable. In between the river of shiny military machines and the crisp, high-stepping soldiers were elaborate performance troupes. Mountainous floats depicted heroic Chinese peasants gathering in a bumper wheat harvest, or heroic workers producing farm implements and industrial goods. The China that would be seen around the world that day was a powerful, prosperous country full of happy people who loved their leaders.

It was a splendid, magnificent display. Standing there with donkey dung under my fingernails and the dust of yellow earth in my nostrils, I was for the first time truly worried about China's future. Would we have to survive on cornbread and pickles forever? If I'd known the whole truth, I would have been horrified. The 1958 harvest had been overstated, and now the 1959 harvest was turning into a disaster. Hundreds of millions already didn't have enough to eat, and a long, cold winter lay ahead. It would be especially harsh in northern China, which is on the same latitude as the northern United States.

Malnutrition leading to edema was common in many areas, and deaths among the rural population increased. According to official statistics, the country's total population in 1960 dropped by 10 million over the previous year. That was the most disastrous result, the most serious lesson of the failed Great Leap Forward and people's commune movement.

Few people present, I least of all, knew of this looming catastrophe as we stood on a lovely fall day atop the Gate of Heavenly Peace. Still, watching that lavish display, I had the strongest urge to speak out about the discrepancy I knew from personal, recent experience.

Back in the office after the parade, I could contain myself no longer. I blurted out to several colleagues that I knew for a fact that on the commune where I worked farmers were spreading plain earth on the fields but reporting it as manure and other forms of fertilizer. "Those people are already hungry all the time," I said. "How are they going to increase production without fertilizer?"

My friends listened with polite expressions. I quickly recognized that I'd crossed a line. Soon afterward, I was called to account by the Party committee at the Ministry. I was informed that I needed to be "helped" to correct my right-deviationist thoughts.

I had to submit to a group-criticism meeting. In a hall at the Ministry, I stood before a crowd of my colleagues, who grilled me: Who was I to challenge the wisdom of the chairman and the Party? Did I think my judgment was greater than his? Wasn't I guilty of revisionist thinking?

The struggle, or "helping," meeting was civilized compared with some I'd heard of, particularly the one I saw against the landlord when I was a student. My Party membership was not at issue. The criticisms were relatively mild, and the "helping" involved encouraging me to acknowledge my mistakes and promise to correct my wrong thinking.

I swallowed my pride and criticized myself, blaming my mistaken thoughts on my bourgeois background and my failure to diligently study Chairman Mao's writing. That was it. I was let off easy. Less lucky were tens of thousands of other dedicated cadres who also dared to speak their minds after being on the front lines of industrial and agricultural production. These "deviationists" were sacked and driven into exile. Meanwhile, the country went through three years of brutal deprivation that ultimately affected everyone. During the "three difficult years" between late 1959 and 1962, there were no fat people in China, not even in government.

In 1960, Xiangtong and I were finally able to move indoors, into an apartment house of one-room studios for Foreign Ministry cadres. We had no kitchen, but we did have our own Western-style toilet, the pinnacle of luxury. After living in the lean-to for three years, and after my commune experience, having a proper roof over our heads was a guilty pleasure.

At the office I was as busy as I had ever been. I was summoned almost daily by the premier to do interpretation work, and to accompany him on overseas visits. My relationship with Zhou Enlai, and my respect for him, deepened. I came to understand that when he corrected me it was not a threat to my career but a reflection of his concern that China—as represented by those of us who were on the international stage—must put its best face forward.

Once, while I was interpreting a discussion with a foreign leader that touched on Latin America, Zhou mentioned several countries whose names I stumbled over. He chastised me afterward, in the presence of some of my colleagues. "You are a Foreign Ministry official and you cannot pronounce the Latin American countries," he said. "You have to be able to recite all of them from memory." The premier then proceeded to rattle off every single Latin American nation, pronounced perfectly.

Now that I was firmly embedded in the Foreign Ministry and showing great promise, my bosses decided that it would be a good idea to raise the foreign doll's political consciousness. I was told that I should study Marxism-Leninism and Mao Zedong Thought. I was sent to a Party school for middle-ranking cadres. Officially, I was a low-ranking cadre, and it was an honor to be selected to study among those of higher rank.

The sessions consisted of government experts lecturing on Marxism and defining a Marxist political economy. I had been deeply interested in Marxism ever since I'd read Edgar Snow's *Red Star over China,* as well as Marx's *Communist Manifesto* in the States. After returning to China, I diligently studied Chinese newspaper and magazine articles on the Chinese revolution and revolutionary policies.

But I had never been as bored as I was now, listening to the lectures and attending the study groups at the Party school. I could not grasp the logic. It sounded like nonsense. It was all I could do just to stay awake. The only part I enjoyed was the food. In contrast to the scarcity of necessities throughout the country, we had three decent meals a day.

The premier rescued me from my torture by calling for me to accompany him on a short trip abroad. When I returned to China, my superiors decided that I was needed too often for my interpretation work to take time for the study sessions.

The early years of the new decade, the 1960s, saw the worst manifestations of the Great Leap and the commune movements, as well as trouble abroad.

In 1960, as the famine deepened, relations between the Soviet Union and China deteriorated. Khrushchev openly criticized Mao for being "oblivious of any interests but his own, spinning theories detached from the realities of the modern world." Officially, China responded in kind, criticizing the Soviets as backsliding revisionists.

Soon after, the Soviet Union announced that all its experts working in China were to return home at once. Russian aid was terminated. All Russian-funded projects, such as factories and research, were abandoned and, worst of all, the Soviets demanded repayment of earlier loans with grain exports. We couldn't feed our own people, let alone meet their demands.

Xiangtong and I, and everyone we knew, were always hungry. It was said that in the communes the people were too hungry to work and the pigs too hungry to stand up. Rationing was strictly enforced. Office workers were entitled to about thirty pounds of grain per person per month, laborers slightly more. The only vegetable was cabbage, also rationed. Per person each month, we could buy just three ounces of meat and two ounces of cooking oil in government-run shops.

Compared with most Chinese, I was lucky because I often traveled with the premier to other countries, where we were well fed. My colleagues and I were given a small allowance, depending on the length of our stay abroad—somewhere between ten and twenty dollars. Every single staff member would use that money to buy milk powder and pork fat to take home to their families. I was especially concerned about the health of my elderly parents and shared some of this bounty with them. Xiangtong, too, had lost weight. On one occasion, I gave some milk powder to one of my old Korean-era comrades, whose wife had just given birth and was too ill to produce enough milk to feed the child.

By 1961, the world had learned that China was starving. We blamed it on a drought, which was only partly true. Canada sent us wheat. Even in the United States, which continued to block our entry into the United Nations and maintained a belligerent foreign policy toward us, there was concern on a human level. The chief justice of the Supreme Court, William O. Douglas, suggested that the United States send assistance to show that Americans have "a bright conscience and a very warm heart." He was right, but the opportunity to build bridges fell on deaf ears. Even if President Kennedy or some private American group had offered aid, I would have been surprised to see it accepted directly or openly. That would have involved an even greater loss of face for Mao.

To lessen the competition for food in urban areas where it could not be grown, some 25 million people were ordered to move out of the cities into the countryside. China's population boom had continued, and we now had another 50 million mouths to feed—650 million in all.

In some places the local militia turned on the citizenry and became bandits instead of protectors. The country was falling apart, and although Chairman Mao had told the Party leaders that he was going to relinquish his primary role, retiring to the "second front," he made it clear that he expected them to govern in a way consistent with Mao Thought. This meant continuous revolution and the beating of drowning dogs.

Our top leaders made extended trips into the countryside to see for themselves just how bad things had gotten. This included Mao's chosen successor, the new chairman of the People's Republic, Liu Shaoqi; Premier Zhou Enlai; and my brother Chaoding's boss, Vice Premier Chen Yun, who was the minister in charge of economic policy.

Quietly, heroically (against Mao's policies), reforms were ordered. Peasants were given back small plots of land for their own cultivation, the mass back-yard production of steel was halted, and big communal dining halls were dismantled because they were inefficient. A ray of realism managed to break through the dark clouds.

But the brutal denunciation of Marshal Peng, a true patriot, had injected new poison into the political atmosphere. More than ever, no one dared speak out or openly challenge the chairman's wisdom, past or present.

A master of changing the subject when he was losing the argument, Mao ordered a new mass movement aimed at destroying the physical remnants of our feudal past. This meant the systematic tearing down of ancient city and town walls, including the great city wall of Beijing. Some of us in the Foreign Ministry were ordered to take part in this operation, going together as a work crew to hack at the ancient massive blocks with picks and sledgehammers.

The walls had been built centuries earlier from bricks and mortared with a mixture of cement and glutinous rice. They were built to last forever. Many had markings on them showing when they were made and by whom, centuries ago. It was heartbreaking to me, a lover of antiquities and archaeology. Most of the bricks were shattered, and intact pieces were trucked away to be used to build latrines and pigsties.

Luckily for posterity, there were some level-headed leaders who resisted, notably Deng Xiaoping, another early veteran of the Party and the war for liberation, and now general secretary of the Party. Then stationed in Nanjing—home of one of the most complete and beautiful ancient city walls in China, built five hundred years earlier—Deng quietly defied Mao, issuing strict orders that the wall not be touched. It remains intact to this day. But practically all other city walls were torn down, along with other irreplaceable structures.

Worse than the destruction of our material heritage was the repudiation of cadres at all levels of the Party and the government, the same people who were trying to fix the problems caused by the Great Leap Forward and the People's Commune Movement. They became the targets of vicious attacks by Mao's sycophants, who took this opportunity to destroy rivals and seize power for themselves.

At a large Party meeting early in 1962, Mao made a tepid self-criticism regarding the Great Leap and the commune debacles, but he expressed no sorrow for the deaths and misery of millions of Chinese. Instead, he demanded that others "who think you are tigers, and that nobody will dare to touch your arse," confess their mistakes. So, dutifully, they did, including the premier.

It is difficult for many foreign historians to understand the mood in China at this time, and they often cite Premier Zhou for what they perceive as his slavish obedience to the chairman. Having spent as much time with Zhou as I did, and seen the two men together, I saw their relationship as far more complex. Sitting together after a foreign guest had departed, the two seemed in every respect like a couple of old war buddies, sharing a joke or a memory. I never observed a harsh word between them.

Over the years, Mao would punish and destroy many of the people who had been with him from the beginning, seeing in them real and imagined ambitions to replace him, or to take China in a direction he disapproved of. The premier received his share of rebukes, but rather than challenging Mao or forming anti-Mao alliances with others, he let the chairman's words roll off him like water off a duck's back. Then Zhou went forward and often did what he felt was right.

While Mao was railing against the Soviet Union in the mid-1960s, for example, the premier made an agreement with the USSR to collaborate on aid to North Vietnam, allowing Russian military equipment to travel over China's rail network. Mao was furious when he found out, but he took no action against Zhou.

Of all China's top leaders, the premier seemed to be the one with the least ambition and the greatest desire to achieve harmony, both within our government and with foreign governments. Harmony is an important concept in our culture. Many ancient sites and buildings are named in praise of it. While Mao saw contradiction in everything, the premier sought harmony. Zhou Enlai had a knack for defusing tension in virtually any situation, or finding common ground where none was apparent. He was China's greatest asset on the international stage, a gifted speaker, an excellent listener, and a sharp wit.

Domestically, the political atmosphere went from bad to worse. As Marshal Peng Dehuai discovered—and many more would learn the hard way in the years ahead—one didn't need to plot and scheme against Mao to court personal disaster. The denunciation of patriots and the destruction of our culture that marked Mao's response to the disasters of the Great Leap and the commune movements were disturbing and dispiriting. However, no one could have predicted that these would prove to be just the first steps toward the main event, which still lay ahead: the Great Proletarian Cultural Revolution.

While China was struggling internally, the world seemed to be teetering on the brink of a third global conflict, this time involving weapons of mass destruction: the atomic bomb. In October 1962, while the United States was going toe-to-toe with Khrushchev over the Cuban missile crisis, China confronted an Indian patrol along a disputed border in southern Tibet, starting a six-week war high in the Himalayas.

We had problems with other neighbors as well. There was a boundary problem with Burma, but we were able to contain it and prevent its escalation into armed conflict. There remained serious problems in the Indo-Chinese states, especially the former French colony of Laos, which was in the grip of a civil war. We sided with an insurgency against a regime supported by the United States. The Americans were demanding an international peacekeeping force to stop the fighting, a position that we regarded as an excuse to support another puppet regime in our backyard.

Once again, I found myself at a Geneva peace conference, in May 1961. Premier Zhou played a pivotal role in brokering a peaceful settlement even after the Americans accused us of trying to turn Laos into a satellite state. Also, during the talks Foreign Minister Chen Yi made a point of supporting "the righteous stand" of Communist North Vietnam, led by the popular Ho Chi Minh, against armed intervention by the United States and South Vietnam.

I assured my colleagues who had never been in the States that the American public would never support a Korean-style conflict in Vietnam, another peninsular-shaped country bifurcated by political strife. Besides, the battlefront of the Cold War was far away, in Berlin. "The Americans aren't so stupid as to make the same mistake twice," I said confidently. "Capitalists have no stomach for war. They are afraid to die."

While we were in Geneva, our delegation learned that there might be another attempt to assassinate Premier Zhou. We young men—secretaries, translators, and interpreters—were organized into a security force and took turns patrolling the grounds of the premier's villa every night, armed with a loaded handgun.

I had learned how to shoot a pistol while I was in Panmunjom, and took my extra duties seriously. I was prepared to take a bullet for Zhou Enlai. I began my first patrol with the pistol cocked, so that I could fire quickly should an assassin suddenly attack. But I realized that, wandering around in the dim light, I might stumble and accidentally discharge the weapon. I might injure myself and cause an embarrassing uproar. I gently uncocked the hammer but kept a bullet in the firing chamber. Happily, I never had to pull the trigger.

CHAPTER 20

Death and Birth

The internal chaos and heightened international tensions brought about major transitions in my family and my work.

First of all, my parents returned to Beijing for good. My father had been serving on a Shanxi provincial committee back in Taiyuan when the Hundred Flowers campaign began. He had taken Mao at his word and openly criticized the Party for using rhetoric to gloss over China's problems. When the anti-rightist backlash broke out, he was verbally attacked for his views. My brother Chaoding knew that it wouldn't take much for the verbal abuse to turn violent, so he insisted that my parents return to their Beijing house next to the Forbidden City, where he and I could keep an eye on them.

I was glad to have them nearby again, at least in the same city, especially Father, who was nearing eighty. Mother was twenty years younger and his third wife, but, even so, she was getting on as well. There wasn't room for all of us to live together, for even if we wanted to, the living space was far too small. What's more, Xiangtong and I were busy with our lives and were obliged to live in Ministry housing, which meant for both of us a nice square meter lean-to, not far from the Foreign Ministry headquarters. Meanwhile my boss was making me stay late every night, whether there was work or not.

I had apparently been too eager to leave as soon as the quitting bell sounded at six o'clock. I was always in a hurry to get home to Xiangtong. But I had a hard taskmaster. My boss, a scholar who had studied in London, spoke the King's English with a thick British accent. He looked down on Yankees like me, seeing me as useful only as his personal typist, for his typing skills were far inferior to his English. One day he saw me tidying up my desk in anticipation of the bell's ringing and gave me a finger-wagging lecture: "You act like a superficial socialist when you are so eager every night to run home to your corrupt bourgeois life!"

It was a ridiculous statement, but in the tense political atmosphere of the time his rebuke constituted a serious reprimand. Even so, I recognized it for what it was: professional rivalry and maybe some transferred guilt, since he, too, had been educated abroad and once enjoyed the bourgeois lifestyle. He got no argument from me, and I began to stay until nine o'clock every night, whether I had to or not. To be fair to the old man, he wasn't so bad. He was not like those "true revolutionaries" who later tried to destroy me.

Unable to care for my aging parents, we hired a housekeeper, Tian Ma, who had been my wife's childhood nanny when the Wangs lived in Beijing. Years earlier, my mother-in-law had hired Tian Ma in order to rescue her from another employer, who beat the poor girl. Tian Ma had led a hellish life up to that point, raised with painfully bound feet in the ancient tradition, and forced into an arranged marriage with a man who essentially abandoned her and showed up only when he wanted money.

She found work as a house servant, often treated worse than a dog. Xiangtong's mother had saved Tian Ma, and Tian Ma ended up raising Xiangtong. They had been as close as mother and daughter. Xiangtong had been devastated to bid her goodbye years ago, when her family fled the Japanese.

Xiangtong rediscovered her old nanny years later in Beijing, after liberation. Tian Ma's cruel husband had died, and we hired her. It was a great relief to know that my parents were safe nearby, and under the care of someone we knew well and trusted completely.

Although there were nights when I had little to do until I left at nine o'clock, increasingly there were others when I had so much work that I didn't make it home until the morning. It was hard for Xiangtong to adjust in the beginning. The premier routinely worked deep into the night, and often required my services.

One evening soon after we married, I worked all night with the premier. It would have been an unnecessary security risk for me to phone home to tell Xiangtong that I would be very late. But, even if it hadn't been, we had no phone to call. So worry Xiangtong did, sitting up all night imagining all sorts of horrible fates that might have befallen me, from a bicycle accident to an assassination. The next morning, as soon as she got to work she phoned my office and was told that I was peacefully enjoying my breakfast at the Ministry canteen. I imagine at that point she wanted to strangle me.

That night I explained to her that she shouldn't worry if I didn't show up on time. It was the way things were done. Enemy spies were still about, so there had to be as little advance notice as possible concerning the movements of our top leaders, and no nonessential communication that might compromise security. There were still spies everywhere. In time, that came to include some of my overseas travel. The only way she knew what was going on was when I came home to pack my Western clothes. I'd give her an extra warm hug and disappear. My destination might be Hong Kong or Cairo, and I might be gone a day or two weeks. All I could say was "See you later, dear! I'll be back soon!"

She was a good soldier, never complaining and never allowing this void in our shared lives to detract from our deep connection. The one area that we were both growing frustrated about was children. After several years of marriage, watching all our peers having babies right and left, we were starting to lose hope.

The premier had picked up the habit of meeting foreign dignitaries and working at night because that was Mao's schedule. The chairman worked nights and slept during the day. Zhou wanted to be on call anytime Mao summoned him.

But, unlike the chairman, the premier could not afford to spend his days sleeping. He was the country's chief operating officer, and, day or night, he received reports of conditions inside the country, along our borders, and as the years went on, around the world, presiding over meetings with his staff and cabinet ministers, escorting foreign dignitaries on tours, and a hundred other details. Somehow Zhou pulled it off without betraying the constant fatigue he must have felt.

One of the premier's great interests was relations with the United States. Over the years he would, from time to time, talk about the missed opportunities that might have resulted in the two nations ending up as friends rather than enemies. Now, unlike the Eisenhower administration, whose vice president, Nixon, was an outspoken anti-Communist and China basher, the Kennedy administration appeared to be adopting a less confrontational approach.

In November 1963, Xiangtong was assigned to interpret for Henrik Beer, the secretary-general of the Geneva-based League of Red Cross Societies (now known as the League of Red Cross and Red Crescent Societies). A Swede, Beer had come to China as a guest of the Chinese Red Cross. While they were touring in Wuhan, the Red Cross entourage went sightseeing to a park.

The Chinese music that had been playing from a loudspeaker suddenly stopped and an announcer came on to report that President Kennedy had been assassinated. Xiangtong immediately told Beer this news. He thought it might be propaganda. But it was announced again and again, and Xiangtong assured him that it must be true.

In spite of the cold weather, Beer broke out in a sweat and appeared nervous. Later, Xiangtong's boss and Beer's host told her with a sigh, "What a pity! Mr. Beer had been received by President Kennedy just before he left for China. He was going to see Vice Premier Xi Zhongxun with an important message from Kennedy. But now . . ." He just shook his head.

Beer never disclosed what it was that he had been asked to convey to the Chinese government, but Xiangtong and I couldn't help wondering how history might have been changed had Kennedy lived.

Conditions in the country gradually improved beginning in 1963. Mao had retreated from public life in the wake of the disasters of the previous few years. Liu Shaoqi, as chairman of the People's Republic, and Zhou Enlai, as premier of the State Council, brought order and stability to our economic and political lives. Food became more plentiful, and daily life slowly returned to a semblance of normalcy.

Meanwhile, the pace of our diplomacy accelerated. More and more heads of state visited China, and our top leaders were often on the road. It was exhilarating and exhausting work, globe-hopping from culture to culture, with the expected odd, awkward, and memorable moments.

One of the most ambitious trips I had the privilege of attending was a fourteen-nation tour of Asian and African countries from December 1963 to March 1964. After that trip with Premier Zhou and Vice Premier and Foreign Minister Chen Yi, I accompanied the premier on separate trips to Tanganyika (before it was united with Zanzibar in 1964 to form Tanzania), Pakistan, Nepal, Burma, and Romania.

China was breaking free of its diplomatic isolation. The premier was eager to find allies among nonaligned nations for all the usual reasons, not the least of which was to put pressure on the United Nations to seat the People's Republic.

First Tunisia, and later Ethiopia, both of which had distrusted China's ambitions, established diplomatic relations with us after the premier visited them. Zhou's theme in his talks continued to be the one he laid out in his successful speech at Bandung years earlier: We were all former colonies or victims of foreign exploitation, and we all shared a need for a prolonged period of peace to develop our countries. To do that, we should seek common ground while setting aside our differences, support and help one another, and never interfere in one another's internal affairs. These words of the premier's were quickly followed with specific deeds.

This won China many new friends. The premier was very popular among foreign leaders—principled but flexible, dignified but gracious, a gentleman but also a realist. He always kept his word and never told a lie or a half-truth. Unlike Mao, he never conducted himself as though he were one of the most-wanted men in the world. He knew that he was a prime target for assassination, but instead of hunkering down he chose to go anywhere and meet anyone he thought could be a natural ally of China.

The premier expected his staff to know enough about the local cultures we visited to make sure that after we left we'd be remembered as perfect guests.

In his periodic chats with us he emphasized that we were to show absolute respect for local traditions and conditions, no matter how odd or disturbing. "When you go to the mountain, you must sing its song," he said. This was a Chinese version of "Do as the Romans do."

For example, we were scheduled to visit Ghana when we got word that a would-be assassin had bitten President Nkrumah during an unsuccessful coup attempt. Our security people advised the premier to postpone his trip, but he insisted on keeping his commitment. To cancel could have serious implications, sending a message that China was losing faith in Nkrumah, which would create more instability. Going in spite of the crisis was a sign of good faith: China keeps its word.

The situation in Ghana was so unstable that it was unsafe for Nkrumah to observe protocol to greet the premier at the airport. The premier offered to meet anywhere Nkrumah chose. We ended up in a castle on the Ghanaian coast, where the president was holed up. Zhou, who had thirty years of experience with civil war and shifting capitals, assured Nkrumah that he was not put off by the conditions and suggested they get down to business.

During the talks, our delegation took meals together around a large dining table with no particular seating arrangement. The premier often ate with us. The Ghanians had placed a large, comfortable chair for him at the head of the table. But his custom, when eating with the Foreign Ministry staff and on other informal occasions, was to sit at different places around the table and chat freely with whoever happened to be seated next to him. He was always asking how our work was going, and often made career suggestions. He especially encouraged me to keep up my studies of the old Chinese historians and philosophers. "Study the past and you will see the future," he told me.

Our head of security, Yang Dezhong, was a tall, solidly built man who held himself in a dignified, self-confident, vigilant pose until everyone else had been seated. Only then would he take a seat.

The premier had chosen a seat other than the big imposing chair the Ghanians had arranged for him, making that the only unoccupied chair left. Yang, the premier's personal bodyguard, took it. The Ghanaian waiters, thinking Yang was the premier, made sure he was served before anyone else and fussed over him throughout the meal. We all exchanged amused glances, watching the premier's bodyguard getting the royal treatment.

When dinner was over, the premier—as was his habit—went around the room and shook the hands of all the waiters, cooks, and servants, thanking them. The Ghanians were both dumbfounded and impressed. "What an amazing premier you have!" one gushed.

We arrived in a very hot Muslim country once to find a beautiful swimming pool at the villa where we were staying. We had a few hours to kill before work, so we younger members of the delegation put on our swimming trunks and jumped in. Among our delegation was a medical team that included a young nurse. She also put on her suit and jumped in with us.

We were splashing around, enjoying ourselves, when the premier appeared at poolside, hands on his hips, scowling. "We're in a Muslim country and you haven't studied the customs? Well, let me help you. Men and women never swim together, and women never go about uncovered. Suppose our hosts saw a woman in a swimming suit in a pool full of half-naked men? When you enter the temple, you must follow the monks!" The red-faced nurse jumped out of the pool, and ran inside to get dressed.

As China recovered from the horrors of the Great Leap Forward and the People's Commune Movement, the Asian and African countries seemed to be in a downward spiral. The poverty we saw was shocking, even for those of us who had seen our share of misery at home.

In Africa, the premier had interpreters for English, French, and Arabic. When English was not the main language, I could do some sightseeing. There were beggars in every city. I saw people walking around with no clothing, their ribs so prominent that it was painful to look at them. In Somalia, some colleagues and I visited a village of huts that was so crude it could have been a museum exhibit of how people lived in prehistoric times.

The Ethiopian emperor, Haile Selassie, invited the premier and Marshal Chen Yi, now vice premier, to one of his secondary residences, where the state guesthouse had one bedroom with a private bath, reserved for the premier. The vice premier and foreign minister of the People's Republic, Marshal Chen, slept with the rest of us on sofas, floors, and in the hallways. Since we had no bathroom, we collected empty soda bottles to use for urination at night. The flies were so aggressive they wouldn't budge until you squashed or flicked them away. One got in my nostril and it took me forever to snort it out.

The real shock came during the state banquet. We were served many different dishes of colorful but indeterminate substances. I didn't like the look of any of it, so I saved my appetite for a piece of the big, luscious-looking chocolate cake sitting on the dessert table across the room.

When the waiters had finished clearing the meal, one of them strode over to the cake holding a fan. He waved it and a swarm of black flies rose off the "chocolate" cake, revealing the large vanilla cake they had just been feasting and pooping on, which the waiters then proudly served to everyone. That night I stuck to the biscuits and soda water our support staff kept on hand for late-night snacks and upset stomachs.

Later, at a state dinner in Nepal, I noticed a large black stain on my plate and asked the waiter to bring me a clean one. The waiter took the dirty plate, spat on it, wiped off the stain with his hand, and set it back down in front me. That night's dinner was stale bread and hot tea.

I commented in passing to our deputy chief of protocol, Han Xu, "I can't wait to leave this wretched place and fly back to China!" In my enthusiasm, I had forgotten how loud my voice could be. Han Xu scowled and placed a finger on his lips. Then he whispered close to my ear, "Always assume there are listening devices wherever we stay."

It was at one of the staff dinners in early 1963 that the premier asked me about my family life, and whether Xiangtong and I planned to have children. I told him that I was happy with my marriage but that Xiangtong had been unsuccessful in becoming pregnant. He smiled benignly and raised his glass. "I, too, have no children," he said. "So here is a toast from one childless husband to another!"

I hadn't given much thought to the exchange, so I was surprised when, a few days later, the premier told me to report to the best doctor in the best hospital in Beijing for a checkup, to see what might be done. The doctor prescribed some medicine. A couple of months later, on a trip with the premier to Pakistan, I received news from home: Xiangtong was pregnant!

When I told the premier, he asked me if we had decided on a name. We hadn't, beyond my agreeing with Xiangtong's determination to abandon the ancient tradition of using the names set aside generations ago, and going with something more modern.

"I'm sure your child will grow up to be a hard worker like you," the premier said. "I've noticed that in Africa the women do the work while the men sit about, but in Pakistan the men do the work while the women stay at home. So if you have a boy you can give him a second name, Tan [which is also a Chinese word meaning "sincere" or "candid"], to honor our friendship with Pakistan, where the men work so hard. But if it's a girl you can give her the name Fei [Chinese for "Africa"], to honor our friends in Africa, where the women work so hard."

The baby turned out to be a boy, and we named him Xiaotan, which translates, roughly, as "little" (a term of endearment) and "candid." And indeed, our son Xiaotan has turned out to be a very candid and trustworthy person. It was a great honor to have a son named by Zhou Enlai. Every time I say Xiaotan's name, it brings back good memories.

The joy I felt at learning that Xiangtong was pregnant was short-lived. A month or so later, on August 9, I was summoned in the early evening to the premier's office to interpret. He looked up and blurted, "Little Ji, why are you here? Your brother has just passed away! Quick, go home!"

I raced to Chaoding's home on my bicycle, choking with emotion. Jingyi greeted me sobbing and I, too, dissolved into bitter tears. When she could compose herself, she explained that my brother had been preparing for one of his many overseas visits, this time to Algeria. The upcoming trip had special significance because he had received permission to make a stop in Switzerland, where he was going to be reunited with his two American sons, now twenty-one and twenty-five years old.

Sixty years old, my brother had been chairing a meeting of the China Committee for the Promotion of International Trade, which he had been positioning to be an engine of economic development for post–Great Leap China. He excused himself to go to the bathroom and collapsed in the hallway.

He was rushed to the hospital. Between his advanced diabetes and high blood pressure, the doctors were unable to stabilize him. By the time Jingyi reached his bedside, Chaoding was in a coma. He lingered through the night and died the following afternoon.

This was a devastating blow. Chaoding was my role model, my hero, my beloved brother, the person who shepherded our family halfway around the world to escape the dangers at home, and a solid-gold patriot of the revolution. I had never gotten a chance to say good-bye. My heart was shattered.

And there was my eighty-five-year-old father, whose heart would also be broken. His firstborn son and his pride and joy was gone. How would we break the news to him? He was going deaf, and it would be difficult just to get him to understand.

"We mustn't tell him," Jingyi insisted. "It might kill him, and then we'll have two calamities to contend with."

I was too grief-stricken to argue, and my sister-in-law's logic seemed sound enough. Months would sometimes pass between visits with our father. I was often traveling with the premier, while Chaoding was globe-trotting himself. Mother and I agreed with Jingyi that we would wait a bit before bringing Father the awful news. This required us to make sure he would not read about it in the newspaper.

The day after Chaoding died, we hid the *People's Daily* and the other newspapers my father ritually read. The *People's Daily* ran the obituary on its second page. I would later learn that initially it was to run on page eight, but the premier insisted that Chaoding's death notice be displayed more prominently. Everything was politics.

Father was perplexed at the absence of all his newspapers, and we told him through his hearing aid that there must have been a problem in the post office. He seemed to accept our explanation.

My brother's death was international news. *The New York Times* ran a full obituary under the headline (spelling his name in the style of the time): "Dr. Chi Chao-ting Is Dead at 60; Red Chinese Economic Expert." Letters of condolence poured in from far and wide.

Unbeknown to me, lost as I was in a fog of grief, the premier was preparing a state funeral for my brother, and using his sudden death to make a political statement. I would learn later that at a cabinet meeting Zhou spoke passionately of Chaoding, telling a room full of high-ranking ministers and vice ministers, "Ji Chaoding made greater contributions to New China than some people sitting in this room today."

This was one of the most controversial and provocative things I'd ever heard the premier say, and it rippled through the establishment for some time after. I think he said it to make clear his disdain for the recent purges and the climate of fear, and he chose to do so by example, confronting the false insinuations of the Mao fanatics that my brother had been a double agent when he had been working undercover and spying on the Kuomintang.

The premier ordered my brother's funeral held at the Capital Theater on Wangfujing Street, in the heart of Beijing. This was a common venue for the funerals of cabinet-level ministers. Mountains of wreaths arrived from around the world, including one from Harriet. Among the high-level mourners were Premier Zhou, Marshal Chen Yi, Mao's security chief Kang Sheng, and Vice Premier Li Xiannian.

Liao Chengzhi, the minister of the Office of Overseas Chinese Affairs, delivered the eulogy, saying of my brother, "For forty years he went through wind and storm, and with great firmness, flexibility, and tact he successfully struggled against the enemy whether at home or abroad." The talk was political as well as personal.

When the ceremony was over, the premier shook hands with everyone and expressed his condolences to my family. But as he was finishing he hesitated and looked around, as if trying to find someone. Then he asked us, "Where is the family elder, Chaoding's father?" Jingyi explained that we were worried that he might not hold up under such a sad occasion, so we had hidden from him Chaoding's sudden passing.

The premier scowled and said in an irritated tone, "You are wrong! The old gentleman would have withstood that terrible blow. What a great pity! I had wanted to see the venerable gentleman and express to him personally my condolences."

I was mortified. My father had been robbed of the chance to honor his firstborn child, to see the respect with which he was regarded, and to be comforted by the premier in person. It was a dreadful mistake, one I have always regretted.

In the days and weeks that followed, Father asked a few times why Chaoding hadn't come to see him. We had agreed as a family that we would continue the fiction, so we told him that his son was on one of his many trips abroad at some international meetings. But after a time he stopped asking and became increasingly downcast and withdrawn.

It was clear that he suspected that Chaoding had been purged as a rightist, or something worse. But he never demanded a clear answer and never learned the truth.

Later that year, there was another memorial for my brother in London, attended by more than one hundred people. At this event, a tribute was read that had been written by the American scholar Owen Lattimore, an Asian expert who became famous during the McCarthy hearings of the early 1950s, when he was falsely accused of being a Soviet agent. Lattimore had been a friend and admirer of my brother's in the States during the 1930s, and had visited my father in Shanxi Province in 1937.

In his tribute, Lattimore praised my brother's ability to straddle two cultures, West and East, and spoke of my "remarkable and admirable father," who had helped China into the present while preserving "the continuity of China's Confucian past."

Chaoding's final honor was to have his ashes accepted for burial at Babaoshan Revolutionary Cemetery, on the outskirts of Beijing. This was the main resting place for revolutionary heroes and high government and Party officials. I wished Chaoding could have heard all the accolades while he was alive.

CHAPTER 21

Our Dark Ages Begin

The economy continued to improve in the mid-1960s as more control was returned to local officials and the peasants. But Mao, who had retreated to the "second front" while Chairman Liu Shaoqi, the premier, and others ran the country, grew restless. Storm clouds were gathering beyond the horizon. They would soon sweep China backward again, into revolutionary chaos.

The Party had launched two new movements that called for government cadres to be sent back down to the farms. The Socialist Education Campaign was supposed to instill political loyalty among the peasants. And the Four Cleanups Campaign was supposed to clean up politics, economy, organization, and ideology. There had been growing complaints about local cadres indulging in corruption, embezzling, cheating workers, and reporting inflated production figures.

I had spent a half year feeding the pigs years before, and now had a full work schedule. But in late 1965 the Party leadership in the Translation Department of the Foreign Ministry decided that I needed to spend some more time getting politically scrubbed by working with the peasants.

One day the political commissar of our department sent me home to pack for an extended stay in far-off Hunan Province, in southeastern China, with some of my colleagues. This distant destination, we interpreters were told, was intended to familiarize us with the Hunan accent, spoken by Chairman Mao and Chairman Liu.

Xiangtong was pregnant with our second child and was due to give birth in early 1966, so I asked for permission to stay until the baby arrived. The commissar glared at me, scolding, "It is your wife and not you who is going to give birth! So go!"

I obediently left with my colleagues by train in a fourth-class hard-seater. After traveling for a day and a night, we arrived in Changsha, Hunan, and caught a bus to Liuyang County, famous for its fireworks industry.

At a production brigade headquarters, we were briefed by a local official and a Foreign Ministry representative, and then sent out the back door. I got my first good look at the lush beauty of the Hunan countryside. In front of me stretched a vast green field of rice paddies, peasant huts here and there, and green rolling hills beyond.

Throughout my stay, I lived with the poorest peasants but I moved several times because I found the stench in the homes overwhelming. I was trying to find a place where the air was tolerable. The problem was the local custom of keeping jars of fermenting urine inside the sleeping quarters. At the first hut, I asked the host if I might move the jar outside.

"No, no, no!" he declared. "It might be stolen!" He explained that the urine was so valuable as fertilizer that leaving it unattended outdoors was much too risky. I decided to sleep in the stable with the horses, where the smell of manure was, by comparison, as sweet as roses.

Our other mission was to find and root out corruption. Peasants were urged to report any suspicions they might have about their brigade and their team leaders—if one of them suddenly had new clothing or new furnishings in his hut, for instance. Nothing much came of our investigations.

We were repeatedly admonished to accept the hardships and conduct ourselves as model, hardworking cadres. I had already proved myself to be an enthusiastic cadre on the farm in 1959, but the hardships in Hunan were even greater. It was dirtier, smelled worse, and was colder in winter because in that southern climate the huts had no sleeping *kangs* or other heating for the short, damp winters.

It seemed to rain all the time, but the peasants worked the fields anyway, and we were expected to do the same. Along with the fact that my revolutionary zeal had subsided considerably since my peasant experience in 1959, a few days of being soaked and cold all the time took its toll. My Ministry comrades and I decided that it would do no one any good if we came down with pneumonia, so we stayed in our huts when the weather was bad. Even so, I woke up one day with a cough that refused to go away.

Falling each year between late January and late February, Spring Festival (or Chinese New Year) was approaching. We were ordered back to Beijing so we wouldn't be a burden to the peasants during their celebrations. Spring Festival is the most important holiday of the year. I was relieved, because the birth of our second child was imminent.

The day I got home following the long trip back, Xiangtong and I had a happy reunion and retired early. In the wee hours of the morning, she woke me up to say that she felt her time had come. We made it to the hospital just as our second son, Xiao-bin, came flying out of the chute. Xiangtong's mother stayed with us to help out, and then I had to return to Hunan.

The train going back was jammed, and the heating broke down. I still had a persistent cough, and by the time I arrived in the provincial capital of Changsha I was so sick that I collapsed on the bathroom floor of the hostel where we were staying overnight.

I insisted on being carried to the hospital. On the way, I became semi-delirious. Worried that I might mutter something reactionary in my befuddled state, I kept repeating, "Long live Chairman Mao!"

I was diagnosed with severe bronchitis bordering on pneumonia, put in a private room, and pumped full of medicine. I was discharged after a week and returned to my brigade to find that there had been a shift in the emphasis of our work.

We'd been sent to ensure clean local government. Now the focus was on class struggle. A new phrase had entered the language of politics. We were now struggling against "those in power who are taking the capitalist road" or, simply, "capitalist roaders." None of my colleagues or I could make sense of what all this was supposed to mean, but we followed our orders.

The storm clouds that had been gathering unseen now rolled into view. Mao had grown increasingly unhappy with the way the country was being run. Toward the end of 1965, in his private dealings with Chairman Liu Shaoqi and the Party's general secretary, Deng Xiaoping, Mao began complaining about Party leaders "taking the capitalist road." At a banquet for his seventy-first birthday, on December 26, he criticized Deng and Liu, directly and indirectly, for holding anti-Marxist views, and warned that a new struggle was coming "to rectify the power holders within the Party taking the capitalist road." Many of the senior leaders didn't take Mao seriously. After all, he was getting old and had retreated to the second front.

But other, unseen developments were about to change the face of China. Mao's wife, Jiang Qing, who had once been an actress and had survived a bout of cancer years earlier, was now playing a major role in Mao's plans. She was universally disliked by those who knew her. Paranoid, controlling, jealous, ambitious, childish, and manipulative, she had long ago ceased being a true wife and had become an attack dog of Mao's. She would later say that she was Mao's dog and she bit anyone he told her to bite.

Meanwhile, Defense Minister Lin Biao, another old soldier from the early days, had been building up an even greater cult around Mao. Lin had orchestrated the publication of a collection of Mao's writings—*The Quotations of Chairman Mao*—which came to be known as *The Little Red Book* and which, in time, would be reproduced in hundreds of millions of copies with shiny red plastic covers.

In mid-May 1966, the Politburo issued a Party circular that, for the first time, attacked "representatives of the bourgeoisie who have sneaked into our Party" and called for a "Great Revolution [to establish] Proletarian Culture." This would come to be known as the Great Proletarian Cultural Revolution.

I was suddenly ordered to wrap up my work in the countryside and return to Beijing, where I discovered that there were now open political attacks being made on Beijing's mayor, Peng Zhen, a close ally of Chairman Liu Shaoqi and other senior leaders. It was clear to all in government that a major political upheaval was about to burst within China.

I had weathered all the previous political movements with only mild criticism, so I wasn't thinking about myself. But I was deeply concerned for our two sons, eager for them to get the best possible education. With the increasingly virulent attacks on "bourgeois and imperialist culture," books for children became scarce.

I made a special effort to find some children's books for our kids before they all disappeared and had purchased several in the village bookstore in Hunan before my return to Beijing. When I got home, all I could find were new booklets showing poor peasant children exposing and struggling against wicked landlords.

Almost as soon as I returned, I was told that the premier needed me to accompany him on visits to Romania and Albania, even though those countries' leaders spoke no English and our Foreign Ministry had good interpreters in both Romanian and Albanian. This was odd. When the premier visited non-English-speaking countries, I generally stayed behind.

My duties on this trip were to take notes, but my shorthand was in English, and my written Chinese was still quite poor. I attended all of the premier's official meetings and assisted our stenographer, together with our interpreters, in drawing up the notes of the meetings. But I had little to contribute and the trip was almost a vacation for me, although I would rather have stayed home with Xiangtong and the kids.

Why the premier took me along on this trip was never explained, but it may be that, knowing what was brewing at home, he wanted to keep me out of harm's way. In any case, our delegation arrived back in Beijing just as the Cultural Revolution was heating up.

In July, Chairman Mao made his famous hour-long swim in the dangerously swift Yangtze River near Wuhan, where my family had lived for a year before going to New York. Photos and newsreels of the seventy-two-year-old swimming in the great Yangtze River appeared around the world. Of course, the photos did not show that he was surrounded by bodyguards and other strong swimmers. Nothing Mao did was casual, and this publicity stunt was calculated to show that he was still strong and vigorous. The effect on his status with the population was electrifying.

Lin Biao, who had been nurturing the cult of Mao, made a speech to the Politburo in which he declared, "Chairman Mao is a genius. . . . One single sentence of his surpasses 10,000 of ours." The *People's Daily* editorialized that "Chairman Mao is the red sun in our hearts. Mao Zedong Thought is the source of our life. . . . Whosoever dares to oppose him shall be hunted down and obliterated."

At Tsinghua University Middle School, a new term came into existence that spring, in response to coordinated efforts by Mao's wife and her collaborators to stir up university students to "eliminate all demons and monsters, and all Khrushchev-type counterrevolutionary revisionists, and to carry the socialist revolution through to the end." The term was "Red Guard," and it immediately became a movement that spread throughout the Beijing schools.

By August, the pot had boiled over. Liu Shaoqi—whom I had personally heard Mao describe to Viscount Montgomery, of Britain, as his successor—was suddenly demoted from second-in-command to eighth. Lin Biao, the defense minister and architect of the renewed Mao cult, became Mao's sole deputy. The premier remained third in rank but with slightly lower status.

To underscore the significance of what was happening, Mao wrote a big character poster, like the ones we had written in the Foreign Ministry back in the late 1950s. His was entitled "Bombard the Headquarters." It attacked the "bourgeois dictatorship" of "leading comrades."

With Mao's blessing, the Red Guard Movement spread nationwide. On August 17, a million Red Guard students from around the country converged on Beijing for a series of orchestrated rallies, the first of which was attended by Mao himself. He walked out through the gate from the Forbidden City just as the sun was rising, wearing, for the first time since 1950, his green army uniform. The crowd went wild. Then he walked back inside and ascended to the reviewing porch atop Tiananmen Gate, where Lin Biao made a speech whipping the crowd into a new frenzy, and, in full view of the throng, a young girl pinned a Red Guard armband on Mao's sleeve. The photo of that moment was widely published, a clear signal that Mao endorsed this new movement.

The night after the chairman wrote "Bombard the Headquarters," he issued the "Sixteen-Article Decision on the Great Cultural Revolution." Xiangtong was breast-feeding Xiao-bin when her colleagues came by to tell her she was to go with them to celebrate this new dictum of the chairman. Not daring to decline, she left the baby with my mother. She was out in the rain marching together with her colleagues, chanting slogans, dancing and singing throughout the night. When she finally returned home, she was exhausted and unable to produce breast milk, which became permanent. My mother was furious, but the atmosphere had grown so tense that no one risked defying orders to participate.

Within days, the slaughter of the innocents commenced. It was the start of China's modern dark age.

CHAPTER 22

Our Lord of the Flies

Entire libraries are filled with personal and official accounts of the Great Proletarian Cultural Revolution—the name given the decade between August 1966 and the death of Mao in September 1976. Millions died, and for every person who died an untold number suffered in some way. Like the European Holocaust of World War II, the Cultural Revolution was so horrific and irrational that people all over the globe wonder how it could have happened. So do we Chinese.

The facts seem to speak for themselves. Mao had come back to town (back from his second-front semi-retirement), gotten rid of anyone who had or might have challenged his renewed primacy, and replaced them with sycophants, fanatics, and yes-people who, with an eye on his inevitable death, jockeyed for political power. Mao had again scored a decisive and subversive victory by arousing the masses— only this time the masses were idealistic students instead of downtrodden farmers with mouths to feed. And they were given free rein.

The police were encouraged not only to stand back but to help foment the carnage. Security Minister Xie Fuzhi issued a memo to his police commanders in which he asked, "Should Red Guards who kill people be punished? My view is that if people are killed, they are killed; it's no business of ours. . . . The people's police should stand on the side of the Red Guards, . . . sympathize with them and provide them with information . . . about the landlords, rich peasants, counterrevolutionaries, bad elements and Rightists."

What resulted from this combination of the youthful instinct to rebel and the utter lack of restraint resembled William Golding's 1954 novel about a planeload of British boys marooned on a tropical island without adult supervision. In *Lord of the Flies,* the youngsters start out bonded together by the desire to survive and end up split into warring camps, with one side trying to destroy the other.

It has been estimated that the Red Guards, some as young as thirteen, were responsible for the beating death of one person on every block in Beijing. This was going on all across the country. To use an American term for hooliganism, it was state-sanctioned "wilding" on a societal scale in the most populous nation on the planet.

People were stopped on the street and interrogated about their backgrounds and often beaten, even if they had nothing to hide. Children turned in their parents, assisting in the mayhem. Colleagues turned on one another. Wives denounced husbands, and vice versa.

One of the early victims of the Cultural Revolution was an eminent sixty-seven-year-old writer, Lao She, who, with more than two dozen other intellectuals, was dragged from his Beijing home by mobs of teenagers wearing Red Guard armbands. These Red Guard victims were taken to a former Confucian temple, where they received the customary yin-yang haircut administered to those deemed enemies of the cause: half of the head was shaved, the other not. Throughout this humiliating process, Lao She and the others were beaten, punched, and screamed at.

Their faces were smeared with black ink, another common indignity ("black capitalist"). They were made to wear signs identifying them as demons and spirits, then beaten literally to a pulp. When Lao She was finally sent home, his wife had to cut off his clothes, they were so caked with congealed blood. Medical treatment was out of the question. No hospital would dare admit him; no doctor would dare treat him. The next day, he managed to walk to a lake near the Forbidden City, where he drowned himself.

The Red Guards were the children of the revolution, most of them born at the time of liberation—China's baby boomers. Now they had, with official encouragement, a revolution of their own to fight for Chairman Mao. Without supervision, they went on a rampage of destruction and death. Teachers were shot, buried alive, made to blow themselves up by sitting on packs of dynamite and lighting them. Husbands and wives were forced to beat each other, sometimes to death. The ways in which people were tortured and killed was limited only by the most sadistic of imaginations.

A casual remark was all it took for the Red Guards to attack the home of a suspected capitalist roader, smash all their "feudal" and "bourgeois" belongings, and thrash the occupants. It didn't matter whether it was an old man or the infant child of a "reactionary family." There was no discrimination, and no one to appeal to.

My friends at work and I were horrified at what was going on, and even more disturbed that there were radical elements within the Foreign Ministry who sympathized with the Red Guards. Everyone knew someone who had been or might be a target.

I wasn't worried for myself, but I was definitely worried for my wife. Xiangtong had been singled out for discrimination before, when I returned from the fourteen-nation African tour with the premier in March 1964. At the airport we were greeted by a big celebration, and all the wives of members of the delegation were waiting for them—all except mine. I was trying to find her when the premier asked me, "Where is your wife?" I was baffled. When I got home, I discovered that my section chief—who was jealous of the work I did for the premier—had instructed his staff to tell Xiangtong nothing about my return date. He had deliberately singled her out to hurt me.

As worried as I was for her, I was terrified for my parents, who would be prime targets. I cooked up a scheme that I thought might inoculate them. It was risky, but I felt sure I could pull it off. Doing nothing seemed even riskier.

Many photos had by this time appeared in the press showing Mao with a foreign guest and, hovering between them, me in my big black-rimmed spectacles. The man on Mao's right, I was the interpreter with no name. I had a large version of one of these photos at my office. As the carnage got under way, I took the photo to my parents' home and hung it on the wall in a prominent spot above the sofa where my father always sat.

I shouted my instructions into Father's hearing aid: he was to sit on the sofa and say nothing. I would be right back. I tracked down the neighborhood Red Guard representative and turned in my father. "He is a capitalist roader of the landlord class," I told him, trying to appear as eager as possible to support the movement to eradicate the "black" elements of society. "He lives nearby. Come with me to my home and help me make a revolution."

The young man took the bait and, my heart pounding, I found myself marching down the street in front of a small crowd of students brimming with righteous rage, ready to smash and beat. When we reached the house, I pushed open the door, which I'd deliberately left unlocked to avoid having my mother or father open it.

As I led the Red Guards down the corridor, one of them said, "Look at this bourgeois furniture!" pointing to my father's battered old reading chair. I kept marching down the hallway and into the living area, where my father sat demurely, peering up at all these strangers through his thick glasses with a bemused expression.

One of the Red Guards noticed his library of books. "We should burn those!" he said. But just as they were getting ready to begin their mischief, one by one they spotted the picture on the wall above my father's head and gasped. Their heads wagged from the photo to me and back again. They looked at me in my big, horn-rimmed spectacles, and then at the picture of me with Mao, in my big horn-rimmed spectacles. The mood shifted like a thrown switch.

"Venerable sir, we are sorry to disturb you," the leader said, bowing slightly. "We did not know you had such a strong revolutionary family. Please forgive us." And out they marched. I finally exhaled.

I warned Father to leave the picture up, and hurried back to the office, relieved and hopeful that my gambit had worked and would protect my parents for the duration. No one knew how long this nightmare would last.

Weeks of insanity stretched into months. For many, just walking in the street was a terrifying ordeal. Everywhere, one saw evidence of homes that had been ransacked, women with their hair shorn, people with bandages or ink-stained faces.

One always had to carry in plain sight a copy of the little red book of Mao's sayings. We had to "ask the chairman for instructions" at ten o'clock in the morning, and then "report to the chairman" in the afternoon.

People answered their phones with Mao's signature slogan, "Serve the people," to which the caller was expected to reply, "Completely and thoroughly." If you failed to answer correctly, the caller hung up and you might be visited by the Red Guards.

A Chinese proverb says, "Once you have jumped onto the back of a tiger, it is difficult to jump off." The Red Guard Movement was the tiger, and Mao and his loyalists were now riding on the tiger's back, a precarious set of circumstances that was causing consternation at the highest levels of government. At one point, a thousand chanting Red Guards showed up at the entrance to the State Council offices demanding to see the premier. They wanted him to produce Liu Shaoqi so they could beat him for "disloyalty" to Mao. The tiger had gotten so out of control that the State Council asked the Red Guards to leave the capital. While the government tried to bring the movement under the control of the military, the chaos continued.

Meanwhile, all primary schools and universities were shuttered, and stayed that way for years. University professors and students were sent to the countryside to be reeducated, and only Mao's writings were taught in high schools. At the Foreign Ministry, we dealt with the radical elements as best we could. I was subjected to struggle meetings, and in time had some of my responsibilities taken away. I was not, for example, to interpret for Chairman Mao but I continued to work for Zhou. Normal activities ground to a halt amid the chaos. In spite of the premier's best efforts to insulate us from the political cyclone, our foreign-policy apparatus was in a state of near-paralysis.

One day after returning home I lay on the floor in my little room, looking at the portrait of Chairman Mao on the wall. I talked to him: "Chairman Mao, are you going mad?"

One of the great ironies that emerged from this maelstrom involved Nancy Tang (Tang Wensheng), the daughter of my father's old newspaper partner, Tang Mingzhao. Nancy, who had brought Xiangtong and me our hot-water thermos when we lived in the lean-to, had completed her education and was working at the Foreign Ministry. In a few years, I would turn forty, the age at which interpreters were expected to move on or up in the diplomatic corps. Because of her excellent English, I had suggested that Nancy would be a worthy successor to take over for me.

As she was a friend of the family and now a co-worker, I had many occasions to talk with her about what was going on in the country and I discovered, to my chagrin, that she was turning into a radical. We compared notes, and then debated. In time, our debates became arguments. Nancy couldn't accept the notion that what was going on was hurting many innocent people and endangering China's future.

Finally, one day she broke down crying, and that was the last time we spoke of these matters. Our friendship ended. In time, Nancy moved into Mao's inner circle and our arguments came back to haunt me.

My father was retreating into his deafness and his grief over Chaoding's disappearance. His health slowly declined. Still, he kept up a good front, and continued to study each day's news in detail. I visited regularly, and we discussed the latest twists and turns in world events, as we had so many years ago in the greasy green kitchen on East Twelfth Street, halfway around the world.

When I was traveling, Xiangtong filled in for me, stopping by to check up on my parents. On one of these visits in late 1966, she found Father in a glum mood. He held up his copy of that day's *People's Daily* and through his heavy lenses looked at my wife with mournful eyes.

"Look at these articles. They make me feel cold, with shivers going up my spine!" Father could read the political tea leaves as well as anyone, and he was deeply disturbed by what was developing. But he said nothing more. Perplexed, Xiangtong simply nodded.

Almost a year to the day that the Great Proletarian Cultural Revolution got under way in earnest, I received a message from my father that he wished to see me. When I arrived at his house, I could see that he was quite ill with fever and needed attention. He motioned me closer, trying to speak, but I could not decipher what he wanted to say. I just nodded my head repeatedly and tried to comfort him. I stayed with him, knowing it was out of the question to try to get him to a doctor. The hospitals, like everything else, were now controlled by Red Guards intent on weeding out "hidden reactionaries" among the patients. I had heard of instances where elderly patients, instead of receiving proper treatment, were forced to endure struggle meetings in the hospital and then allowed to die for lack of care.

Among the ideas the Red Guards had picked up from Mao was that the greater one's academic credentials, the more reactionary one must be. In the hospitals, the Guards often ordered doctors to clean toilets and sweep floors while the nurses and sometimes even the janitors took over the job of treating patients.

A young revolutionary from the Russian section of the Translation Department at the Ministry, who had no medical training, once boasted to me that he had just operated on a patient, and that it was "so simple and easy."

If Father was going to die, it would be better that he died at home with me, not in a hospital being butchered or humiliated in struggle meetings. With as much tenderness as I could muster, trying my best to hide my rage and frustration, I stayed with my father until, with a final sigh, he passed away.

I sobbed violently for what felt like hours. My brother, a true patriot, had worked himself to death for China. My father, also a patriot, had sacrificed so much for his country, and, in the end, China turned its back on him.

Now it was happening to me, too. I had been branded by the radicals at the Foreign Ministry a "steel-clad royalist with the head of President Kennedy." I did not risk asking for mourning leave, nor would I dare to wear a black armsleeve to show my grief. Doing so would have given the radicals yet another excuse to hold a struggle meeting against me for being the son of the "decadent exploiting classes." I held my tears until night. I hoped he forgave me.

The final insult was that I could not get a proper death certificate from the radicals in the Foreign Ministry, so that I could have him cremated. At the time of his death, my father was the president of the Shanxi Provincial chapter of the Chinese Red Cross, so Xiangtong managed to get one issued from her unit.

Xiangtong was stoic throughout. Even when it looked as if I would once again be sent to the countryside to feed the pigs, she said, "Don't be afraid. Remember, a dead hog does not fear being thrown into boiling water, and a deaf man does not fear the clap of thunder." Her words gave me strength, again and again.

A week or so after Father died, there was another spasm of Red Guard activity. The most rabid young radicals from the Foreign Language Institute decided to storm the Foreign Ministry, to sweep away all the "royalists."

The Red Guards had been encouraged in their attack by Yao Dengshan, a middle-aged Chinese diplomat who had been expelled from Indonesia after leading a radical rebellion within our embassy. He'd encouraged a protest by the many Chinese residents of Jakarta against discrimination by the Indonesian government, which promptly revoked his diplomatic status and kicked him out.

Yao had broken all the rules of diplomacy, and had angered Premier Zhou. But he had been welcomed home with open arms by Chairman Mao and Mao's wife, Jiang Qing, who had emerged as one of the most powerful and feared architects of the Cultural Revolution.

When hundreds of shouting youngsters appeared one day at the gates outside the Ministry, demanding to be let in, Yao was delighted. My moderate friends and I were determined to stop them. We knew that we must, at all costs, prevent the storming of the Ministry, which, like the Ministry of Defense, held vital state secrets.

If the rabid students got inside, irreparable damage could be done to our national security. The Red Guards would smash everything in sight, but in the case of the Ministry the students had another, even more sinister agenda: they wanted to raid the archives to find evidence to use against the deposed chairman, Liu Shaoqi; Foreign Minister Chen Yi; and the premier himself.

I joined hundreds of other Foreign Ministry officials racing down the halls to the front gate to stop this assault with our bodies. But they outnumbered us and forced open the gates, pushing us steadily back. With a sudden rush, they broke through our ranks and entered the building, where they were welcomed by Yao and his cohorts, which now included Nancy Tang.

We braced for the worst, but Yao and his gang had bigger plans. They wanted to capture and stage a struggle meeting against Marshal Chen Yi himself. The foreign minister and the premier had offices in the Great Hall of the People, on Tiananmen Square.

The students reorganized to march on the Great Hall, while my colleagues and I raced ahead to try to stop them. This time we formed a human chain. Arms interlocked, we created a human barrier across the marble steps leading to the tall ornate doors. The mob arrived, shouting obscenities and demanding that we produce the foreign minister.

Then, unexpectedly, the door opened and the premier himself appeared, his bushy brows knit together, his face like a fist, angry and ready for an argument. He had been fighting this same battle all over China. In the south, Red Guards had disrupted a major rail hub and even stolen guns and artillery destined for our friends in Vietnam.

"Is China ruled by you or by Chairman Mao?" he shouted, a fist on one hip and his other hand pointing at the crowd, scanning the faces with hawklike intensity. "You have broken into government offices in your attempts to drag out so-called evil elements and have taken away many important documents of the Party and the government. Such thoughtless acts have given nothing but great pleasure and advantage to enemy countries."

The students hesitated, heads wagging, voices muttering. But their leaders repeated the demand that the premier produce the foreign minister.

The premier folded his arms over his chest, widened his stance, and said, simply, "Over my dead body."

The crowd fell still for a long moment, pondering the consequences if they persisted. Then began a tense negotiation between the students and the premier, who agreed that they could have a proper meeting to voice their views but he would be there beside the foreign minister.

A delegation from the mob was ushered inside, into one of the large meeting rooms. The foreign minister and the premier sat for hours, listening to the rhetoric and the accusations of political crimes and bad thoughts. When the students finally seemed to be running out of steam, the premier stood to go to the toilet. Just as he did so, a couple of the protesters rushed the rostrum and tried to grab the foreign minister and drag him down. But Chen Yi's bodyguard was alert and quickly whisked him backstage and into a waiting car that Zhou had arranged just in case.

The premier had high status, but his political credentials were constantly being questioned by the radicals. He was accused of pandering to China's enemies, of being too friendly with the imperialists—all the usual nonsense. But the true power brokers made it clear, in their statements and in newspaper editorials, that the premier was considered to be as "clean" as Mao, Lin Biao (his new chosen successor), Kang Sheng (security czar and a Cultural Revolution power broker), Jiang Qing, and Chen Boda, another old military hero who now headed the Cultural Revolution Group. Although they couldn't control the Red Guards, they held tremendous political power.

Protected by his status and his reputation for loyalty, Zhou worked hard behind the scenes to protect veteran government officials, including some who had already been tortured and beaten. He had some ministers whisked away to safe hiding places, refusing to divulge where they were even to Jiang Qing, whose main purpose seemed to be to constantly stir up trouble.

The diplomatic chaos was just beginning. Yao and his gang organized attacks on foreign embassies and encouraged radicals in the south of China to make direct assaults on British-held Hong Kong, a symbol of imperialist oppression.

The Red Guards attacked the Soviet, Indian, and Burmese embassies, each assault more violent than the last. They first screamed and hurled insults at the Soviet Embassy and repainted the nameplate of the street on which the embassies were situated from Legation Street to Anti-Revisionist Street. They smashed the windows of the Indian Embassy.

Encouraged by what was happening at home, and by Mao's open support of Yao, radicals in our various diplomatic missions abroad felt they had permission to indulge in equally outrageous behavior. In London, radical Chinese diplomats staged a public demonstration, shouting, "Down with British imperialism!" and scuffled with the police. In Rangoon, radical Chinese diplomats provoked bloody clashes with the Burmese police. Reports of Chinese casualties in Rangoon aroused outrage back home. Yao planned a reprisal attack on the Burmese Embassy in Beijing.

This alarmed all the levelheaded people in the Foreign Ministry, but there was no authority that we could turn to for help. The premier was fighting another fire somewhere else in the country. And, now that they had been targeted by the Red Guards, Foreign Minister Chen Yi and his vice ministers were keeping a low profile. The person with all the remaining clout, straight from the top, was Yao Dengshan, whose official Foreign Ministry title was conveniently vague: deputy head of the General Services Department.

A group of us went to Yao's office to beg him to call off the students. These attacks were gross violations of the most basic diplomatic rules. In some cases, they would be considered acts of war. China seemed to be sliding backward in time and evolution, to the 1899 Boxer Rebellion (the Righteous and Harmonious Society Movement), when a Chinese physical-fitness cult started a rampage to destroy all foreign legations, and killed thousands of Chinese and foreign religious leaders in the process.

Yao ignored us. He continued to give orders to the young rebels inside the Burmese Embassy. One boy reported that the students had started looting it. Yao suddenly turned stern and declared, "I'll tolerate no looting! Smash up the place, but no looting or stealing will be allowed!" Looting was decidedly capitalistic. Revolution was about destruction.

These diplomatic fiascoes reached a crescendo in August of that year—1967—when Yao planned to storm the British Office of the Chargé d'Affaires after demanding immediate return of the colony to China. The Red Guards gave the British diplomats in Beijing forty-eight hours to comply. The demands had no official status, so the British ignored them.

Local radicals in Hong Kong were already out in the streets in force, and radicals on the mainland were making preparations to invade. In Beijing, the attack on the British diplomatic compound began on the evening of August 22—the deadline the radicals had set for their demands to be met.

I had been such an outspoken critic of the madness that I had been sidelined from all my duties. With nothing to do, I returned early that day to our new, larger flat, around the corner from the British chancellery (their diplomatic compound of offices and living quarters). I'd been home for a while when a commotion broke out in the streets. Outside our apartment, I saw hundreds of people—possibly thousands—rushing toward the British compound.

I ran outside and heard waves of shouting followed by cheers. Just before eleven o'clock, long tongues of flame and clouds of sparks shot into the night sky above the trees. I saw with my own eyes but could scarely believe what was happening. The Red Guards had set fire to the British Consulate. The world was spinning out of control.

Arriving fire trucks were blocked by throngs of screaming people. The police tried to keep order, but the students ignored or, in some cases, attacked them.

Xiangtong was bicycling home after working late, when a convoy of fire trucks raced past her in the direction of our apartment compound. Terrified that the radicals had set fire to our quarters, she pedaled with all her might, weeping with relief when she saw that our building was unscathed.

This time Yao had gone too far. Not only did the Red Guards gut the British compound, they beat up the chargé d'affaires, Donald C. Hopson, for refusing to bow his head and admit guilt for the exploitation of the Chinese people. They also beat several members of his staff.

Not only was Zhou Enlai furious; Chairman Mao finally put his foot down, declaring that those responsible were counterrevolutionaries and would be punished. Now a new political wind began to blow, to purge the government of these troublemakers.

The situation in the Foreign Ministry changed overnight. The radicals headed by Yao and his followers went from being "true revolutionaries" to counterrevolutionaries. Overnight, "royalists" like me became the "true revolutionaries" for opposing the excesses.

My troubles and China's were far from over, however. While the worst of the violence and destruction had ceased by early 1969, untold

October 20, 1971: A new chapter opens—Henry Kissinger's second visit to Beijing to negotiate the details of Nixon's visit to China a few months later, the first by an American president. *(Xinhua News Agency)*

July 1971, Beijing: During Kissinger's first, top-secret visit, Premier Zhou Enlai hosted a banquet for Kissinger (far left). I am at the right, next to Zhou. With Kissinger were his top aides, John H. Holdridge (to Kissinger's immediate right) and a young Winston Lord (next to Holdridge), who would later become U.S. ambassador to the People's Republic. *(Xinhua News Agency)*

Now you see me, now you don't: Nixon's February 21, 1972, arrival in Beijing was covered by the world press, broadcast live around the globe. I was standing just behind the premier, on his right, as Nixon said, "This hand stretches out across the Pacific Ocean in friendship." Nixon would later write, "As our hands met, one era ended and another began." *(Nixon Presidential Materials Project, National Archives)*

The next day, in virtually every television news broadcast and on the front pages of newspapers around the world, the moment was memorialized, with me leaning toward the premier's ear, trying both to hear Nixon speak and to make myself heard by Zhou over the whine of jet engines. In one of those absurd turns of Chinese politics at the time, the photo was altered by the government press, who airbrushed me out and inserted the image of Mao's grandniece, Wang Hairong. In recent years I have been "rehabilitated"—photos of Chinese history now use the original image, with me in it. *(Xinhua News Agency)*

■ 上圖是一九七二年二月二十二日新華社發的周恩來迎接尼克遜圖片，經過處理，去掉冀朝鑄，突出王海容；下圖是美方拍的眞實照片

Beijing, 1997: Julie Nixon Eisenhower (right), who had accompanied her father on his 1972 visit, returned to Beijing with my close friend Virginia Kamsky (center) to observe the event's twenty-fifth anniversary on a televised panel discussion.

February 1972: Zhou Enlai (right) and Nixon (middle left) during their talks. Our foreign minister, Qiao Guanhua, is to my right. Kissinger faces Zhou, and Brent Scowcroft, deputy assistant for National Security Affairs, is to Nixon's left. *(Xinhua News Agency)*

Nixon and Zhou share a toast with the Chinese liquor maotai, a traditional, clear, vodka-like drink served in small glasses. *(Xinhua News Agency)*

"Mr. President, I know how you feel": As an American-educated Chinese man who grew up disdaining rice, garlic, and other Chinese staples, I watched Nixon with great empathy as he contemplated a morsel of indeterminate origin. *(Xinhua News Agency)*

August 1972: a busy, stressful year. On a hot summer day in the Great Hall of the People, during a break in a meeting with a Canadian official, the premier showed the strain of a year in which the Nixon visit was initiated, arranged, and successfully completed; the internal political strife of the Cultural Revolution continued to rage; and his health began to decline as his bladder cancer advanced. This was one of the last times I interpreted for Zhou. (© *Bettmann/Corbis*)

July 6, 1973: hitching a presidential ride. Ambassador Huang Zhen (center), the chief of our first Liaison Office in the United States; his wife; and I arrive at San Clemente, Nixon's California estate, with Henry Kissinger, after a ride in Marine One, the official presidential helicopter. *(White House Photograph)*

Meeting with Nixon in his California home. *(Nixon Presidential Materials Project, National Archives)*

April 30, 1976: Mao's final days. I was assigned to interpret for his last few official visits, including this one with New Zealand prime minister Robert Muldoon. *(Xinhua News Agency)*

May 1976: Mao's last visitor—Prime Minister Zulfikar Ali Bhutto of Pakistan. *(Xinhua News Agency)*

January 1979: the man on Deng's right. Three years after my last interpretation for Chairman Mao, I was honored and excited to be asked to escort our new, progressive, de facto leader, Vice Chairman Deng Xiaoping, on his first visit to America. Unlike on my previous trip from Beijing to Washington, none of the engines fell off. *(Xinhua News Agency)*

America gives face: Jimmy Carter pulled out all the stops for Deng's visit, including this White House state dinner, at which he charmed actress and Chinaphile Shirley MacLaine (lower left corner). *(Jimmy Carter Library)*

Three who reshaped the world: a historically challenged moment in Chinese-American relations. The man who brought an end to the acrimonious past (Nixon) sharing a lighthearted moment with the men who hoped to forge a harmonious future. *(Jimmy Carter Library)*

January 29, 1979: All of Washington turned out for a Kennedy Center performance and gala in Deng's honor. Among the many incongruous moments was when he shook hands onstage with some of the performers, including these towering giants from the Harlem Globetrotters basketball club. Deng's genuine delight and enthusiasm belied his long periods of political exile and seventy-four years. (© Bettmann/Corbis)

Western wear, Eastern style: Deng captured America's heart with his natural charisma—and by being a good sport. Here we are at a rodeo in Texas. (© Bettmann/Corbis)

March 1981: my special mission. It was a great honor to be summoned by President Reagan. He received Ambassador Chai Zemin and me in the Cabinet Room with Vice President Bush, White House chief of staff James Baker, Secretary of State Alexander Haig, presidential adviser Edwin Meese, and National Security Adviser Richard Allen. *(White House Photographs)*

1985: Xiangtong and me with our youngest son, Xiao-bin, at the New York home of Henry and Nancy Kissinger.

1980: I was assigned to accompany a delegation to America to study the U.S. economy and was told I could stay another week or so to see Xiangtong at the United Nations, where she worked, and accompany her to Los Angeles to visit her father. She had not seen him in three decades, so it was an intensely emotional reunion.

Early 1980s: home, sweet home. The living room of our two-bedroom flat in the Foreign Ministry apartment compound in Beijing. Xiao-bin, our youngest, is at left, and Xiaotan is on the right.

1984: ambassador to Fiji.

Reviewing the Fijian troops, in one of my first official duties as a full-fledged ambassador. *(Official Chinese Photograph)*

June 1988, London: with Xiangtong, on our way to the Royal Ascot horse race in our decidedly imperialistic embassy Rolls-Royce. *(Official Chinese Photograph)*

October 1987: Xiangtong and I pose for a photo after I have presented my diplomatic credentials to Her Majesty, the Queen. The carriage was provided to and from Buckingham Palace. *(Official Chinese Photgraph)*

May 1, 1989: British prime minister Margaret Thatcher and her husband, Sir Denis Thatcher (foreground), after a dinner in her honor at our official residence in London. *(Official Chinese Photograph)*

1988, the British Museum: another incongruous moment in my career, but one I had imagined since childhood—the chance to actually wear the medieval armor of an English knight and brandish a sword.

March 1988, London: During my tenure as ambassador to the Court of St. James's, Shanghai mayor Jiang Zemin, who would later become president of the People's Republic, paid an official visit and met with former British prime minister Edward Heath (left). *(Official Chinese Photograph)*

1995: accompanying then secretary-general of the United Nations, Boutros Boutros-Ghali, on a visit to China. *(Official United Nations Photograph)*

November 1995: As under secretary-general of the United Nations, I delivered a speech at the Kremlin, in Moscow, before an audience of six thousand. *(Official United Nations Photograph)*

1993, New York: Xiangtong (left) and I met President Clinton at an event at the Waldorf-Astoria. *(White House Photograph)*

1994, New York: with former president George H. W. Bush at a benefit for AmeriCares International, a disaster-relief organization.

My parents' tomb: These glassed-in cabinets are typical of modern Chinese tombs. This one, where the ashes of my father and mother reside, is in Taiyuan, where I grew up, and is reserved for those deemed to have served the nation in patriotic ways. *(© Foster Winans)*

April 2006: On certain holidays, and whenever possible, Xiangtong, myself, and our son Xiaotan visit my parents' tomb and perform the ritual three bows of respect. *(© Foster Winans)*

Ritual tidying up: In accordance with Chinese tradition, when we visit our ancestors' tombs, we open the cabinet, remove the small caskets containing the ashes and the other objects, and dust everything with loving care before returning them to their places, after which we perform the series of ceremonial bows. This is always a deeply emotional experience. *(© Foster Winans)*

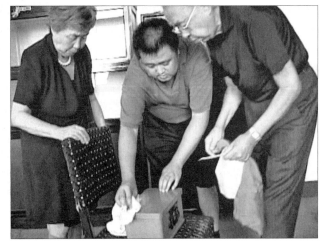

2003, Beijing: at home with Xiangtong.

2006, Tiananmen: still the man on Mao's right. *(© Foster Winans)*

damage had been done nationwide—not only to people but also to many of our most precious cultural sites, buildings, and artifacts. Hardly a pagoda, statue, or temple was left unscarred.

There was also considerable political damage to be repaired within the Foreign Ministry. And my status as a true revolutionary would be challenged again and again by a new crop of ambitious and power-hungry sycophants.

CHAPTER 23

Nothing Public Without Purpose

Xiangtong had been comparatively lucky during the Cultural Revolution, although she did have a close call. One day she overheard her chief telling her co-workers about her "suspicious" Taiwan relations. Colleagues later told her that the man seemed to be trying to provoke an attack on her. But they knew that if the premier trusted me he must also trust my wife.

As a part of Mao's clamping down on the anarchy, military representatives were sent into government units to help restore order. The Chinese Red Cross Society was a nongovernmental agency, but it reported to the Health Ministry, which sent three military officers to take care of both the Chinese Red Cross and the Chinese Medical Association. The team leader, Colonel Kuo Xingguo, was a man in his mid-thirties who had joined the army from a peasant family as a teenager. His political credentials were immaculate. He had received medical training and had been sent to North Vietnam as the leader of the Chinese medical team.

Kuo was a straight shooter who spoke his mind and had no political grudges. On learning that Xiangtong was being discriminated against because she had family in Taiwan, he told the staff, "Xiangtong has been working diligently for more than a decade. That should be long enough to test her loyalty."

An insecure bureaucrat, her boss was jealous of intellectuals, especially those with multilanguage skills, which he lacked. He told Colonel Kuo that Xiangtong was no longer needed and should be dismissed. To protect her, Kuo had Xiangtong transferred to his home unit as a translator and interpreter, where she worked for the next year.

In the summer of 1970, she was ordered to one of the new May Seventh Cadre schools: a farm where urban cadres could shed their bureaucratic tendencies and "integrate with the masses." The school was run by the Health Ministry in Jiangxi Province, in southeastern China, about as far away as I had been in Hunan Province. Some three million ended up in these cadre schools, which got their name from the date the first one was created, May 7, 1968.

With her Medical Association colleagues, Xiangtong left from the railway station on July 2, 1970. I took Xiaotan, our elder son, with me to see her off. Xiao-bin was only four and had lived for several years with my mother while my mother-in-law lived with us and helped care for Xiaotan. It was an imperfect arrangement necessitated by lack of space and scarcity of food.

For years Xiangtong had spent many nights wondering where in the world I was and if I was okay. Now it was now my turn to be left behind. We had no idea how long she'd be gone, but I forced myself to appear stoic. Some people ended up in these cadre schools for many years before they were allowed to return to the cities and their original jobs. Some less fortunate souls lived in the remote countryside for the rest of their lives.

Xiangtong was a hard worker, so I wasn't surprised when she wrote some months later that she had received an official honor for excelling, and then another soon after. But instead of being sent home because of her good work she was assigned to a remote mountain village to help the peasants with medical attention.

Mao had directed the Health Ministry to start teaching aspects of both Western and traditional Chinese medicine. The mission was to serve the people with "one needle [acupuncture], one handful of grass [herbal medicines], one pair of hands, and one loving heart." People like Xiangtong, who had received no proper medical training, were dubbed "barefoot doctors," supposedly taught just enough about acupuncture and herbal cures to treat simple conditions.

Before Xiangtong left for her barefoot-doctor assignment, an unsympathetic official took her aside and told her that she and several others were being sent to the poorest mountain villages, where many people were dying of an unknown disease. They were dispatched to these places without any medical equipment or supplies. "I suggest that you work away as long as you still have a breath left in you," he told her. "And when you die, that's it!" Xiangtong tidied up her belongings and destroyed her personal papers in case she didn't make it back.

She later recalled that she and her colleagues were shocked when they sat down to their first meal at a poor peasant's house and had unwashed dishes placed before them. Noticing their hesitation and startled looks, their host explained that the dishes were okay because they had just been licked clean! When Xiangtong looked into the kitchen, she understood: the only water available for washing was filthy.

Her cadre group showed the farmers how to build better chimneys for their stoves so that their eyes weren't constantly red from smoke irritation. Xiangtong also helped deliver a pair of twins, and earned the nickname Dr. Wang after successfully curing an old man of a nagging cough with acupuncture needles.

Then Xiangtong came down with hepatitis A, which was the easiest form of that disease to treat but required bed rest. She was sent to recuperate at a small clinic run by the cadre school.

This news worried me. I recruited one of my colleagues, Wang Hairong—the deputy protocol chief, who happened to be Mao Zedong's grandniece—to see if Xiangtong could be released to come home. Wang Hairong sent a letter to the Chinese Medical Association saying, "If you do not want Wang Xiangtong, please send her back. We shall have her here." Everyone knew of Wang Hairong's relationship to Mao, so they took the request seriously. As soon as Xiangtong was deemed well enough to travel, she was sent back to Beijing to recuperate. She arrived home the same day I received instructions to move in to the state guesthouse for a top-secret assignment. I had just enough time to take her home, pack, and leave.

Xiangtong was gone for an entire year, but it was a year that would change my life and history. With the backlash against the Red Guards' excesses, I once again became the man on Mao's right.

Relations between China and the Soviet Union had deteriorated following renewed border disputes in the north. For the first time, the

Russians appeared to be more of a threat to China than the United States was. A number of small developments looked hopeful, however. The new U.S. president, Richard Nixon, had publicly expressed a desire to visit China. The United States relaxed its ban on Americans traveling to China. And in October 1969 two American destroyers that had been patrolling the Taiwan Strait were withdrawn.

On December 3, 1969, the U.S. ambassador to Poland, Walter Stoessel, spotted our chargé d'affaires at a Yugoslav fashion show at the Warsaw Palace of Culture. Stoessel tried walking up to him to deliver the message that the United States was ready for serious talks with China. But our timid chargé had no desire to appear to be consorting with the enemy and no idea how to handle the situation. He ran away, down a flight of stairs. Stoessel then followed the chargé's Polish interpreter as he ran into a men's room to hide. It was there that he conveyed the message to the terrified interpreter.

To assure us that Stoessel's message was official and not just a personal whim of his, the U.S. State Department announced at its regular noon briefing the next day that Stoessel and our representative had exchanged a few words.

Shortly afterward, our senior vice foreign minister, Luo Guibo, summoned me to his office and informed me that China and the United States had begun secret contacts. I was among the select few who had been designated to take part in this work. "All your other responsibilities should be subordinated to this," Luo said. "You should immediately start reading up on the necessary materials, which will be provided to you."

From then on, my work—the use of my technical skills in the service of policy—began to focus more on policy itself. This was a challenge, because I was still the premier's interpreter. One day I would be interpreting for a meeting with an African head of state, the next day the guest might be a European ambassador, and the third day I might be required to accompany the premier on a visit to an Asian country. With this new secret initiative, I was being summoned at all hours. I was not allowed to tell anyone, including Xiangtong, where I was going or where I had been.

The working group included one of my "three Musketeers" buddies from Korea, Guo Jiading; Chairman Mao's grandniece Wang Hairong; Nancy Tang; and a few others. We were led by Zhang Wenjin, who had been educated in Germany and was a graduate of Tsinghua University. He had also been one of the premier's other interpreters.

The outcome looked dicey in early 1970, after the United States launched its infamous secret bombing attacks on Cambodia in an attempt to interrupt the North Vietnamese supply lines. But in August 1970, right after Xiangtong left home for her cadre school year, Premier Zhou met the American writer Edgar Snow, who had put the Chinese Communists and Mao on the map with his 1938 bestseller, *Red Star over China*. Snow thus enjoyed special status to visit China. He and Zhou sat next to each other at a Beijing Ping-Pong tournament. The premier asked Snow many questions about the current state of U.S. politics.

He was curious to know how Snow thought the Americans were going to extricate themselves from the Vietnam quagmire, which China had helped create by our assistance to Hanoi, and by allowing Russian supplies to move along our rails. He mentioned to Snow that while the U.S. threat seemed to be subsiding to the south and the east, China still faced a threat from the north. Snow asked, "Would the possibilities be better for negotiating détente with Russia or with the United States?" "I've been asking myself the same question," the premier answered with a coy grin. I was delighted by his response. Maybe, just possibly, after all those years and all the missed and bungled opportunities, my two beloved nations would again find common ground.

A little more than a month later, I was summoned to interpret for the October 1 National Day celebration atop the Gate of Heavenly Peace, with Mao, the premier, and Mao's presumed successor, Lin Biao, the defense minister. As always, I stood at the ready a few steps behind our leaders. I spotted the premier approaching with Edgar Snow and Snow's wife in tow, headed toward Chairman Mao. I quickly walked up and interpreted for Mao and Snow. Mao expressed a warm welcome to the Snows, explaining how the parade was progressing. He then told the writer that after the celebrations were over he would like to chat more with him.

The fact that Mao was hobnobbing with an American atop Tiananmen on such an important day was unusual in itself. But then something else equally odd happened. Marshal Lin Biao, who had been standing next to them, suddenly skittered away when photographers began snapping pictures. The next day, on the front page of all the Chinese newspapers, was a large photo of a serene Mao and a white-haired Edgar Snow standing side by side atop Tiananmen Gate, with me in between.

It was the first time anyone other than heads of state and Communist leaders—and an imperialist at that!—had been shown standing next to Chairman Mao atop Tiananmen Gate, the most sacred place in China.

Snow had spent time with Mao and Zhou in the old days when they were at their mountain retreat in Yan'an. He understood the moment's significance, and later wrote, "Nothing China's leaders do publicly is without purpose." The Chinese news agency released the picture and it ran in newspapers worldwide.

The message to the Chinese people couldn't have been clearer. Chairman Mao was showing an interest in Sino-U.S. relations. Unfortunately, as Henry Kissinger, Nixon's national security adviser later joked, our "crude Occidental minds completely missed the point."

This photo, more than any other, raised my public profile in China and abroad. I could only imagine the gasps of recognition it evoked in the States among all my old school friends from City and Country, Horace Mann–Lincoln and Harvard. Now everyone knew the answer to the question they had no doubt asked one another at reunions: "What ever happened to our pal Chao? You know, the Commie with the funny tooth who went back to China?"

With my new duties, I was no longer Mao's principal English interpreter. Nancy Tang had moved into that role. But I was still busy with the premier. Zhou granted Snow an interview that lasted all night and covered a lot of territory—not the least of which was Taiwan. China, the premier told Snow, was ready to negotiate America's role in protecting Taiwan's rogue government.

Later, Mao himself told Snow that he would be happy to welcome President Nixon "either as a tourist or as president." Whether or not that message ever got back to the White House, we received a message from the White House indirectly. On November 10, 1970, I was interpreting for the premier with Pakistani president Yahya Khan. There were, as usual, note-takers and other Foreign Ministry support staff in the room, along with Khan's staff.

The discussion involved matters of mutual interest, nothing extraordinary until the Pakistani president said, "I would like to have a private discussion with the premier, with just one interpreter present." This was an unusual request, but the premier immediately consented. "Come with me, Little Ji."

In a private meeting room, with the door closed and just the three of us present, Khan said that on a recent visit to Washington he'd met with President Nixon in the Oval Office and had been asked to convey a special message. I felt a slight adrenaline flush. A message directly from the president of the United States to the premier of China! This was a first.

"Mr. Nixon asked me to convey to China that the Americans regard Sino-American rapprochement as essential," Khan said. "Further, the president said that the United States will not join an alliance against China, and that he is ready to send a high-level secret emissary to Beijing to discuss all outstanding issues between the two countries, and to eventually move toward friendship with China."

The premier kept his composure, but I don't know how. For both of us, this appeared to be a dream coming true. It was personal for me, but I knew Zhou's view had long been that China and the United States should have been allies from the beginning. Now, finally, it appeared possible.

The premier's reply, sent a month or so later, was that China "has always been willing and has always tried to negotiate by peaceful means. In order to discuss the subject of the vacation of Chinese territories called Taiwan, a special envoy of President Nixon's will be most welcome in Peking." The message noted that while there had been many other messages received from the United States through various sources, this was the first time that one had come "from a Head, through a Head, to a Head. The U.S. knows that Pakistan is a great friend of China and therefore we attach importance to the message."

The big public breakthrough came in the spring of 1971, at an international table-tennis tournament in Japan. For the first time, China had sent a sports team abroad. One of the American Ping-Pong players casually mentioned to the Chinese players that he would like to visit Beijing. The premier heard about it and conferred with Mao, who at first decided that it was a bad idea. Mao then changed his mind. The Foreign Ministry immediately invited the American players, and we rolled out the red carpet. It was front-page news around the world: "Ping-Pong diplomacy."

Premier Zhou received the players himself in the Great Hall of the People, a meeting that I attended as interpreter. Once again, my picture appeared everywhere. The premier told the young Americans that they were opening a new chapter in relations between the United States and China. "I am confident that this beginning again of our friendship will certainly meet with the majority support of our two peoples," he said. The American athletes sat in respectful silence, unsure what to do or say. The premier gazed expectantly at the young faces for a moment, then said, "Don't you agree with me?" They burst into applause.

That summer, the premier met with a number of foreign journalists, including Seymour Topping of *The New York Times* and reporters for *Newsday* and *The Wall Street Journal*. Zhou's humanity seemed to win them over, and he was honest about some of China's problems, such as overpopulation.

The stage was set for the next move, which has been well documented by any number of historians, including participants such as Henry Kissinger and President Nixon. So I will present a shortened version reflecting my direct role, and the context that led to Nixon's famous visit in 1972.

On July 1, 1971, Henry Kissinger left from Andrews Air Force Base in Washington, D.C., on an announced trip to Saigon, Bangkok, and New Delhi before going on to Islamabad, Pakistan. The plan was for him to secretly slip into China for the initial talks aimed at establishing relations.

Kissinger pretended to fall ill with a stomach virus, and President Khan of Pakistan, who was in on the ruse, made a public show of concern and said that he was shipping Kissinger off to a mountain retreat where he could recover in comfort.

Instead, just before dawn the next day, July 9, 1971, Kissinger and his aides arrived at Chaklala Airport in Pakistani military vehicles. A British correspondent there for other purposes spotted Kissinger and immediately cabled his superiors in London, who decided that their correspondent was mistaken. They ignored his report.

Kissinger boarded a Pakistani Boeing 707 that had just been to Beijing to pick up a Chinese escort that included Nancy Tang as interpreter.

Along with other essential staff, I had moved nearby into the Diaoyutai State Guesthouse in Beijing before Kissinger's arrival, leaving Xiangtong, who was still recovering from hepatitis, in the dark. For all my wife knew, I was halfway around the world.

The plane arrived and taxied to a private section of the airport, where our delegation welcomed Kissinger and his party.

Marshal Yie Jianying, a high-ranking member of the Politburo, and I accompanied Kissinger to the state guesthouse in a black Red Flag limousine with curtains drawn. On the way, the marshal said little beyond telling Kissinger that the premier would see him later that day.

That afternoon, the premier arrived at the guesthouse. Thanks to our advance notice, Kissinger and his party stood at the gate. Kissinger looked tense when the premier got out of his car. Zhou's faint smile and his aura of composure and dignity further warmed the mood. Kissinger extended his hand, and the premier took it. The two men then walked together into the sitting room. After tea and small talk, they moved into a conference room next door, with staff.

As the meeting began, the premier said a few words of welcome and then asked Kissinger to begin. Kissinger took from his briefcase a thick pile of typewritten sheets, shuffled them a bit, and began to read. The premier had before him a piece of blank paper.

Kissinger had been waxing eloquent for quite a few minutes when he read, "Many visitors have come to this beautiful and, to us, mysterious land."

The premier interrupted him with a faint smile, saying, "When you have become familiar with it, it will no longer be as mysterious as before." This broke the ice.

The first day's talks—which included a working dinner—lasted almost seven hours. It was nearly midnight when the first meeting ended, and the premier, as always, returned to Zhongnanhai to report to Chairman Mao. As both Mao and Zhou always worked throughout the night, the next morning was left free for Kissinger to visit the Forbidden City.

Nancy Tang and I alternated the interpretation work at the conference table. When Kissinger—and, later, Nixon—went sightseeing, it was generally just me.

In the second meeting, the premier outlined all the outstanding differences between China and the United States. He asked whether, in view of these vast differences, there was any point in having the U.S. president visit China. Kissinger looked surprised. But he calmly replied that it was for the Chinese side to consider whether or not to issue an invitation.

During lunch the premier launched into a long description of the Cultural Revolution. Kissinger assured Zhou that Nixon considered that to be China's internal affair. But Zhou said that in order to understand China it was necessary to understand the Cultural Revolution. In his long discourse, the premier seemed to be criticizing himself for not being able to keep up with the thinking of Chairman Mao. In retrospect, I think he was signaling to Kissinger that he did not entirely agree with Mao.

After lunch the premier told Kissinger that the following summer—1972—might be a good time for Nixon's visit. Kissinger grinned, clearly relieved that Zhou's earlier remark was not a statement of fact. In the end, it was agreed that the visit would take place in the spring of 1972, so as not to interfere with the U.S. election.

In the negotiations to announce all this, there were two principal concerns. First, would the visit take place because Nixon had asked to go to China or because China had invited him? This involved a major question of "face" on both sides. Second, and even more important to the Chinese people, was what—if anything—should be said about the Taiwan issue? Without resolving these two questions, there could be no joint announcement and no Nixon visit.

The next morning Huang Hua, our vice foreign minister, returned with a new draft that solved both problems with no face lost on either side. Kissinger immediately accepted it with minor changes. The announcement took the world completely by surprise:

> Premier Chou En-lai and Dr. Henry Kissinger, President Nixon's Assistant for National Security Affairs, held talks in Peking from July 9 to 11, 1971. Knowing of President Nixon's expressed desire to visit the People's Republic of China, Premier Chou En-lai, on behalf of the Government of the People's Republic of China, has extended an invitation to President Nixon to visit China at an appropriate date before May 1972. President Nixon has accepted the invitation with pleasure.
>
> The meeting between the leaders of China and the United States is to seek the normalization of relations between the two countries and also to exchange views on questions of concern to the two sides.

The first paragraph solved the first problem. With "knowing" of Nixon's desire to visit, the issue of who initiated it was skirted with a passive, vague word.

The second paragraph, by not mentioning the word *Taiwan,* was our concession. To suggest the possibility of any change in American support for Taiwan would have exposed Nixon to election-year attacks for going soft on Communism. Of course, "questions of concern to the two sides" included Taiwan by definition. In the practice of diplomacy, every word counts and is therefore agonized and argued over.

The country that seemed most surprised by the announcement was Japan, America's principal Asian ally. Japan might have been distressed by the news, but the Japanese responded immediately by recognizing the People's Republic of China as the sole legitimate government of China, and accepting that Taiwan was part of China. Many other nations followed suit and, in a matter of months, Taiwan lost its seat in the United Nations and China's rights were established. Huang Hua, who helped negotiate the Nixon visit, became the head of the Chinese mission to the United Nations.

Three months later, in mid-October, Kissinger made a second, public visit to China to work on a joint communiqué to be issued after the conclusion of the Nixon visit. I worked on the preparations and the talks to iron out the language of the communiqué.

Amid all this developing international goodwill, one of the most shocking events in modern Chinese history occurred. Lin Biao, the vice chairman of the Republic, who was in line to succeed Chairman Mao, tried to flee the country. There are many theories about what happened. At the base of them all was the fact that Lin Biao had lost Mao's trust, and Premier Zhou also had little use for him. According to one account, earlier that year he tried to have the premier assassinated. Lin's son, an air force officer, was implicated in a crazy scheme to assassinate Mao. It has also been speculated that Lin Biao was planning to start a rival regime in Canton.

The fact—as I have come to believe on the basis of what I heard within the government and elsewhere—is that Lin Biao learned that he was marked for purge, and he did not want to wait around to face his fate. His son arranged for a military jet to fly from Beijing to the coast, where he was vacationing. The plane picked up Lin, his wife, and their driver. The Lin family planned to escape China by the shortest route possible: north toward Russia.

News that Lin's son had commandeered the plane reached the premier and was passed on to Mao. Asked whether the plane should be shot down, Mao reportedly said, "Let them go." It was a brilliant decision. Shooting down the vice chairman of the Communist Party could have been seen as an assassination itself, and might have sparked a revolt.

Instead, a miracle of sorts intervened. The plane ran out of fuel and crash-landed in Mongolia. All aboard were killed. Soviet forensics experts confirmed the identities.

By all accounts, Mao sank into a deep depression. Virtually every one of his old comrades and closest colleagues had been denounced as renegades, sham Marxists, counterrevolutionaries, or any number of other political crimes. The nation's intellectuals had been burned by the Hundred Flowers and Anti-Rightist campaigns. The Cultural Revolution had ruined the lives of millions and decimated the Party hierarchy. Those who remained loyal to Mao were the youngsters who had been Red Guards, and his immediate circle of aides, who were ambitious for power and had been able to use the poisoned atmosphere to remove political rivals.

The next time Mao appeared in public, shown on television greeting the new premier of North Vietnam, everyone was shocked at how much he appeared to have aged. His shoulders were stooped and his legs were wobbly. In January 1972, my beloved Marshal Chen Yi, whom I held in as high esteem as my father, succumbed to cancer. I was devastated and wept bitter tears. Here was another innocent victim of the Cultural Revolution who had died without political redemption. Mao attended Chen's funeral in subzero weather. The chairman seemed barely able to walk.

According to those who were present, Mao was in such a bad state, so sick, that afterward he told the premier, "I don't think I can make it. Everything depends on you now. . . . You take care of everything after my death. Let's say this is my will."

The premier protested, and Mao's vicious, calculating wife, Jiang Qing, blew her top. She had ambitions to either replace Mao or control his successor. She decided there was a "spy ring" around the chairman. Jiang, who was now a Politburo member, forced a late-night meeting of the ruling body, during which she claimed, "The chairman is in good health," and accused Premier Zhou of "forcing [Mao] to transfer power to you."

Mao's wife had been plotting to undermine the premier since the start of the Cultural Revolution. Now Zhou presented the ultimate threat. Had Mao died then, and the torch passed to Zhou Enlai, Jiang Qing and her circle would have been in a bad spot. In that moment, the premier's ultimate fate was decided, along with a fresh set of troubles for his allies, including me.

In the middle of Mao's crisis, and only a month after Lin Biao was killed, Kissinger arrived in Beijing on his second visit. The situation in China, that fall of 1971, was tense. Upon arriving at their guesthouse, the U.S. delegation was greeted with anti-U.S. posters in all their rooms. Who put them there was never determined, but it would not have been the premier. Nor do I believe it was done at Mao's direction. It would not surprise me, however, to learn that Jiang Qing was behind it in some fashion.

She was conducting her own private war, and the last thing she wanted was a successful Kissinger visit that would make Zhou look good.

Kissinger was visibly agitated by this insult, but he handled it with characteristic grace. He had his delegation collect all the posters and brochures and hand them over to the protocol officer. He gave us face by offering the speculation that they had been left there by the previous party.

This tension was immediately lifted when Zhou received the delegation later that day in the Great Hall of the People. The premier poured on the charm and warmth. At the banquet that followed, he delivered a welcoming speech, which was not officially published but laid the foundations for a successful second meeting with Kissinger:

> A new chapter will now be opened in the history of the relations between China and the United States after they have been cut off for twenty-two years, and we should say that the credit for this should go to Chairman Mao [Zedong] and President Nixon. Of course, there must be someone serving as a guide, and it was Dr. Kissinger who courageously made a secret visit to China, the so-called "land of mystery."
>
> Our two peoples are great peoples. Although our two countries are separated by the vast Pacific Ocean, friendship links our two peoples together. After receiving the U.S. table-tennis team this year, we received a number of other American friends. We hope that this new era will be approached in a new spirit.
>
> I propose a toast to the friendship between the great American people and the great Chinese people, and to the health of Dr. Kissinger and all our other friends!

After dinner the premier walked around the banquet hall and clinked glasses with all the members of Kissinger's party, including his secretaries and the aircraft crew. The next day's *People's Daily* published a photo of Premier Zhou and Kissinger, the first time that an American official had ever been pictured together with a Chinese leader.

Taiwan remained a big problem. It was Kissinger who came up with the wording that paved the way to an agreement: "The United States acknowledges that *all Chinese on either side of the Taiwan Strait maintain there is but one China and that Taiwan is a part of China.* The United States does not challenge that position." Further modifications were made, but this clever wording led to a solution.

Even as Kissinger's plane was taxiing for takeoff after that second visit, we received the news that Taiwan had finally been expelled from the United Nations and the People's Republic had been granted its rightful seat. We were elated, but there was no time for celebrations. We had to prepare for President Nixon's visit, which was just a few months away.

CHAPTER 24

The Two Young Ladies

What a long way we had come and in such a short time! Three years earlier, when Richard Nixon was inaugurated for his first term as president, he had spoken, on the steps of the U.S. Capitol, of his aspirations for "a world in which no people, great or small, will live in angry isolation."

The *People's Daily* had wasted no time in articulating the official response to this implied insult: "Although at the end of his rope, Nixon had the cheek to speak about the future. . . . A man with one foot in the grave tries to console himself by dreaming of paradise. This is the delusion and writhing of a dying class."

Three years later, it was Mao who appeared to have one foot in the grave, and we were slogging through a political struggle over who would inherit the mantle once it fell from his shoulders.

For years Mao had spoken of his mortality as if his demise were imminent. I had interpreted for many foreign dignitaries and heads of state who tried to engage the chairman in discussions of substance. But Mao considered himself the philosopher, and Zhou the manager. Mao's trick for changing a subject that he didn't care to discuss was to wave dismissively and say, "Oh, well. Why should I worry? Heaven is calling me," coyly suggesting that he had some terminal condition and the difficult issues at hand were ultimately out of his control.

This had been a political ploy until the end of 1971, when he nearly answered heaven's call, and it became clear that he would soon enough. But as the Nixon visit drew closer Mao bounced back like an aging, out-of-shape boxer who gets one last shot at a title bout. His mood improved, and he finally allowed his doctors to treat him properly for a lung infection and heart disease. He practiced standing up and sitting down, and walking a few steps with help. He became increasingly excited about receiving Nixon. It would be another historic moment to add to his legacy. Like the ancient emperors he had studied and emulated all his life, this emperor's name would live until the heavens and the earth grew old.

But decades of stress and smoking had taken their toll. He was bloated with edema and had trouble even mustering the strength to clear his throat of phlegm. He was wary of traditional medicine, believing it was wrong to tell people when they had cancer. "Don't tell the patient, and don't perform the surgery. Then the person can live longer and still do some work," he'd said.

Typically, Mao's approval was sought whenever a member of his staff or a high-ranking Party leader needed major surgery. When his old friend and security chief, Kang Sheng, was diagnosed with bladder cancer around this time, Mao ordered that he be "spared" the discomfort of surgery. Whether Mao thought he was doing Kang a favor or doing Kang in, Kang died a few years later. In the years since, an army of witnesses have testified to Kang's role in the injustice, persecution, and brutality committed in Mao's name.

In addition to the heavy workload and the political storms raging across China prior to the historic visit of President Nixon, I had a few crises of my own. Xiangtong was still mending from her bout with hepatitis. Her mother had been living with us for a number of years, helping to care for our first son, seven-year-old Xiaotan, while our second son, Xiao-bin, lived with my mother near the Forbidden City, in the little house where my father had died.

Our financial situation was dire. In spite of my responsible job, government salaries remained at subsistence levels. Meanwhile, Xiangtong and I were so preoccupied—she living with the peasants and getting sick, and me traveling with the premier or working late—that we rarely had time to visit little Xiao-bin, who was now five years old. One of the saddest moments in my wife's life occurred once when she went to see our younger son and he didn't recognize her. Xiao-bin ran away crying to hide behind my mother.

Xiangtong's mother had been depressed for decades over the lost years with her sons and her husband in Taiwan. A heavy smoker, in 1971 she began to lose weight and was then diagnosed with lung cancer. Because of her Taiwan connections, she was ineligible for the best medical care, but we did what we could. She quickly went downhill, became bedridden, and finally, one day, asked to be taken to the hospital. She didn't want to die at home, in pain.

A sympathetic surgeon we knew was able to bypass the usual political screening to get my mother-in-law a bed. She died within days, with Xiangtong and our older son, whom she had practically raised, at her side. I was unable to get away from work, so I couldn't be there to comfort any of them.

Like millions of stories from that period, hers was a cruel, sad death, made even more so because no one other than our family dared bid her farewell. Only Xiangtong and Xiaotan accompanied her remains to the crematorium.

During this time, there was considerable political stress. At the beginning of the Cultural Revolution, I had been denounced. After Yao's disastrous embassy attacks and the backlash against the excesses of the Cultural Revolution, I was "rehabilitated" and promoted, along with many other veteran cadres and political leaders who had been attacked by the Red Guards. Even Mao made an effort to bring back some of those who had been wrongly expelled or exiled.

But within the Foreign Ministry political plots continued to smolder. I was repeatedly criticized by a radical and jealous faction of my colleagues for having been soft on the counterrevolutionaries. When people like Yao were treated like heroes, and before they became villains, I hadn't complained loudly enough about their destructive behavior.

Unlike some of my colleagues, I was difficult to control and was not an easy target. I had the premier's full confidence, and my role in our government's foreign policy–making was growing. Very few people in the Chinese government had served the premier as long and as personally as I had, having spent hundreds and maybe thousands of hours participating in his conversations. I knew every mole on his hands, I knew when his old arm injury was causing him pain, and I could read his every sigh.

I was also the only one in our government who could converse with Kissinger and the other Americans with the ease of a couple of Harvard students talking over lunch in the university cafeteria while simultaneously retaining Zhou's full trust. This had made me indispensable.

There was more to this office friction than professional rivalry. I had become the premier's eyes and ears within the Foreign Ministry. He often asked me what was going on, who was trying to discredit whom, how his enemies were trying to undermine him and our foreign-policy goals. I frequently brought him messages and pleas from or about good people who had been unfairly denounced and deserved to be rehabilitated or protected from further harm.

My principal adversary was Nancy Tang. Now that she worked directly with Mao, she had fallen under the spell of Jiang Qing and the other careerists and opportunists in Mao's inner circle, all of whom must have shuddered at the possibility of Zhou's being the chairman's successor.

The premier had defied Mao behind his back, helping to protect the politically condemned, and he had defied Jiang Qing to her face, refusing to disclose the whereabouts of the people she considered to be her enemies. She, in turn, had accused the premier of plotting to squeeze out Mao, even though she knew better. Zhou had no interest in assuming Mao's role. Mao was the stern father of China, and Zhou its nurturing mother. But, at seventy-four, Zhou was getting along in years himself. In fact, some of my colleagues and I had expressed concern about him—he seemed to be losing weight.

Nancy Tang had become Jiang Qing's eyes and ears in the Foreign Ministry, helping Mao's wife keep track of and interfere with adversaries such as the premier and his loyalists, including me. As time progressed, Tang recruited to her side Wang Hairong, the Ministry's protocol chief and Mao's grandniece. The two became fast friends, and always seemed to be finding fault with something I'd done or said. In my conversations with Xiangtong, I began to refer to them as the "two young ladies." They were both around thirty years old, and were up to their necks in political intrigue between Mao, Jiang Qing, and Mao's henchman, Kang Sheng, who was also hearing the call of heaven. The two young ladies were my dedicated foes.

My life became especially complicated and nerve-racking as I assisted Huang Hua, now our foreign minister, Deputy Minister Qiao Guanhua, and Zhang Wenjin—the principal advisers to Premier Zhou—in ironing out the most important detail of Nixon's visit: the joint statement that would be issued at the meeting's end. Kissinger worked out the final draft of what came to be known as the Shanghai Communiqué, after the place where it was announced. It was the starting point and remains a foundation of present-day Sino-U.S. relations.

While Mao was trying to muster the strength to stand and hold a conversation with Nixon, the premier was preparing his troops to make the visit a diplomatic success. He gathered us together one day to speak at length about past U.S.-Chinese relations. Zhou Enlai said he believed that the two countries should have been natural allies from the beginning, but every time an opportunity came along something went awry. This time we were going to get it right.

He spoke of the American generals Stilwell and Patrick Hurley, both of whom had spent time in China before and during the war. Stilwell understood the situation in China and was critical of the corrupt regime of Chiang Kai-shek, the premier explained. Hurley—who had arrived unannounced on Mao's Yan'an doorstep shouting Indian war whoops—was a narcissistic blowhard. But in 1945 Mao and Zhou gave a message to Hurley for President Roosevelt: They would meet with Roosevelt at any time and place of his choosing. They would travel to Washington if necessary. Stilwell had fallen ill, and Hurley was the most convenient conduit.

The Russians had proved themselves treacherous friends, and Mao and Zhou thought China would fare better if the country balanced the Russian threat with an American alliance. But Hurley never forwarded the message. He was an ardent anti-Communist. Roosevelt died soon after.

Another opportunity was lost immediately after liberation in 1949, when the Soviet ambassador—China's supposed ally—ran away with the Kuomintang. The American ambassador, Leighton Stuart, and other Western ambassadors had stayed behind with the Communists in Nanjing, the city made famous when the Japanese slaughtered an estimated three hundred thousand people in what became known as the Rape of Nanking.

Stuart had an important message to convey to Mao and Zhou: the United States was ready to provide the People's Republic with a long-term low-interest loan of up to $2 billion. This was an enormous sum in a country as poor as China.

But, instead of delivering the message to Beijing himself, Stuart asked a go-between—a Chinese official who had access to Mao and Zhou—to do it for him. The premier told us that this person was en route to Beijing the day Mao announced, on the twenty-eighth anniversary of the founding of the Party, that China was allying itself with the Soviet Union, and that the Soviets had agreed to provide China with $300 million in aid.

The message from Ambassador Stuart was never delivered. Stuart was immediately recalled to Washington to face howls of outrage over Truman's State Department's having "lost" China to the USSR. The Korean disaster followed, and then the infamous snub by Secretary of State John Foster Dulles at the Geneva peace talks in 1954, when he refused to shake the premier's hand.

This was all about to change, and it began on the cold gray morning of February 21, 1972, when Air Force One landed at Beijing Airport. The crowd was small: about two dozen of our officials and a bank of television cameras, photographers, and reporters. However, the entire world was watching, live, on television.

Kissinger had previously acknowledged regret at the old Dulles insult in Geneva, and Nixon was anxious to create a new, hopeful symbolic moment. The plane taxied to the welcoming area and the door opened. Nixon emerged alone. He had instructed his entire delegation, including Mrs. Nixon, to hold back until he had deliberately and enthusiastically shaken the hand of Premier Zhou Enlai.

I stood just behind the premier, on his right, as Nixon said, to the best of my recollection, "This hand stretches out across the Pacific

Ocean in friendship." Nixon later wrote, "As our hands met, one era ended and another began."

The premier replied, "China welcomes you, President Nixon," and asked about his flight. Then the First Lady was introduced and the rest of the Nixon entourage came down the stairs. The official visit was under way.

The next day, in newspapers around the world, the moment was memorialized on front pages, with me leaning toward the premier's ear. (The sound of the jet engines had made it difficult to hear what was being said.) In one of those absurd turns of Chinese politics, the photo was altered for the Chinese press; I was airbrushed out of the picture, and where I had been standing there was Wang Hairong! The two young ladies had been busy.

As I had when Kissinger visited, I attended all of Premier Zhou's meetings with Nixon. Chairman Mao's meetings were interpreted by Nancy Tang.

The lengths to which the premier went to guarantee the success of the trip were extraordinary. We knew that Nixon had deliberately excluded his secretary of state, William Rogers, from many of the important meetings. Nixon kept Rogers busy with minor meetings and sightseeing, while he and Kissinger met with Mao and the premier. The State Department disagreed with the White House on some aspects of the negotiations, and Rogers had complained in our presence.

It would not be in China's interest to have Rogers return to the United States in a disgruntled mood, as that could affect future Sino-U.S. relations. The premier wanted to somehow turn the situation around, without making the White House unhappy.

Zhou personally inspected the accommodations for Nixon and his staff in advance. He didn't want a repeat of those anti-American posters that had greeted Kissinger. Rogers was to stay on the thirteenth floor of a hotel in Shanghai during the president's stay. I told the premier of the American superstition about thirteenth floors—"Many buildings don't have them"—and he immediately ordered Rogers reassigned. He also went out of his way to invite Rogers to a private lunch at which I interpreted. The premier treated the secretary of state as a respected official and friend, thanking Rogers for his contribution to Sino-U.S. understanding and the success of the Nixon visit. Rogers pointed out a major inconsistency in the final draft of the communiqué and we were able to fix it in time. The premier had given Rogers back the face his own government had taken away.

The Shanghai Communiqué, the short document that would define Nixon's visit and future U.S.-China relations for decades to come, included the following core language. China declared:

> The two sides reviewed the long-standing serious disputes between China and the United States. The Chinese side reaffirmed its position: The Taiwan question is the crucial question obstructing the normalization of relations between China and the United States; the Government of the People's Republic of China is the sole legal government of China; Taiwan is a province of China . . . the liberation of Taiwan is China's internal affair in which no other country has the right to interfere; and all U.S. forces and military installations must be withdrawn from Taiwan and the Taiwan Strait. The Chinese Government firmly opposes any activities which aim at the creation of "one China, one Taiwan," "one China, two governments," "two Chinas," an "independent Taiwan" or advocate that "the status of Taiwan remains to be determined."

The Americans declared:

> The United States acknowledges that all Chinese on either side of the Taiwan Strait maintain there is but one China and that Taiwan is a part of China. The United States Government does not challenge that position. It reaffirms its interest in a peaceful settlement of the Taiwan question by the Chinese themselves. With this prospect in mind, it affirms the ultimate objective of the withdrawal of all U.S. forces and military installations from Taiwan. In the meantime, it will progressively reduce its forces and military installations on Taiwan as the tension in the area diminishes.

I would never have predicted that, nearly four decades later, little has changed.

The events of the preceding several years had taken their toll on my health. Although I was taller than anyone else, and had been well fed in the United States during my growing years, I had begun life with a weak constitution and occasionally I worried that I might collapse again at an inconvenient moment. As a result, I officially retired from my job as an interpreter and went to work helping to develop and write the many documents and communications necessary to establish our new Sino-U.S. relations and our role as a voting member in the United Nations.

Meanwhile, in a more subdued fashion, the Cultural Revolution continued. The two young ladies—who had emerged as two of Mao's top half dozen or so protégés—both worked in the Foreign Ministry, so they focused their meddling power plays on me and their other co-workers. Their motives were dark and their methods treacherous, playing people against one another. Permission to do so, under the premier's nose, came from Jiang Qing, whom many have openly described as insane and insufferable.

I had on occasion interpreted Western movies while they were playing on-screen for Mao's wife. She especially loved Garbo films. She barely acknowledged my presence as I sat on a stool beside her sofa, except to complain if I spoke too loudly or too softly. There are hundreds of stories about her bizarre, erratic behavior and her treatment of others. Displeasing her could mean prison or exile.

The drama playing out in Mao's villa in the twilight of his reign was straight out of Chinese dynastic history, or Shakespeare. Like Lady MacBeth, Jiang Qing summoned dark forces to fill her with "direst cruelty," and tried to manipulate her husband into assassinating his rival for the throne. The two young ladies were tools in her schemes.

I had been promoted to the position of deputy director of the Translation Department, but one day I was informed that I needed another round of peasant reeducation. I had no doubt who was responsible. I was again to labor in the fields and assist in "weeding out hidden counterrevolutionaries." The only thing I had to look forward to was the location. I was assigned to a May Seventh cadre school in my old province, Shanxi.

During the Great Leap Forward, paddy-rice cultivation in Shanxi had been developed through irrigation. My first duty in the fields was to transplant rice. As a student in the United States, I had spent several summers laboring on farms in Connecticut, but I had never taken off my shoes. There were leeches in the paddies, as well as nasty parasites that entered the body by burrowing into your feet and legs. Although it was May, the water was still frigid. We cadres were expected to embrace such hardships as a chance to experience peasant life. Into the paddy I sloshed, shivering and wondering what horrible creatures were attacking me as I slithered around in the murky, calf-deep muck.

I was so slow at transplanting the rice seedlings that everyone finished far ahead of me. This made it difficult to exit the paddy without trampling the hard work of others. The team leader noticed and assigned me instead to carry the rice seedlings on a shoulder pole to the fields. But I was physically so weak that on one occasion I stumbled, seedlings and all, into a paddy.

As our work crew returned to our dwelling that afternoon, I felt and no doubt looked like a crippled street beggar hobbling along, struggling to keep up with the other trainees. The farm had two fierce guard dogs that followed along and seemed to be stalking me like wolves, baring their teeth and growling. I couldn't tell if they wanted me to hurry up or to slow down so they could eat me. Either way, I was relieved when one of my fellow laborers noticed and called them off, which set off gales of laughter among the crew.

The authorities at the cadre school saw that I was in no condition to do any good in the paddies, so I was told to concentrate on weeding out the politically impure. I did my best to appear as if I were doing my duty, pretending to snoop around in the business of others, asking a few innocent questions about people's politics. But the effort was without any enthusiasm or desire to catch anyone.

It wasn't long before the premier rescued me, asking in the office, "Where has Little Ji gone? I need him!" So I was summoned back to Beijing in the late summer of 1972.

On my way, I stopped to visit my family's hometown, Fenyang, which I'd left in 1938. I received a hearty local-boy-makes-good welcome from Party and government leaders. They had all heard about my work for the premier, and seen my picture in the paper standing on Mao's right. I spent a night in the very house from which we'd fled thirty-six years earlier as the Japanese approached. My principal mission was to visit the remains of my grandfather, who had died the year we lived in Hankow, during our exodus to New York. After returning to China, Chaoding had gone to the trouble of moving my grandfather's remains from Hankow back to our home village, a small agricultural community near the county seat.

When I inquired about visiting Grandfather's tomb to pay my respects and perform the customary ritual bowing and cleaning, the red-faced Fenyang county officials told me that his tomb had been destroyed by the Red Guards during the early years of the Cultural Revolution. Along with the remains of other landlords, the students had smashed the cases and urns and discarded the ashes to be swept away by the winds. Now he was gone forever, another victim of the Cultural Revolution. The officials were profusely apologetic, telling me how upset many people were, especially families my grandfather had helped in the old days. I left my old hometown feeling a mixture of pride and bitterness.

Although I was supposed to be retired from interpreting, I continued to serve as Premier Zhou's English interpreter as well as deputy to my boss, Ambassador Ma, in the Translation Department, working on important documents.

By late autumn of 1972, feeling weak as a dishrag, I checked myself in to the hospital. The diagnosis was grim: liver cancer. Poor Xiangtong did her best to keep a stiff upper lip, and I did my best to show her my optimistic side. But when I was alone I fell into a dark mood. It was painful to contemplate Xiangtong alone, without my political protection, trying to raise two little boys and earn enough to feed them.

The premier had arranged a private room for me in one of the best hospitals. I stayed for more than two months. As the test results came back, the doctors began to doubt their diagnosis. Finally, they decided that I had no cancer, not even hepatitis. I had just needed rest, which I was getting, and had therefore begun to recover. I had dodged yet another bullet.

Kissinger made multiple trips to Beijing to discuss the particulars of normalizing relations between our two countries. This included setting up our first diplomatic office in the United States, and vice versa: an American diplomatic presence in Beijing.

The two men got along like old pals. Zhou admired Kissinger's intellect, humor, and objective approach, often referred to as Real-politik—diplomacy without ideological overtones. Ironically, Kissinger's non-American background made him a good representative for the United States. His Jewish family fled the Nazis in Germany and came to New York a year before my family arrived after fleeing the Japanese. The three of us had a lot in common, and the sessions were civil and earnest. There was no table-pounding or discourteous behavior, as I'd seen in Korea.

One day in the spring of 1973, I was interpreting for the premier at a Women's Festival reception when, in a private moment, he delivered big news: he was sending me to the United States as part of the advance delegation team to establish our first liaison office in Washington.

I knew that I was qualified and had hoped to be asked, but the news gave me a jolt of energy nonetheless. After more than two decades, I would be returning to the other land I loved. And the news got even better: the premier said he and Chairman Mao agreed that Xiangtong would be allowed to go along.

I nearly wept with joy. After years of being marginalized and gos-siped about because of her Taiwan connections, Xiangtong was finally going to be vindicated. The two most important people in China had decided that she was trustworthy enough to be sent abroad. This would send a clear message to all that the discrimination against her had been unjustified and that she was just as patriotic as anyone else.

Our delegation would be gone for a year or more. Now Xiangtong and I could be together and share the experience of making history. When I got home and told her, I could barely speak, I was so happy for her. She beamed with pleasure, her eyes shining. The children could not go, especially on such a sensitive first mission. We recruited a cousin of Xiangtong's in Beijing to live at our apartment and look after the boys while we were gone.

Xiangtong and I each received a lump-sum stipend to purchase or make the clothing we would need. Xiangtong attended a Foreign Ministry study class for those going abroad, while I prepared by reading important documents. I would be traveling with a small contingent of about ten people, who were to scout out offices and places for all of us to live. The ambassador and other top officials would arrive later, with our wives.

I couldn't wait to stand again on American soil, and to show Xiang-tong the world I had been describing to her for so many years. I felt more hopeful than I had in a long time.

CHAPTER 25

A Circle Closes, Another Opens

The advance party to Washington was led by the deputy head of the Liaison Office, Han Xu. He had been moving up in the ranks, from protocol officer to ambassadorial rank. Our task was to find proper living and working quarters for the staff and families. After we had accomplished that, Ambassador Huang Zhen, as the chief representative of the People's Republic, would arrive with the rest of the staff and spouses.

In April 1973, a few days before we were to leave, the premier invited the delegation to his residence for a simple lunch of steamed pork dumplings and soup. He made a few announcements before dropping a bombshell. "This will be my last time to see you, and the last time we will have a meal together."

It was a thunderbolt from the blue sky. A dish clattered in the stunned silence. Someone gasped. One of the counselors dabbed at his eyes with a napkin. I experienced a storm of emotions that coalesced around fear. Zhou Enlai had been looking gray and thin lately. Was the premier sick?

As much trouble as I'd had with the two young ladies, the political battles the premier had been engaged in were epic, pitting him against Jiang Qing and her gang of thugs. Even Mao was becoming fed up with Jiang. According to some accounts, he considered divorcing her. Was the premier being purged? What would this announcement mean for me and my family? For China? Strange things had been happening; disquieting rumors had been whispered.

The premier had recently given a reception for Western experts living in China. All the attendees had been Communists, and many of them worked for our government editing and translating propaganda. While translating Mao's works into English in the early 1960s, I had worked with some of them, including Americans such as Sol Adler and Frank Coe. A Marxist economist who had worked in the U.S. Treasury, Coe fled to China during the McCarthy anti-Communist investigations. Adler was a British-born American, also an economist, who had worked with Coe.

With passion and embraces, Zhou had apologized at that reception to Coe, Adler, and others for the injustices they had suffered over the years. The gesture seemed to be cause for optimism at the time, but in light of Zhou's remarks, now took on the color of a man organizing his affairs, settling his debts while he still had time.

The premier offered our delegation no further comment or explanation for his remark, and it would have been improper to ask questions. That he'd said even as much as he had was evidence enough of big changes to come. The unspoken agony hung in the air the rest of the meal. Another one of my father figures and mentors—a dear friend, in a professional way—was exiting my life. But I was hardly the only one who revered Zhou Enlai.

This announcement was much discussed among my colleagues, but no one knew anything concrete, except that our beloved premier appeared to be aging quickly. He didn't smoke, but he was acquiring the same weary, drawn look of my mother-in-law in her last years. Fortunately, I was so busy preparing to leave for Washington that there wasn't much time for idle gossip or contemplation.

On a warm spring day, our delegation flew to Tokyo for an overnight layover. The following afternoon we boarded a Boeing 747, my first flight in one of the relatively new jumbo jets. Its inside was massive. I marveled at the ingenuity required to fling a thing that big and heavy into the air and have it stay aloft a dozen or so hours at a time. It was like a floating hotel lobby.

We lowly Communist cadres found ourselves ushered to the upper deck to first class, no doubt a goodwill gesture by the airline. We were treated like royalty. The ambassador's chauffeur was with us, to secure a car, get a license, and learn the traffic rules. He was easygoing, middle-aged, and plump, but as the servant of an important personage he carried himself with dignity.

The cabin attendants assumed from his bearing that he was the ambassador and addressed him as "Your Excellency," fussing over him as if he were a potentate. The chauffeur understood no English and just smiled and nodded his head gravely. We all had to stifle our laughter every time an attendant asked "His Excellency" if he wanted another pillow or something to drink.

Our destination was Los Angeles, which I had last seen almost twenty-three years earlier from the stern railing of the *Cleveland*. I was returning a middle-aged man, world-weary from living so long in a culture at war with itself, and with a heart aching from loss of father, brother, and soon, mentor. But I remained optimistic, looking forward to the adventure of returning to the States. It would be a welcome break from the stress of China's continuous revolution. And I would get to share the experience with the love of my life.

The sun quickly set as it raced west and we raced east. We were served a dinner that qualified as a banquet back home. The movie had just ended when the intercom crackled to life:

"Ladies and gentlemen, this is the captain speaking. Some of you may have noticed that one of our port engines is on fire. Please don't be too alarmed. The 747 is designed to be able to fly with as few as two engines. The plane is also designed so that I can jettison the engine that's on fire. You may feel a bump and a little turbulence when that happens. Do not be alarmed. Please remain in your seats with your belts fastened. We will be making an emergency landing in Hawaii, where you'll transfer to another plane."

Moments later, the plane shuddered and shimmied. I couldn't see from where I was sitting, but I could imagine the flaming engine uncoupling from the wing and falling to the vast ocean far below. Some of my co-workers broke out in nervous sweats, their eyes big as plums. The stewardess was shaking so badly that she spilled a glass of orange juice on my new Western suit.

I was more upset about the suit than I was about the engine trouble. I'd escaped Japanese bombers, strafing by an American fighter, a close encounter with an unexploded artillery shell, and an assassination attempt. It occurred to me that this might be another. But I'd flown all over the world with the premier, and had always returned in one piece. I'd survived illness, physical stress, and mental exhaustion. I had no reason to think my luck would change now.

Frantic and apologetic U.S. State Department officials who'd been rushed from Los Angeles met us at Honolulu Airport, along with local officials who'd heard about the emergency. I could just imagine the horror on the faces of American officials when they learned that the plane carrying China's first diplomatic mission to the States might go down in flames in the middle of the Pacific Ocean. Had we disappeared into the deep blue Pacific, the conspiracy theories would have been debated for aeons.

After a brief rest, we changed planes and continued on our way to Los Angeles without further incident. We were hustled off to a hotel near the airport. Everyone was exhausted and retired early, but I had trouble sleeping.

I would have given anything to go outside and walk around. But discipline was always tight when we traveled. We were not allowed to walk around alone in any foreign country, let alone the United States. I stayed in my hotel room and looked out the window at the city lights glittering as far as I could see, remembering the past and reviewing the years in between. One circle seemed to be closing, another opening.

The next day, we flew to Washington with two State Department minders who briefed us on the arrangements. We landed at Dulles International Airport—named for the man who snubbed the premier in 1954 in Geneva. As I exited the ramp I recognized, in spite of the years and the graying hair, my Harvard roommate Herb Levin. We shook hands and exchanged broad grins.

"You smell better than you used to," he told me. "And your suit isn't full of burn holes from chemistry lab! You've come a long way, comrade." It felt so good to be able to talk again with someone from my youth, and to be able to tease and laugh the way we had as college boys.

A bank of television cameras had their lenses trained on Herb and me, as though we might be discussing matters of great diplomatic import. So I said to Herb, with exaggerated gravity, "There are great problems to be discussed. For example, is it true that women are living in Thayer Hall, in our old dormitory?"

"Yes, I'm afraid so," he said, laughing.

Herb, who had learned some Chinese, had brought with him a copy of a Taiwan-subsidized Chinese-language newspaper published in Washington, with an article about how the Liaison Office delegation included "the bandit Ji Chaozhu, a Harvard-educated Chinese Communist." I laughed and showed it to my co-workers. It was an honor to be insulted by the likes of the Kuomintang.

We stayed at the Mayflower Hotel, just five blocks up Connecticut Avenue from the White House. Among our little troop, I was the only one who felt completely at home. Beautiful throne toilets! Soft beds! And I couldn't wait to sink my teeth into a steak, and to dive into a dish of high-calorie ice cream. But my poor colleagues suffered. They had no palate for the taste or texture of American foods. It took some time, but the State Department found us a "real" Chinese restaurant. Owned by a man who had emigrated from China around the time of liberation, the restaurant delivered superb Chinese meals to us every day. We poor, malnourished cadres quickly plumped up.

Herb and other officials from the State Department also helped us with our real-estate search. We had instructions from home to find a freestanding building, so we wouldn't have to worry about eavesdropping through adjoining walls. Because of my perfect English and my familiarity with American culture, my colleagues often turned to me for advice: "How does that sound to you, Ji?"

One day we were about to drive across the Rock Creek Bridge in northwest Washington when I spotted an elegant old Victorian hotel called the Windsor Park, near a number of embassies. It was for sale, and I thought it looked perfect. Ambassador Huang gave us the green light and we bought it for just over $5 million. The real-estate agent assured us that we would make a big profit when we sold it. We also found two old estates nearby, one with an outdoor swimming pool and a tennis court, for the higher-ranking officials.

As helpful and solicitous as our State Department hosts were, we had arrived in Washington in the middle of the greatest crisis in the history of the American presidency since the Civil War: Watergate. The day before our arrival, the president had made his first public admission that someone in his administration might have been involved in a dirty-tricks campaign against his political enemies. Our new friend Richard Nixon was in trouble, and as I interpreted for my colleagues what was being reported on television, panic set in.

"Do you think he might be purged?" I was asked. I tried to remember my constitutional history, but I couldn't recall how a president could be removed from office.

I reported these fears to Herb, and he and the State Department staff tried to reassure my colleagues. Personal relations have the highest value in our culture, and the relationship with the United States was Nixon's personal achievement.

"Tell your people to take it easy," Herb counseled. "The government's policy toward China is not what's got Nixon in trouble, even though there are right-wingers who criticized it. Don't get involved." Nevertheless, our delegation watched with dismay as the Watergate scandal unraveled, followed in a few months by a bribery scandal that led to the resignation of Vice President Spiro Agnew.

Ambassador Huang Zhen arrived at the end of May, wearing a rumpled Mao suit and a soft cap. Han Xu and I, along with the rest of our staff, met him at the airport. I interpreted his initial perfunctory remarks about establishing good relations. Huang Zhen was an unusual veteran diplomat, one of the good guys, politically speaking, and someone with whom I felt safe and respected.

Before his many postings abroad in places like Indonesia and France, he had been a People's Army general who participated in the famous Long March. Huang had fought the Japanese aggressors as well as Chiang Kai-shek's army. He was well educated and a talented artist who had painted the only surviving images of the People's Army on the Long March. Significantly, he was the only Chinese diplomat who was also a member of the Central Committee.

Because our lodgings and our offices had not been formally delivered and renovations made to suit our needs, we stayed on at the Mayflower. A hotline telephone had been installed here, directly linking Han Xu and myself to General Brent Scowcroft, Kissinger's deputy at the National Security Council. There were frequent meetings in

272 · JI CHAOZHU

those early months. We carefully avoided mentioning the political disaster unfolding in the White House. When we finally got into the Windsor Park Hotel, Han Xu and I each had a hotline phone in our rooms.

The wives of some of the other officials in our growing staff began to arrive, but Xiangtong was not among them. When I inquired when she was expected, I got vague answers, blank looks, and shrugs. At first, I assumed that the wives of higher-ranking officials had been given priority, but after a few months I began to get a bad feeling. Xiangtong wrote that she'd inquired at the Foreign Ministry, and was told that there was no information on her departure date.

While I grew ever more impatient for her arrival, Ambassador Huang kept me busy. He had frequent meetings with Kissinger, as well as meetings and dinners that included President Nixon, during all of which I served as interpreter. We flew to Nixon's home in San Clemente for one of those sessions.

One of the things I had very much looked forward to was seeing some of my old friends from City and Country School, as well as my two compatriots from Horace Mann–Lincoln. However, under rules established by Jiang Qing and her gang back in Beijing, we were prohibited from having "private" foreign friends.

Anne Tonachel, one of my closest friends in school, had learned of my arrival in Washington and invited me to dinner at her New York apartment. Like the premier, Ambassador Huang Zhen was open-minded and trusting of me. He said that I could accept her invitation but, because of the regulations, I should find a friend in our Chinese mission at the United Nations to go with me. I knew a woman there who was an interpreter, and she agreed to be my chaperone. I telephoned Anne and asked if I could bring a lady friend. Anne sounded a bit scandalized, knowing that I was married, but she agreed.

Anne and her husband treated us to a steak dinner. My escort was a gregarious young woman with excellent command of English. She was also married, and charmed our hosts. I didn't want to reveal to Anne that her presence had been forced on me, and I didn't want to give the impression that I was being a playboy, so I made sure to repeatedly refer to my dear wife and children, assuring her that I loved them very much. I also heaped praise on my escort's husband, assuring Anne that he was a good friend. Anne got the joke.

Ambassador Huang Zhen's trust and support included a strong interest in my making new friends in the American establishment. I was assigned to the political section of the Liaison Office as its deputy chief, dealing principally with the China Desk of the State Department. But Ambassador Huang also wanted me to make friends in the U.S. Senate and the House of Representatives.

We had numerous conversations that centered on identifying the crucial lawmakers, and we drew up lists of whom to call on, or invite to dinner. Ever since liberation and the United States' decision to support Taiwan, the Kuomintang had established a powerful lobbying effort in Congress. Ambassador Huang understood that we needed to fight fire with fire.

We arranged meetings with a number of political leaders, including Senator Mike Mansfield, a Democrat from Montana, and Senator Ted Stevens, a Republican from Alaska. Huang found the regulation against any of us having one-to-one meetings with foreigners ridiculous, understanding that it inhibited foreigners from speaking frankly. He had such political clout that he could order us to meet individually with certain people. For example, he sent me to meet with *New York Times* columnist James Reston for a background interview and, of course, to learn what I could about what was going on with the Watergate investigation that might not have been reported in the press.

Han Xu, the number-two man in our Liaison Office, was as observant of the one-on-one prohibition as Ambassador Huang was dismissive. I often accompanied Han Xu to receptions and he never left my side, scowling at me if I wandered off even a few feet to shake someone's hand. Paranoia was endemic in our political culture in 1974, as the Cultural Revolution in China heated up again. Radicals at the Liaison Office had even begun to criticize Ambassador Huang Zhen. Once again, I also found myself on the receiving end of suspicion because of my American friendships and the ease with which I got along with American officials.

In January 1974, I was in New York on a mission to meet with some of our officials at the United Nations when I heard that Deng Xiaoping—

one of the old generals who had been purged at the beginning of the Cultural Revolution—had been rehabilitated by the premier, and welcomed back into the Politburo. I did a victory dance in my room, I was so happy. Deng was a good guy, one of the premier's allies. But, even with Deng's restoration, China's internal politics remained in turmoil as Mao's health declined.

The goodwill and optimism that had resulted from the Nixon visit now lay in ruins. Crippled by Watergate and the disgraceful exit of his vice president, Nixon would soon resign.

In the meantime, back in China, the premier, the country's greatest asset on the world stage, seemed to be fading. Mao's wife and her gang took advantage of Mao's failing health to do everything they could to undermine Zhou's influence and revive the most destructive tactics of the Cultural Revolution: the so-called tearing down to build up. The heroes of the revolution—especially those who spoke out against the mass movements—were systematically being purged, exiled, killed, or driven to suicide. Peng Dehuai, the general who had commanded our side in Korea and who had been a People's Army marshal, had been viciously beaten by Red Guards and died grievously wronged in November 1974.

It began to dawn on me that the reason Xiangtong hadn't been sent to join me had everything to do with Jiang Qing and the two young ladies, who exercised control over the Foreign Ministry. My heart ached. Xiangtong was still being punished for her Taiwan relations. The fact that she had been kept back was seen by her co-workers as a political curse, so they shunned her.

From halfway around the world, the long tail of absurdity reached us when the Ministry of Culture sent a delegation to visit the Corning Glass Company in upstate New York to discuss a possible joint venture to produce televisions in China. This was a direct order from Jiang Qing, who had written some strident "model revolutionary" operas that she wanted promoted throughout the country on TV.

At the end of the delegation's visit, Corning Glass presented the visitors with a gift of a piece of handmade glass art in the shape of a snail. When the delegation returned to Beijing, a young radical in the Foreign Ministry wrote a letter to Jiang Qing "exposing" the "traitorous" action of the delegation head in accepting the gift. It was an insult, the letter writer declared, mocking China for moving at a snail's pace.

Jiang turned her wrath on the premier, who had approved the visit, and demanded that the Liaison Office lodge a formal protest. On this question, even the radicals in the Liaison Office disagreed. We sent back a long cable explaining the situation, and the "snail incident" was quietly put to rest.

By early 1974, my friend Herb Levin had left the State Department and returned to Harvard to teach. Between the two of us, we arranged a visit to Harvard by Ambassador Huang and some of our delegation. Herb flew down to Washington to escort us to Cambridge. We met him at National Airport and were in the process of checking our baggage when Ambassador Huang declared to Herb, "I don't have to go through the security check."

Herb explained, "You do have diplomatic immunity as far as pouches, but the carry-on baggage check is for weapons or bombs and everybody has to go through it. It's for your own safety."

But the ambassador, an old general unused to taking orders, balked. "I don't see why," he groused. "I don't have a weapon or a bomb."

"I'm sure you don't," Herb said. "But still, that's what we all have to do. Even us Americans."

After a few awkward moments, the ambassador gave up his carry-on bag and it slid into the X-ray machine. The machine operator stopped the conveyor belt and pointed at the screen. Herb peeked and announced, "It looks like a large knife."

Ambassador Huang drew himself up. "I've carried that since the Japanese war," he said. "I sleep with it under my pillow. I've always done it."

I was shocked. I had shared a room with him! I had no idea he put a knife under his pillow. It turned out that even his wife didn't know. Why he did, I could only guess. Perhaps it was a superstition or a good-luck charm.

Herb solved the problem by assuring the ambassador that he would give the knife to the pilot and it would be returned at the end of the flight. I wondered what the story was behind that weapon. How much Japanese blood had it spilled?

We arrived safely at Harvard Yard, and I immediately asked Herb to show me our old dormitory. Although he'd warned me, I was still scandalized to find women living in our old suite, with boys living right across the hall. This arrangement would never have passed muster in China.

One of the women students asked me, "Who are you?"

"At a prehistoric time, I lived here," I said, laughing. "But it is much nicer now, all fixed up."

In our tour of Cambridge, we happened to be present during a reenactment of the Battles of Lexington and Concord, when, in April 1775, the British sent a detachment to destroy a colonial supply depot. A descendant of the original regiment was participating, wearing the British Army's old red uniform. The Minutemen fired their muskets from behind trees, the British returned fire, and men in period costumes fell to the ground, pretending to be shot.

Ambassador Huang was astonished. "Why would the British willingly come here to remind everyone of their loss and humiliation?" he asked.

Herb patiently explained, "It was two hundred years ago, and we're friends now. In less than two hundred years, you and the Japanese will be doing the same thing!"

"Not in a thousand years!" Huang nearly shouted.

There was no similarity between the American rebellion and the Japanese slaughter of women and children. The American Revolution was fought to establish an independent, self-governing nation, and the combatants shared a similar heritage. Japanese militarists were intent on the genocide and subjugation of the Chinese people. I hope no one ever wants to reenact the bayoneting of babies and men being burned alive in locomotive fireboxes. Not in ten thousand years!

As supportive as Ambassador Huang was of me, I was constantly reminded by his deputy, Han Xu of the Liaison Office, that I had been sent to the States as a "trainee," and that I should observe how other Chinese veteran diplomats (meaning himself) behaved. I was admonished to strengthen my sense of discipline and watch my "bourgeois liberalism."

I did my best to appear to take Han's advice seriously while continuing my work according to Ambassador Huang's open style. But my frustration and unhappiness had steadily grown during my time in the States. In spite of Premier Zhou's explicit instruction that she and others should go, Xiangtong was prevented from joining me, even though the chairman himself had approved the name list. After two years, my hair had turned much grayer and my general health had deteriorated from the stress and unhappiness.

Then came more unhappiness. Han Xu returned from a home visit to Beijing and privately told me that the premier had been diagnosed with cancer and was urinating blood. I was upset at having my worst fears confirmed. But he told me not to worry, that the cancer was "not serious."

I neither trusted nor believed him. I was exhausted, miserable, and lonely. I told Han Xu that I felt it was time I returned to China. He gave me a look of surprise. "How did you know?" he said. "You will receive your summons to return very soon."

Ambassador Huang strongly opposed my being recalled. But, as the Chinese like to say, an arm cannot beat a leg.

Hearing of my impending departure, Kissinger invited me to his office for a private visit, at which he revealed that he knew about the premier's declining health. "If it would be accepted, I can arrange for America's best cancer specialist to travel to Beijing to treat Premier Zhou," he told me. I felt that I had been handed a great privilege and an opportunity to give back to the premier a little in exchange for all that he had given me. I returned to the Liaison Office more eager than ever to leave for home.

In mid-April 1975, Han Xu, along with some other senior staff members, called me in to give me an evaluation of my work before I returned to China. Chiang Kai-shek had just died, and after some discussion about avoiding any public statement about his death, Han Xu began, "As a trainee"—how I disliked that expression—"you did pretty well, comrade."

Others complimented me on my strong sense of responsibility, my humility, and my commitment to hard work and simple living. Their criticisms were principally that I tended to see things in a simplistic way. I preferred to think of myself as clearheaded and direct. But in Chinese politics, nothing is clear and everything is indirect.

I returned to China frustrated, struggling to keep up my spirits. I had cabled Kissinger's generous offer of medical help for the premier, but now learned that it had been ignored. The premier was quite ill, and it was beginning to look as if I might never see him again, just as he had predicted two years earlier. Furthermore, I was immediately removed from all work concerning Sino-U.S. relations.

In my absence, the two young ladies in the Foreign Ministry had solidified their direct access to Chairman Mao and used it to issue directives in his name that were to be carried out without question, or else. At the age of forty-seven, there was no future for me in the Foreign Ministry or anywhere else. I was a lamb in the slaughterhouse.

My greatest sorrow was having lost the struggle to right the injustice done to Xiangtong. She had suffered terrible social and political isolation in my absence, stained by the vicious gossip surrounding the failure of the Foreign Ministry to send her abroad to be with me. People she worked with avoided speaking with her unless it was absolutely necessary, and when they were required to interact with her they kept their distance, as if she had a highly contagious, deadly disease.

Our reunion ought to have been pure joy, but it was marred by the bitterness of betrayal, and anxiety about what miseries awaited us around the next corner.

CHAPTER 26

An Empty Seat on the Stage

In the spring of 1975, I entered the terminal at Beijing Airport after a two-year overseas assignment to find the smiling face and red-rimmed eyes of Xiangtong, with our two boys. Shockingly tall, at nine and eleven, my sons were just about the age my brother Chaoli and I were when we fled China for New York thirty-six long years earlier. Our copious tears and long embraces were a bittersweet blend of relief, hope, and exhaustion.

One manifestation of hope was a special household gift I brought back with me: a color television I had bought on a stopover in Tokyo. Xiangtong and I might be political underdogs, but our television made us overnight celebrities—very bourgeois and rightist!

Our tiny living room became the local children's theater each evening as kids from all over our Foreign Ministry apartment compound came knocking on our door at about seven o'clock, the start time of the once-a-day broadcast session. Xiangtong enjoyed having the youngsters around. Being distracted by the future was a break from mourning the past. Sometimes she and I were tired and wanted to go to bed early, but the kids were mesmerized and we hadn't the heart to send them home until the broadcast period ended at around ten P.M. Otherwise, I think we would have had to carry them out.

The attraction was the miracle of color, not the content. The state-owned broadcast channel aired newscasts and politically sanctioned entertainment, dominated by Jiang Qing's eight "model revolutionary" operas and ballets, which had titles such as *The Red Lantern* and *Red Detachment of Women.*

Mao's fourth wife, Jiang had been a young actress when he married her in 1939 over the earnest objections of Zhou Enlai, among others. She was paranoid, with good reason. Mao had parted ways with his first three wives and Jiang had a tawdry personal history that, by some accounts, included being a teenage prostitute in Shanghai and having collaborated with the Kuomintang. The possibility that her past might show up in her present must have given her many sleepless nights.

Jiang's model operas were popular at first, but they were wooden propaganda pieces and the only theater permitted during the Cultural Revolution, so the public grew bored with them. Still, the neighborhood children were transfixed by anything in color on TV.

It was good to be home, and a bit of a jolt to see my lover and soul mate for the first time after two stressful, middle-aged years. We had both aged. My eyesight wasn't as sharp and we both had more gray hair. Xiangtong looked weary. But the children were oblivious to our burdens, simply glad to have Mom and Dad together again, to sit down to real family dinners and go to Grandma's house to be fussed over and spoiled.

Back at work, I repeatedly asked about, and asked to see, the premier. I was told that his health was none of my business and that he was too busy with important affairs to squander time on social visits from underlings.

Rumors flew, and the air crackled with anxiety. No one doubted by now that Zhou was dying. He had been spotted in November at the Beijing Hotel dining room, working on some papers while he ate, looking painfully frail and drawn. Word spread that Mao had at first refused to grant permission for Zhou to receive surgical treatment for bladder cancer but then relented.

Jiang Qing and her three closest cohorts had come to be known as the Gang of Four, which included two writers who ghosted many of Mao's pronouncements, and a Korean War veteran who some thought might be Mao's choice to replace the premier. All four were top Party officials who had gotten where they were by doing Mao's bidding: biting those Mao told them to bite, plus anyone else who threatened them. To maintain their positions of power after Mao's death, they needed Chairman Mao to be the last man standing, to outlive Zhou.

If Mao died first, they'd lose his protection and face a backlash from the many people whose lives they had ruined or made miserable. They'd been trying to get rid of the premier for years. Now, by interfering with his medical care, they were helping Mother Nature deliver the final solution. Jiang had once reportedly ordered doctors to interrupt a transfusion, claiming that she had to discuss with the premier important state business that in fact had no urgency.

The premier was so well liked that intense political pressure was brought to bear, even from abroad. He finally began to receive proper treatment, both Western and Eastern—many surgeries, plus herbal and other traditional Chinese methods. But it came too late to extend his life by any great measure. Along with thousands of other cadres who were plugged in to the rumor mill, my colleagues and I held our collective breath, bracing for the grief and turmoil lurking around the road's next bend.

Almost as soon as I returned from the States, the two young ladies tried to have me put me out to pasture, ordering my transfer to the Foreign Language Institute to teach English. That was a long descent: from the top of Tiananmen Gate to a dusty classroom.

Our new foreign minister, Qiao Guanhua, was another one of the premier's old trusted aides. He reported to still another, Vice Premier Deng Xiaoping, the military officer who had twice been purged and reinstated. Deng famously challenged the Party's obsession with political witch hunts to weed out the "black" elements of rightism and deviationism and so on, declaring that the most important goal was to "feed the people. . . . It doesn't matter whether the cat is black or white, as long as it catches the mice."

Qiao Guanhua had a few years earlier married the daughter of a wealthy lawyer who had played an important role in financing Mao's People's Army in the early days. Zhang Hanzhi was well educated, a language expert who had lived abroad when she was younger, before coming to work at the Foreign Ministry. She was one of a number of experts who taught English to Chairman Mao, and she had been one of the interpreters during the Nixon visit.

Instead of sending me into professorial exile as ordered, Foreign Minister Qiao made me deputy director of the Department of International Organizations and Conferences, coordinating our relations with the U.N. Security Council and General Assembly. Just as I was beginning to settle into my new job, I was for the fourth time ordered down to the farm, to the pigsties and rice paddies of the Foreign Ministry's May Seventh Cadre School on the outskirts of Beijing. At least this time I was close enough to home to see the family regularly.

Each time I'd been sent to the countryside, the waste of my skills and experience, and the attempts to break my spirit, seemed more incomprehensible than the last. This time it came after twenty years in the diplomatic corps. In spite of my experience and accomplishments, I was still being treated like a recovering capitalist roader who'd fallen off the wagon while abroad, and the only known cure was pig manure.

With a sigh of resignation, I made a genuine effort to learn to work as a true peasant. Being close to nature was relaxing, and I was laboring and living with other Foreign Ministry people who knew, and occasionally confided their agreement with me, that the world was upside down.

My rice-transplanting skills had not improved, but I kept at it through the stifling Beijing summer, my bare torso running with sweat. The job was harder now because of my age. I had to bend down low in the paddies to work the roots into the mud, trying not to disturb the work I'd finished or that of my neighboring laborers. The heat and the strain left me limp at the end of each day. We had our own kitchen and plenty of food, though, so we worked on full stomachs.

My new tour of duty at the cadre school was interrupted from time to time when I was summoned out of a rice paddy to be driven home, where I'd rush into our flat, clean up, dress, bid a quick goodbye to the family if anyone was around, and rush out to interpret for some official. When I was done, I made the reverse transformation: from diplomat back into tired old peasant.

Zhou Enlai's struggle ended on January 8, 1976. The announcement of his death the next day was preceded on loudspeakers in public places and on radios everywhere by a funeral dirge. The entire nation seemed to burst into tears. A whole trainload of People's Liberation Army troops were said to have wailed when the news came over the intercoms. People walking the streets openly wept.

There had never been a cult around Zhou, as there was around Mao, and his enemies had worked hard to discredit and destroy him. But China's eight hundred million people had grown to love Zhou Enlai. He was seen as the compassionate parent who showed up at natural disasters or dropped in on farmers to find out what was going on in the countryside. He was the smiling, charming, urbane diplomat who had won China many new friends abroad.

When I heard the news, I was on the rice farm, feeding the pigs in the middle of a cold winter. My grief was profound: for my personal loss, for the premier's physical and political suffering, and for China. A beacon of hope in a storm-tossed sea had suddenly gone dark. Except for the Nixon visit and other diplomatic successes, the country had been slowly sliding backward for almost a decade, since the start of the Cultural Revolution. China's future was now in the hands of a dying emperor isolated by a court of incompetent opportunists.

I received permission to return home during the official mourning period. The announcement of the premier's death, aside from the usual propaganda about his heroic efforts to advance the cause of Communism, reported that he'd received "meticulous" medical care and that he had died "despite all treatment." These disingenuous comments were thinly veiled attempts to answer growing criticism of the premier's shabby care and treatment, and the shameful official disrespect with which his death was treated.

The premier's body was prepared and left to lie in private in the hospital where he died. Zhou had requested cremation, but there was to be no public viewing first. I was angry when I learned that many other government officials had been permitted to visit him in his final days, even if it was just to spend a few moments standing at the foot of his bed while he lay in a semiconscious state. I had been robbed of that opportunity.

But on the second night after the premier died I received a phone call at home from his principal bodyguard, who had been present during the time I worked with the premier, and who had treated me as a member of the family. I liked Zhou's bodyguard, and the feeling seemed mutual.

After we exchanged condolences, he said, "The premier is being taken to the crematorium tomorrow. If you'd like to pay your respects, you can meet me in Tiananmen Square and I will take you there now."

I pulled on my warmest coat and heavy fur hat and dashed out the door. The bodyguard drove me to the hospital and slipped me in a side door to the room that served as a private viewing chamber. It would have meant big trouble for us both if I had been spotted by any of the premier's enemies. I had to keep my visit short.

I remember little of the surroundings beyond a burning candle and the simple black coffin in which the premier lay. But I clearly recall how emaciated he looked in death. I fought a reflexive sob.

For the last time, he and I were alone together. Through my constricted throat I managed to croak a muted "Farewell, Premier. I will keep and honor your memory until the earth and heaven grow old." I bowed deeply the customary three times and, after a short pause, turned and left the room.

The premier's remains were to be moved to the crematorium without ceremony the following afternoon. The Gang of Four announced that there would be no public mourning, but many people were expected to show up along Chang'an Boulevard, the main street that runs in front of Tiananmen Gate, alongside Tiananmen Square. The next day, an enormous throng—more than a million people, by some estimates—crowded Chang'an Boulevard. Many of them had been there since before dawn on a bitterly cold, snowy day.

The next evening, Xiangtong and I were at home with our children. We had been repeatedly told by our superiors that we were not allowed to go out to the streets to pay homage to the premier as his remains were taken from the hospital. Watching the evening news on television, tears in our eyes, we saw the hearse—white with blue stripes, draped with black and yellow streamers—slowly rolling down the boulevard. Lining the streets in the freezing winds were people of all ages, parents with children, young students, factory workers, peasants, housewives, mothers with babies. Everyone wept as the vehicle rolled past, bidding a final farewell to our beloved premier.

I was allowed to attend Zhou's state funeral at the Great Hall of the People a few days later. Vice Premier Deng Xiaoping delivered the eulogy, expressing what many of us felt about Zhou: "modest and prudent, unassuming and approachable, setting an example by his conduct and living in a plain and hardworking way." When Deng began by saying "Our premier," his voice broke. Everyone was sobbing.

Overwhelmed by a desire to make my own public case, I wrote an article commemorating him and sent it to the *People's Daily*. After many weeks had passed and the article failed to appear, I phoned the newspaper to find out if I could get someone to print it. I was told that my article was lost, after which the person on the other end abruptly hung up.

The end of January brought the Year of the Dragon, believed in Chinese culture to be a year in which bad things happen. At the beginning of February, wall posters appeared denouncing Deng Xiaoping as an unrepentant capitalist roader. This was depressing news to those of us who had hoped that this rehabilitated reformer would emerge as Zhou's successor.

In March, just before the annual Qing Ming festival—the Day of Pure Brightness—when the Chinese traditionally visit and clean the tombs of their ancestors, a Shanghai magazine published a scathing attack on Zhou Enlai. Within hours, by word of mouth and through slogans scrawled on the sides of express trains crossing the country, a protest movement quickly spread.

I had returned to the cadre school, where colleagues coming from Beijing reported that people had begun to carry wreaths and silk chrysanthemums to Tiananmen Square, building a new mountain of tribute to the premier. A trickle turned into thousands. More eulogies and poems were posted, with phrases such as "We weep but the wolves laugh."

The Party Committee of the Foreign Ministry sent explicit instructions forbidding the copying and propagation of poems and tributes to Zhou, but no one paid any attention to the sanction. The "wolves," the

Gang of Four, denounced the demonstrations as a plot by Deng. But the people of China did not need a leader to show them how to express their frustration. The crowds in the square grew as the days passed. Strolling among the throngs and sharing the sorrow and outrage became a daily ritual for thousands.

One morning in early April, the people of Beijing awoke to find all the wreaths and flowers gone, Tiananmen Square swept clean, and the monument surrounded by a cordon of police to prevent the placing of any new wreaths or posters.

One evening, Xiangtong decided to take a detour on her homeward bicycle route from the office to pass through Tiananmen Square. She stopped to read some new posters. As she was reading, a sudden gust of cold air blew across the plaza. She felt uneasy, and she hopped back on her bike and pedaled home.

Within an hour, on orders from Beijing Party officials, the floodlights ignited, bathing the huge square in harsh light. The great doors of Tiananmen Gate opened, disgorging thousands of men wearing red armbands and swinging wooden truncheons. Hundreds of people were beaten bloody and carted off in trucks. By morning, a hose squad had washed away all the stains and other evidence of violence.

A week or two later, a car arrived at the cadre school from Beijing with orders to take me without delay or detour to Qiao Guanhua. The car deposited me at the door to the foreign minister's private home on Shijia Alley, a villa that had belonged to the father of his wife, Zhang Hanzhi.

Qiao personally greeted me at the gate, and hustled me into his study. Three steaming cups of tea were waiting, along with Zhang. The foreign minister and his wife seemed nervous.

"Little Ji, you know there is a big problem in the Foreign Ministry with Nancy Tang and Wang Hairong," Qiao began. "The situation has become impossible. I can do nothing without their approval. They are making a mess of things with their meddling and struggle meetings and accusing me of being a rightist and all that."

I said nothing, but I began to feel as nervous as Qiao appeared. Zhang said she had been writing letters to Mao complaining about the two ladies, thinking that her family's long history of supporting Mao would give her pleas weight. But the letters were being intercepted. In any case, she had received no response.

"I believe the chairman does not know about the viciousness of those two ladies, and it is important that he does," Qiao said. The determined tone in his voice made my blood race. I had never been recruited into any sort of political plot, but I was prepared to help fight the young ladies.

"I need a personal audience with Chairman Mao so we can get our messages to him and rid ourselves of the scourge of these ladies," Qiao went on. "But with them in charge it is hard for me to get in. They won't let me. If you go to Mao's villa as an interpreter, the one the chairman himself requested, there's no way they can stop you. I will go along, and no one can stop me, since I am the foreign minister. So I have arranged for you to interpret for the chairman again."

"I haven't interpreted for the chairman in years," I said. "He has Nancy. Why would he now ask for me?"

Qiao said they had made arrangements with Mao's private secretary, a woman named Zhang Yufeng. Not part of the cabal angling to succeed Mao, she got the chairman to agree. It made no sense, and I knew the young ladies would see right through it.

Qiao explained that Nancy and Wang Hairong had been quarreling with Jiang Qing, and the power struggle going on around Mao had become increasingly fractious as his health declined. "The only way to get rid of those two is to curry favor with Jiang Qing, to influence Mao," he said.

I couldn't believe how reckless this sounded. "This is extremely dangerous," I said. "Everyone hates Jiang. She is the worst of the worst!"

Qiao looked at me with a crooked smile. "You know, Little Ji, this is what we call attacking poison with poison." He told me he could no longer tolerate the situation: bearing the heavy burden of being foreign minister while constantly ordered about by the "two young ladies." I repeated that his plan was much too dangerous.

But Qiao and Zhang were determined. "This is the last fight," Qiao said. "You just don't understand the complexity of all this." Indeed, I did not; nor did I wish to.

But I had no choice. I had been ordered by the foreign minister to work again with Mao. It had been six years since I'd stood atop Tiananmen Gate to Mao's right as he entertained Edgar Snow. Qiao and his wife kept me hidden in their home for several days, filling me in on all the political battles that were being fought in secret, from the Politburo on down.

Finally, I was driven to Mao's villa with Qiao to interpret for Prime Minister Robert Muldoon, of New Zealand, on his first official visit to China. I was aghast at how feeble Mao had become. His speech was reduced to mumbling. He would mutter something and wait for Zhang Yufeng to repeat it in clear Chinese. If she had heard him correctly, he would nod his head, and then I would repeat what he'd said in English to Muldoon. If Zhang had misunderstood, Mao would shake his head and write a few words on paper until she got it right.

Now eighty-two, Mao could no longer stand on his own. When the time came to say goodbye, Zhang Yufeng and his bodyguard lifted him by his arms and held him up. They even had to support his arm so that he could offer a limp hand to shake. As physically weak as Mao was, I was astonished that his mind seemed to be working just fine. He may have been mumbling, but he was not babbling.

So I was again the chairman's interpreter and now at risk of being implicated in the plotting of Qiao Guanhua and Zhang Hanzhi. When I finished my interpretation, I returned with relief to the pigs and paddies.

The last time I interpreted for Mao was during a visit by Zulfikar Ali Bhutto, the Pakistani prime minister, on May 27, 1976. Mao could no longer hold his head up properly, and when he saw the official photo of himself—bloated, slack-jawed, eyes swollen, head lolling against a badly stained spot on the back of his chair's green plaid cushion—he declared that Bhutto would be his last official visitor.

Several months later, after the downfall of Jiang Qing, Hua Guofeng, Mao's supposedly handpicked successor, began a campaign to undermine Qiao Guanhua that eventually involved my having to suffer through repeated struggle meetings aimed at expelling me from the Foreign Ministry. Qiao Guanhua was repeatedly condemned by Hua Guofeng and the "two young ladies" for his complicity with Jiang Qing. Some years later Qiao died of cancer. His "attacking poison with poison" did not work. Years after Qiao's death, his wife, Zhang Hanzhi, would admit: "Qiao and I were naïve!"

The Year of the Dragon lived up to its reputation. On July 26, a powerful earthquake struck Tangshan, an industrial city about 125 miles east and south of Beijing. Nearly 250,000 people were killed and nearly as many injured, in the worst such disaster to hit China in four centuries.

I happened to be in Beijing at the time. The city was shaken, but damage was light. There was widespread fear that more quakes could strike, so I immediately arranged for my family to fly to the ancient city of Xi'an, far away in Shaanxi Province. Xiangtong had relations they could stay with until things calmed down. I remained behind to hold the fort, joining millions of others who were camping out in the capital's streets, just in case.

In Chinese legends, the deaths of emperors are foretold by natural disasters such as tsunamis and earthquakes. On September 9, forty-five days after the Tangshan earthquake, Mao Zedong died in his villa, just as Jiang Qing returned from one of her elaborate journeys by special train.

In contrast to the spontaneous mourning for the premier in spite of Jiang Qing and her cronies, Mao's funeral was rigidly formal. On September 18, the entire Tiananmen Square plaza was packed with cadres ordered to be there from government offices and organizations, along with schoolchildren, workers, peasants, soldiers, and so on. Each wore a black armband and was assigned a place to stand on the pavement. I had to stand with my Ministry colleagues, and Xiangtong had to stand with her co-workers.

It was early autumn, still quite hot, and the ceremony dragged on for hours. A few people were crying, but most of us were thirsty and tired. When it finally ended, I began walking home when I heard Xiangtong calling my name. She approached smiling, holding two ice pops she'd just bought from a vendor. Both she and the ice pops were a welcome sight.

CHAPTER 27

China's Second Liberation

Mao's continuous revolution continued in death. No moment illustrates the darkly absurd side of his legacy like the scuffle that took place beside his coffin between Jiang Qing and Wang Hairong. A high-ranking official who was present later described the spat that broke out over a wreath Jiang had placed at Mao's bier in the Great Hall of the People. Wang Hairong had taken some offense and the two women flew at each other. Wang grabbed a fistful of Jiang's hair, except Jiang had none. Her wig came off in Wang's hand, leaving her naked scalp exposed for all to see.

Soon after Mao's death Hua Guofeng announced the "Two Whatevers"—whatever Chairman Mao had said was correct, and we were to continue to carry out whatever policies he had set. Hua had none of Mao's credibility, but his pronouncement signaled that radicals would remain in control of the government.

There were people in the country who genuinely mourned Mao. He was a godhead in an ancestor-worshipping culture. He had freed China from foreign domination. But there were many more who wept with rage at the suffering and sadism associated with his mass movements, the Great Leap Forward and the Great Proletarian Cultural Revolution.

There were many who wept in fear. Now what? Who was really in charge? Hua Guofeng had emerged as the new chairman, but he had been virtually unknown to the public before turning up in the last act as the chairman's successor. His anointment was tainted by rumors that it was based on a deliberate misrepresentation of Mao's final instructions.

For the first twenty-seven years of the People's Republic, Mao *was* China. Now that the anchor line had been cut, no one could say with certainty in what direction the country might drift. Anything was possible, even civil war. In Shanghai, the Gang of Four and their cronies controlled the Shanghai Workers' Militia and were preparing to mobilize them to consolidate their power. The people were still angry over the treatment of Premier Zhou, and the nation's economy was stuck in neutral.

Meanwhile, diplomatic matters beckoned. Right after Mao's funeral ceremony, I was told to pack my bags for New York, where I joined Qiao and the rest of our delegation at the thirty-first session of the U.N. General Assembly. I left home hoping the situation in China would remain stable and my family would be safe.

Kissinger, whom I had admired since we'd first met and with whom I had spent many hours, spotted me at one of the opening events and strode over to say hello. We hadn't crossed paths in more than a year. "Mr. Ji, vat happened to you?" he blurted in his deep voice, giving me the once-over. "You have become so thin. Have you been ill?"

I looked around and found that I was separated from the others in our delegation. With all the uncertainty and treachery in the air, I had to restrain my usual outgoing nature when speaking to foreigners without a fellow Chinese witness to vouch for me. I wanted no gossip that I was sneaking off to consort with the enemy. I just smiled at Kissinger, now secretary of state under President Gerald Ford, and declared, "Nothing is wrong with me. I am fine!" Then I turned and walked away. I felt terrible snubbing him, but I couldn't risk chatting the way we had in Beijing and Washington.

A few days later, I was alone in my room at our U.N. mission in New York when I heard the news that Jiang Qing and the three other members of the Gang of Four had been arrested and charged with anti-Party crimes. They, and others who had collaborated with them, faced execution.

There was no one to hug, so I clapped loudly and cheered, feeling for the first time a great sense of relief and hope. But the celebration was premature. Foreign Minister Qiao received a summons to return home at once. Soon afterward, I also received a summons home, delivered with a worried look by our U.N. ambassador, Huang Hua.

"The criminals responsible for the Cultural Revolution are behind bars," I said. "Why are you worried?"

"Well, Little Ji, things are more complicated than you think."

I shrugged off his remark as excessive caution.

Just before I left New York, a colleague took me aside one day and asked me, "What do you think about those two ladies back in the Foreign Ministry?" I was not the only person who called them the two ladies. Nancy Tang and Wang Hairong were two names almost always spoken of as one. They worked together like predators.

I told my colleague exactly what was on my mind—very un-Chinese. Maybe it was the excitement of being back in my other home, New York, where I had been encouraged from childhood to seek the truth and speak my mind. I told him that the ladies, like cockroaches, thrived in dark, filthy places. Their harassment had contributed to the premier's ill health and early death. Their meddling had interfered with China's developing good relations abroad. After years of being criticized, forced to self-criticize and defend my patriotism, I held nothing back. Mao was dead. Jiang was in prison. The Cultural Revolution was over.

I was overly optimistic. My comments sped ahead of me, back to the Foreign Ministry, where I was once again called to account before mass criticism and struggle meetings. My colleague had betrayed me, and the cockroaches hadn't been exterminated.

"You'd better confess honestly and quickly," they said, "because we know exactly the reactionary words you uttered at the U.N. So repeat them to us now." I was furious.

The bright spot was being welcomed back by Bi Jilung, my new boss in the International Department. He'd been a colonel in the Chinese People's Volunteers in Korea and was a good guy, a supporter of Qiao. We were dumbfounded when one day the two ladies ordered us to lead the department in criticizing First Vice Premier Deng Xiaoping and the "rightist attempt to overturn the correct verdicts" of the Cultural Revolution.

Things weren't adding up. The Gang of Four had been overthrown. Why should we criticize Deng Xiaoping, who'd been unpurged again? Why were the "verdicts" of the Cultural Revolution still considered correct when the criminals responsible for that dark decade sat in prison cells awaiting appointments with the executioner?

Qiao was also to be publicly criticized, repudiated, and purged from his position as foreign minister. All those who had supported him would be politically "helped."

I refused to cooperate. One day I was told that I could no longer meet with foreign officials, participate in diplomatic functions, or even read diplomatic cables. I was so choked with rage that I leaped out of my chair and headed up to the roof to get a breath of fresh air. I needed to get away for a few minutes and calm down. The bearer of this news followed, apparently fearing I might do something rash, like jump off the roof. Nothing could have been further from my mind.

I paced the roof while this fellow followed close behind, an insincere grin pasted on his face, trying to engage me in small talk. I ignored him until I realized that the only way to get rid of him was to go back down the stairs. I returned to my desk, fuming.

A few days later, when I went to use the toilet, two branch chiefs I knew followed me, whispering as we washed our hands what Nancy and Wang were cooking up next. Another struggle meeting, reassignment to some remote post, and so on. When I was alone in my office, some of the younger members of the staff popped in under the pretense of bringing me my daily newspaper and offered quick words of support and comfort. "We're with you, comrade," they said.

I suffered several months of this until, frustrated by my lack of cooperation, the ladies ordered me back to the countryside with instructions to contemplate all my nefarious deeds and to recall the crimes of Qiao Guanhua. I was told that my only hope was a full confession. I made it clear that I had nothing to confess.

I was welcomed back at the cadre school by a new crop of young graduates from the Foreign Language Institute. They were cheerful, supportive, and eagerly shouldered the heavy work so that we old folks could coast a bit.

At the cadre school I was now a celebrity, well known for my long years working with the premier and treated with genuine respect. Almost all my elders were gone. I was no longer Little Ji. I was becoming Old Ji.

The cult of Chairman Mao—aside from his legacy as the nation's founder—was quickly fading. In its place, Zhou Enlai was emerging as a folk hero, a modern, modest Confucian gentleman who valued the best aspects of Chinese culture. He was being recognized for having been shrewd without scheming, forceful without brutality. A documentary film about his life débuted in early January 1977, just four months after Mao's death. *Eternal Glory to Esteemed and Beloved Prime Minister [Zhou] Enlai* included scenes of the protests the previous April, when plainclothes thugs were sent out to beat up and arrest the premier's mourners.

Articles in regional newspapers recounted telling anecdotes, such as the time Zhou's chauffeur accidentally sideswiped a young girl on a bicycle and Zhou made sure the child got the best medical care and then personally went to her home to apologize to her parents. The Party committee in his native county wrote an article recalling how, in the early 1950s, he had ordered that the house where he was born be kept a secret, to keep tourists from visiting it. But people made the pilgrimage in droves anyway, so he told the locals to tear the house down. But they never did. Mao's birthplace, meanwhile, had been turned into a major national monument and tourist attraction during his lifetime.

It saddened me that Zhou Enlai never got to enjoy all the face he was getting, but the example he set in death was powerful medicine for a beaten-down people whose leaders had misled them into the jaws of one catastrophe after another.

Cadres working at the rice farm were permitted furloughs to go home every other weekend. The Monday morning ritual was receiving the latest gossip and wall posting reports from those coming back from city furloughs. Topic A was whether and when Deng Xiaoping would reappear. Rumors were rife.

One Monday morning in the spring, a returnee reported that a Foreign Ministry driver had delivered a former Ministry official to a courtyard house near the Imperial Palace. To the driver's amazement, like a genie from a bottle, Deng Xiaoping appeared at the door. The elated driver jumped out of the car and ran over to shake hands with Deng— a short, squat, seventy-two-year-old—and asked after his health. Deng took his hand with a big, confident smile and said that he was very well.

This tidbit had my rice-farm comrades cheering. Deng was alive and healthy, not sitting in prison or laboring in a factory, where he'd previously been sent for "reform."

Everyone heard stories of condemned low-level cadres, stuck for years on impoverished farms, putting down their buckets of human waste and walking away, like soldiers spontaneously laying down their arms and leaving the field of battle. No one tried to stop them.

There was excitement in the air, like the anticipation of a child who smells dinner cooking and realizes how hungry he is. At the farm, we had a small transistor radio that we listened to almost constantly, not wanting to miss a scrap of news. We assigned one person each day to stay behind at our quarters and monitor the broadcasts.

This paid off on a sweltering day in July 1977. The radio monitor came running down the path between the paddies, shouting and waving, his face one huge grin. We dropped our tools and ran toward him. Out of breath, barely able to speak, he cried, "Deng has been liberated! He has been restored!"

Almost overnight, everything changed. Nancy Tang and Wang Hairong were stripped of their power and reassigned. I was free to go back to the Foreign Ministry, where I had long conversations with the new leadership about the injustice those two had inflicted on so many, including denying Xiangtong permission to join me in Washington.

"As proof of my total innocence, as well as that of my wife," I demanded, "I want to be posted abroad again, this time with Xiangtong, whether it be in the Liaison Office in Washington or at the U.N."

My new bosses assured me that I had nothing to worry about, but it was another six months before I was officially recalled to the Foreign Ministry and all my duties as vice director of the International Department were restored.

Meanwhile, I continued to spend some of my time at the cadre school, where, to my surprise, Nancy Tang showed up. I saw her hoeing in a field. As soon as she noticed me, she turned away.

She was working at the edge of the field, next to a large truck whose engine was idling. The driver was sitting at the wheel. Suddenly he put the truck in gear and started to back up, as if he might run over her. She jumped aside, scowling, and the driver turned off the ignition.

Nancy went back to hoeing. The driver turned on the ignition again and started to back up toward her. Again she jumped, and again he shut the engine off. When he started it up a third time, she realized he was harassing her and glared at me. Nancy had a knack for getting under the skin of most anyone she encountered.

She dropped her hoe and marched over to me. "Maybe we should have a talk," she said.

I shook my head and resumed hoeing. "There is nothing to talk about." I wasn't interested in anything she had to say, and I knew that if I said what I felt we would end up in an argument. For the remaining time we were there together, we studiously avoided each other.

Just as I was resurfacing from political exile, I received a letter from my Harvard roommate and the former Kissinger aide, Herb Levin, along with an article about me from the Toronto *Globe and Mail*. The writer was author and China expert Ross H. Munro, a Canadian I had met during the two years I spent in the Liaison Office in Washington.

Published at the end of 1977, Munro's article was entitled "Impressions of China." I read it sitting at my old desk, back in my old job, finally out from under Nancy Tang and Wang Hairong. I chuckled at the irony and beamed with pride.

It is almost impossible for foreigners to discover the precise fate of Chinese officials who suddenly drop from sight.

Such is the case with [Ji Chaozhu], a Foreign Ministry official who impressed many with his relaxed manner and his knowledge of U.S. affairs when he was stationed at the Chinese Liaison Office in Washington a few years ago.

But Mr. [Ji] dropped from sight soon after the purge of the radical "Gang of Four." When a foreigner recently asked a former colleague of Mr. [Ji] about his whereabouts, the colleague gruffly declared, "I think he is in very bad health," and then walked away, terminating what had otherwise been a pleasant conversation.

The person who actually laid it on the line was a lowly functionary who distributes official photographs of Chinese leaders to foreigners. When asked why there was no picture available of [Ji Chaozhu] translating for Chairman Mao, he said that Mr. [Ji] is "a running dog of the Gang of Four."

I burst out laughing. I couldn't wait to show it to Xiangtong. Munro ended his report on a dark note:

We can conclude that Mr. [Ji] is, indeed, in trouble, but there is no way of knowing when, if ever, he will reappear.

I had not only reappeared but would soon burst onto the international scene.

By the end of 1978, the mood in the country had dramatically lifted. We began to see more foreign visitors, including American tourists. There were also increasing cultural and commercial exchanges. Deng launched a massive push for economic development. In the process of being politically marginalized by Deng, Chairman Hua Guofeng officially recanted his "Two Whatevers" order.

The Central Committee of the Chinese Communist Party scrapped the slogan "Take the class struggle as the key link," declaring economic growth its prime issue. It urged schools and universities—which had essentially closed up shop during the Cultural Revolution—to get back to the job of educating China's youth.

Most important, Deng Xiaoping was now recognized as the de facto leader of the Party and an outspoken reformer. Poverty, he argued, is not the goal of socialism, and the pursuit of prosperity is patriotic (although the Western press twists this slightly for ironic effect—"To be rich is glorious").

The conclusion of the Party's Third Plenum meeting in December marked the sealing of the tomb of the Cultural Revolution, and the opening of a new period in our history. Happily for me, it coincided with the end of official relations between the United States and Taiwan, and the start of official relations between the United States and the People's Republic of China.

For the first time in two decades, I now had the mental space to devote myself fully to work. The United States and China had previously set January 1, 1979, as the official date for the start of formal diplomatic relations. The Liaison Offices in our capitals would become full embassies in March. The delay was intended to give the U.S. president, Jimmy Carter, time to get his nominee for ambassador to China approved by Congress. Carter, who had defeated Gerald Ford in 1976, was expected to run for reelection and conservative Republicans criticized him for ending formal recognition of Taiwan (then referred to by the United States as the Republic of China).

Deng Xiaoping had been invited to the United States to mark the start of this new era, and needed a competent interpreter. I was now forty-nine—overripe for an interpreter, according to the late premier's forty-and-out rule. But when I was asked if I would be willing to accompany Vice Premier Deng to the States, I immediately agreed.

On January 1, I interpreted for him at a special ceremony in Beijing at the U.S. Liaison Office, where toasts were drunk with champagne and Coca-Cola, the first U.S. product to be manufactured and sold in the People's Republic. Leonard Woodcock, a former American labor leader, headed the U.S. Liaison Office and would later be confirmed as ambassador. He and Deng wore lapel buttons bearing crossed Chinese and American flags that had been supplied impromptu by an American legislator.

It was an extraordinary event by any measure. Three decades of acrimony over the Korean War, the Taiwan issue, the Vietnam War, our U.N. status—all that bitterness seemed to melt away, forgotten like the snows of winter on a warm spring day.

As I had many times before, I packed for an overseas trip with one of China's top leaders. But I was now feeling the aches and pains of years of mental and physical stress. Direct from our seventeen-hour flight, we were driven to the home of Zbigniew Brzezinski, the U.S. national security adviser, for a buffet dinner attended by about two dozen officials.

I was discovering how hard it was to interpret for a man who was just five feet tall. To compensate for my height, I had to half crouch or spread my legs to lower my head so that he could hear me and I could hear him. At the Brzezinski dinner, there were fewer seats than guests. Deng sat and I stood behind him, bending down almost double. I hadn't slept for a day and a half. By the time it was over, my legs felt like stumps and my head like a sack of raw wool.

Although ours was not an official state visit, President Carter treated us royally. We were put up at Blair House, the official state guesthouse, which was palatial compared with anywhere I had stayed while traveling with Premier Zhou.

The food was excellent, except for dessert. We were served sherbet, which, to a lover of dairy products, is a pale shadow of the real thing. I grumbled in Chinese to some of my colleagues that I was disappointed we hadn't gotten ice *cream*. The next day, at both lunch and dinner, and for the rest of our stay, the waiters produced a huge plate of assorted flavors of ice cream. We marveled at the great efficiency of the American Secret Service and their eavesdropping skills.

Sleep deprivation and fatigue finally caught up with me after a couple of days and I collapsed with a heart rate of 150 beats per minute. The White House doctor showed up and gave me medication that worked like a charm. After a day's rest, I was back on duty.

President Carter's public fuss over Deng's visit included a speech in the Rose Garden, a state banquet, and the usual official and private talks on subjects such as trade, security, and Taiwan. Carter and his administration made it clear, publicly and privately, that the United States had divorced Taiwan to marry China.

On this visit I played a dual role, interpreter and diplomat, introducing Deng to members of the U.S. government and Congress whom I had met during my Liaison Office days. Everyone was gracious and starry-eyed. Everyone wanted to talk about Taiwan, on which our position remained firm but amicable. We agreed that the United States should honor its hands-off commitment and respect our goal of peaceful reunification.

For all his years, Deng was full of energy and a good sport. One of the most famous pictures of the two of us was taken at a rodeo in

Texas, where tiny Deng and tall Ji (in my geeky horn-rimmed glasses) donned ten-gallon cowboy hats. The only thing more incongruous than a Chinese cowboy is a Chinese gnome and a giant Chinese nerd playing cowboys. Everyone had a good laugh, including us.

Deng had come a long way from the dark years when, like many others, he found himself transformed in a matter of days from valued, honored, founding hero to enemy of the state. He toiled for several years of his exile in a small-engine factory, squatting to eat his meager rations, sleeping on a hard board with dozens of others in an unheated, barren dormitory. I admired his humility. It must have helped pull him through, and now it was serving him well as the new face of China.

Time magazine had made Deng its Man of the Year for 1978, with his picture on the cover of the January 1, 1979, issue. He was featured on the cover again during his visit in February. We were told that this was the first year in which the same person had been on the cover twice. Deng was a hit with the media.

During our visit, I "reemerged" in a very visible way in a *New York Times* editorial entitled "The Indispensable Mr. [Ji]":

[Ji Chaozhu] is hardly a household word in America. Yet Mr. [Ji] has been an indispensable man. If [Deng Xiaoping] had not brought the former Harvard man from the Chinese Foreign Ministry as his interpreter, his discourse with President Carter might have gone uncomprehended. The United States Government, it turns out, does not employ anyone fully qualified as a simultaneous interpreter from English to Chinese.

That painful condition is the culmination of chronic neglect. Unless complemented by academic training in the history, culture, economics and politics of a given society, the knowledge of its language alone becomes a dull instrument—practically useless in delicate diplomatic situations. Indeed, the translators at summit meetings have often observed that they cannot properly convey nuance of meaning unless they are familiar also with the private views and policies of the principals.

In 1972, President Nixon was able to speak with the Chinese leaders in [Beijing] only through *their* interpreters. Seven years later, the humiliation—and perhaps damage—continues on American soil. Absurd, in any language.

One of the defining moments of that visit for me occurred at the state banquet that President Carter hosted at the White House. The president had turned out the troops for us. The guests included cabinet members, congressional leaders, and a few celebrities, such as the actress Shirley MacLaine, who sat with us at the head table.

MacLaine had produced a documentary film in 1975 based on a tour of China she arranged, with the government's invitation and close supervision. For *The Other Half of the Sky: A China Memoir,* MacLaine had flown a group of American women to China to witness surgery being performed under acupuncture anesthesia, and to experience the "glory" of life on Chinese farms, in schools, and at model day-care centers. The film, beautiful and touching, reflected the idealized vision her government handlers allowed her to see, and was dismissed in the West as propaganda.

MacLaine charmed Deng, and they chatted amiably until she recounted one of her experiences in China. With good intentions and innocent enthusiasm, she said, "I was so moved when we visited a village where I met a university professor who was planting tomatoes in a field.

"I asked him if he didn't feel a loss, having to do physical labor in the remote countryside, divorced from his scientific research at the university. And you know what he said? 'Quite to the contrary! I am very happy to be with the poor peasants. I can learn much from them.'"

Deng listened with a look of polite interest as I translated. But when I got to the end, a shadow flickered across his face. He paused for a moment and then declared, unsmiling, "That professor was lying!"

MacLaine's jaw dropped. Carter, who had been listening, nodded gravely. I knew then that China's true liberation was finally at hand.

CHAPTER 28

The Reagan Crisis

Vice Premier Deng and I returned from a triumphant tour of the United States to a China that was rapidly opening to the West, building export factories, relearning how to be capitalist, and dealing with the psychological and societal damage of the last decade of Mao's rule. Our shrines and antiquities had been smashed, our spirits trampled, and we'd lost our Confucian sense of self, articulated by the Chinese philosopher twenty-five hundred years ago: "Do not do to others what you do not want them to do to you." There was widespread disillusionment, many scores begging to be settled, and many wrongs begging to be righted. That painful process was well under way.

One of the most symbolic and emotional moments of the early post-Mao years involved the fate of Liu Shaoqi, the Long March veteran who had been Mao's chosen successor until the 1960s. Liu had been Mao's ally for more than thirty years when he criticized the Great Leap Forward and the chairman's other experimental mass movements. Liu's wife had become a public figure with him, going into the countryside to investigate corruption. They were "rewarded" for their honesty when the Cultural Revolution began.

Liu, until then highly respected, was labeled a traitor, a scab, and the "biggest entrepreneur in the Party." He was expelled from all his positions and from the Party with much fanfare. Color posters were hung depicting workers shoveling Liu's body into a dung heap.

Liu disappeared in October 1968 and was never seen again. His wife, Wang Guangmei, was also declared a capitalist roader. Attacked by the Red Guards, she was kept under house arrest until Mao's death, when the horrible truth was finally reported in the press. Liu had been repeatedly tortured and interrogated, confined to an unheated cell, and denied medical care. He died in November 1969, his remains surreptitiously cremated under a false name. His death was kept from his wife for three years, and from the public for a decade. Liu was politically rehabilitated in 1980, with a state funeral at which his recovered ashes were handed to his wife. She hugged the small flag-covered wooden box to her cheek as she received it. Few who lived through those years can look at the photo of that moment without a lump in the throat.

In spite of all that the Chinese people had been through, the truth was more important than revenge. After a public trial at which Jiang Qing loudly blamed everyone else and repeatedly burst into tears of self-pity, she and one of the other members of the Gang of Four who denied wrongdoing received death sentences that were later commuted. Jiang lived for years in Qincheng Prison. She developed throat cancer and was released on parole for medical treatment. She eventually hanged herself. The remaining Gang members received long prison sentences, along with some of their high-level supporters. Some never repented. Zhang Chunqiao, backbone of the Gang of Four, said in prison that he had no regrets for what he had done, claiming his mistake was simply that he had overestimated Jiang Qing's power and strength.

With my career in high gear, I had no time or interest in settling scores. My new title after the Deng visit to the United States was vice director of American and Oceanic Affairs. I interpreted a few more times for Vice Premier Deng and Chairman Hua Guofeng, but now that the United States and China had full diplomatic relations, my interpreting work was handed over to a younger colleague.

As far as righting wrongs, the opportunity for Xiangtong arrived in short order. She took a competitive examination for a post working at the United Nations as a translator, passed easily, and was shipped off to New York in January 1980. It was her turn to shine. We also hoped that being in the States might provide an opportunity for her to see her father and a brother who were now living in Los Angeles. They'd had no contact for more than thirty years.

A few months later, Vice Foreign Minister Zhang Wenjin assigned me to return to the States with a delegation headed by Vice Premier Bo Yibo to study the U.S. economy. After the vice premier had concluded his visit, I was permitted to stay another week to see Xiangtong and accompany her to Los Angeles to visit her father.

The reunion was intense. Through his tears, her father said, "You were a teenager when we parted. Now you are over fifty and the mother of two sons!" He was now in his eighties, so we felt fortunate that Xiangtong had the chance to see him while he was still alive.

Although the United States and China had established formal diplomatic relations, below the surface of goodwill and expanding trade there remained the question of Taiwan. The Kuomintang lobby had been strong and entrenched, anxious to regain access to the White House. In the presidential election of 1980, Ronald Reagan sided with them in accusing President Carter of selling out America's "friends" to us Commies.

When Reagan won, he declared his intention to help upgrade Taiwan's military strength by selling the regime the most sophisticated American warplanes. This reversal of U.S. policy was a betrayal of the Shanghai Communiqué and caused almost as much consternation in the U.S. State Department as it did in our Foreign Ministry. No one wanted another Taiwan Strait confrontation, yet Reagan seemed determined to create one.

The American career diplomats who had experienced the opening of China from the days of the Nixon visit were so concerned that, within weeks of Reagan's inauguration, Vice Foreign Minister Zhang told me to pack my bags for Washington again. This time, the Americans had asked me to come and try to defuse the tension.

Zhang said the Foreign Ministry had received a letter signed by two high-ranking American diplomats suggesting that the Chinese government send me to "explain" China's foreign policy to the new administration and to key members of Congress. I was the only one, they said, who could bridge the cultural gap.

The letter-writing go-betweens were Michel C. Oksenberg, assistant national security adviser under Carter, and Stapleton Roy, a State Department official who was born in China while his father was working there as a missionary. Roy had been in the U.S. Foreign Service for years, including a stint in Moscow. He had recently been deputy chief of mission in Beijing, so we had met many times.

Foreign Minister Huang Hua thought sending me was a good idea. Over the next few days, I met with Deng Xiaoping and a number of our top diplomats to discuss how to present our case: that the continued sale of arms to Taiwan by the United States would make our goal of *peaceful* reunification difficult. As I had learned well from Zhou Enlai, it was important to be firm without being bellicose, and to be agreeable while disagreeing.

I flew to New York in March 1981 for a short reunion with Xiangtong, and then on to Washington, where I reported to Ambassador Chai Zemin with the instructions I received from Vice Premier Deng. Regulations requiring us to travel in pairs had been lifted, so I set out on my own, calling on about two dozen officials. They included senators and congressmen, mostly right-wing Republicans, as well as senior and middle-ranking officials of the State Department, the Department of Defense, and the Central Intelligence Agency, and Henry Kissinger.

To those who needed persuading, I explained the Taiwan issue in the context of Chinese history, and by example in the context of American history. Yes, we fought you in Korea and, yes, we helped Ho Chi Minh fight you in Vietnam, I said. But we were not the ones interfering in the domestic affairs of another nation. "Imagine if the Soviets had prevailed in the Cuban missile crisis, and for decades now you'd had their nuclear missiles pointed at you from just a few minutes' flight time away," I continued. "Taiwan is only a hundred or so miles off our coast. We feel just as vulnerable as you did in October 1963."

I also reminded some of those I spoke with that the force that had brought the United States and China together was a common irritant: the Soviet Union. The Chinese had no more affection for the Russians than the Americans did, especially as we shared a long and often disputed border.

I was about to leave Washington when Ambassador Chai and I received an invitation to meet with Vice President George H. W. Bush, who had been chief of the United States Liaison Office in Beijing, and then director of the CIA, before becoming Reagan's running mate. I repeated China's position to the vice president, although he appeared to need no persuading. He had drunk the Chinese water, so he understood us better than most.

I returned to our embassy to cable my report back to Beijing, and then flew to New York, where I went straight to our U.N. mission to visit Xiangtong. I arrived to find a message ordering me to return to the airport and fly back to Washington. President Reagan was about to receive Ambassador Chai and wanted to meet me as well.

It was flattering to have been summoned by the U.S. president. My discussions around Washington had apparently filtered upward, and I'd succeeded in leaving a good impression. Zhou Enlai's example was always in my mind. The goal was not to win but to find common ground.

Reagan received us in the Cabinet Room. Also there were Bush, White House Chief of Staff James Baker, Secretary of State Alexander Haig, presidential adviser Edwin Meese, and National Security Adviser Richard Allen. The number of ranking officials made it clear that we were being taken seriously. How I wished my father could have seen how far this ant had climbed!

Once again, Ambassador Chai and I reiterated China's policy with regard to the Taiwan question. I found Reagan's demeanor, considering his hard-shell anti-Communist politics, surprisingly cordial and amiable. His advisers leaned forward attentively, some taking notes.

I rattled off my presentation: Taiwan was and always had been part of China, and we desired peaceful reunification. We could not accept foreign interference, such as selling weapons to Taiwan. Reagan mostly listened, asking a few historical questions. Unlike Carter, Ford, or Nixon, Reagan had run as an ideologue. It was important to demonstrate to the president that playing the anti-Communist card with Red China was misguided policy and a repudiation of the spirit of Nixon's visit.

Haig seemed the most eager and engaged of the group. When we left, he took me aside to emphasize that Washington had no desire to spoil Sino-U.S. relations. I sensed he wanted to send the message that the new administration wasn't about to tear up the Shanghai Communiqué.

I returned to Beijing to report to Deng and other top officials. They congratulated me on all the contacts I'd made, and were especially delighted that I'd gotten to see Reagan and deliver our message to the top.

My efforts appeared to have paid off when, two months later, the Taiwan regime complained bitterly to *The New York Times* that Reagan was not keeping his promise to provide Taiwan with sophisticated new aircraft. The head of the downgraded Taiwan regime's mission in Washington bravely claimed, "Reagan will show his hand later. His heart is on our side."

While the Taiwan regime complained, negotiations began in Washington and Beijing. I participated in meetings held in Beijing between Vice Foreign Minister Zhang Wenjin on our side and U.S. Assistant Secretary of State John Holdridge. Nothing of substance came of these sessions, since, in our view, the matter had been settled in 1972, when Nixon and the premier signed the Shanghai Communiqué.

Meanwhile, China's evolution following the Mao years continued to pick up steam. I had been back in Beijing a month after my Reagan adventure when the Central Committee of the Communist Party adopted and published a resolution that praised Mao as "a great proletarian revolutionary, strategist and theorist," and China's "respected and beloved great leader and teacher," but admitted that "the Cultural Revolution, initiated by a leader laboring under a misapprehension and capitalized on by counterrevolutionary cliques, led to domestic turmoil and brought catastrophe to the party, the state and the whole people."

It continued:

Chief responsibility for the grave extreme leftist (ideology) error of the Cultural Revolution, an error comprehensive in magnitude and protracted in duration, does indeed lie with Comrade Mao Zedong.

Comrade Mao Zedong's prestige reached a peak and he began to get arrogant at the very time when the party was confronted with the new task of shifting the focus of its work to socialist construction, a task for which the utmost caution was required. He gradually divorced himself from practice and from the masses, acted more and more arbitrarily and subjectively, and increasingly put himself above the Central Committee of the party, [which should also bear a certain degree of responsibility].

The Central Committee confirmed what many people felt about those years, and it went a step further in distinguishing Zhou Enlai's record from Mao's in a way that truly captured the dilemma that defined the last decade of the premier's life:

> Comrade Zhou Enlai was utterly devoted to the party and the people and stuck to his post until his dying day. He found himself in an extremely difficult situation throughout the Cultural Revolution. He always kept the general interest in mind, bore the burden of office without complaint, racking his brains and untiringly endeavoring to keep the normal work of the party and the state going, to minimize the damage caused by the Cultural Revolution and to protect party and nonparty cadres.

It struck me as a rather modest epitaph for the man who had kept China from devolving into total chaos.

A year after my March 1981 Reagan visit, Chinese-U.S. relations had deteriorated. There were fences to mend. Hua Guofeng, Mao's designated successor, had been eased out of office by Deng Xiaoping, and in his place Zhao Ziyang had become premier. Zhao was a reformer who advocated government transparency and foreign investment, and was popular with the peasant masses. During the Cultural Revolution, he was considered such a threat by the radicals that they made numerous attempts to assassinate him.

Premier Zhao traveled to Washington to meet with President Reagan and Secretary of State Haig seven months after I did. The visit produced no breakthrough on Taiwan. The administration had refrained from selling the sophisticated aircraft, but it agreed to sell spare parts for existing planes and was proposing to sell updated versions of older jets. Meanwhile, U.S. spy planes had been making reconnaissance flights over North Korea, in our backyard.

Our government responded with a harder line at the beginning of 1982. Any arms sales to Taiwan were objectionable. "There is no other way," we said. "Those who insist on selling arms to Taiwan encroach

THE MAN ON MAO'S RIGHT · 309

on China's sovereignty and interfere in its internal affairs. The United States is no exception in this matter."

It was no bluff, as the Dutch had discovered the previous summer, when the Netherlands sold Taiwan two submarines. We recalled our ambassador from The Hague and downgraded our embassy to a liaison office. We were now warning the Americans that sales to Taiwan would be a "severe test" of whether Washington valued its relationship with Beijing.

We left a door ajar: "The United States . . . must seek . . . a solution to the issue of selling arms to Taiwan." But I knew from my participation in negotiations on the issue in Beijing that we were a long way from any solution.

In the middle of this stalemate, I was permanently reassigned to our Washington embassy as minister-counselor, responsible for political relations between China and the United States. My return set off alarms in the U.S. State Department. Within days of my arrival, Assistant Secretary of State Holdridge invited me to lunch in a private home with several other State Department China experts. I was the only Chinese official present.

Once we had all filled our buffet plates and found seats, the mood turned businesslike. Holdridge began by asking me straight out, "Is China preparing to recall Ambassador Chai and downgrade your embassy status?" The other men leaned forward, forks poised in midair.

"I've received no such instructions," I said. "My assignment is to be the number-three man in the embassy, to assist in political relations between China and the U.S."

What followed was a tense ten-minute grilling, as my hosts peppered me with questions about China's intentions with regard to Taiwan, and how serious the situation really was. These were people I considered to be professional friends, but I needed to be firm.

"The prevailing situation between the two countries is grave," I said. "Arms sales to Taiwan are a serious violation of the fundamental principles underlying our agreement to establish full diplomatic relations.

"All of you here are fully aware of the history of the normalization process between China and the U.S., and you have all made important contributions to the success of that process. I hope you will prevail on the administration to abide by the agreements we all worked so hard to achieve."

"So China is not about to recall Chai, and you are not here to take over as liaison chief," Holdridge pressed. "Is that correct?"

"As I said, I have no instructions to that effect."

The tension immediately dissipated. My hosts sighed, sat back in their chairs, smiled, and tucked into their lunches. I took it as a good sign that they had been worried enough to ask. They also must have realized that if Chai had been about to be recalled, I would have known enough to decline the invitation.

The rest of the luncheon was confined to small talk. As soon as I got back to the embassy, I reported the conversation to Ambassador Chai so that he could get a cable off to Beijing right away. It was important for officials there to know how terrified the Americans were of a diplomatic break. The threat alone gave us a strong bargaining position.

The two sides continued negotiations in Beijing, and on August 17, 1982, an agreement was finally reached that produced the third joint communiqué between China and the United States. It reaffirmed the previous two communiqués, and the United States agreed to gradually reduce its military support for Taiwan. There was no timetable, however.

The United States' willingness to reaffirm our sovereignty and its prior agreements had averted a crisis. From then on, I was able to get down to the business of promoting a good working relationship between my two beloved countries.

The situation improved when my good friend and role model, Vice Foreign Minister Zhang Wenjin, was named China's chief representative for our U.S. talks. Like me, Zhang had been an English interpreter for Zhou Enlai. He had played an important role in the early days of Chinese-American relations, and he was the official in the Ministry who granted permission for Xiangtong and me to visit Los Angeles so that she could be reunited with her father.

Han Xu, whom I had worked with in the Liaison Office from 1973 to 1975 and who had been afraid to let me out of his sight, moved up into Zhang's job in Beijing as vice foreign minister in charge of Sino-

U.S. relations. Of all the senior officials I had worked with in the United States, my relationship with Han Xu had been the least friendly.

Han's English was not as good as mine, which put him at a disadvantage. He often pulled a long face when I, a lower-ranking cadre, had to explain to him the American cultural references and idioms that naturally came up in our meetings. "There's more than one way to skin a cat" translates poorly into Chinese, and when someone made a joke about another official being an Eli, I had to explain that it was a pejorative nickname given to Yale students by Harvard men.

Like many Chinese diplomats Han was very cautious politically. He was anxious not to say or do the wrong thing for fear he'd be criticized and lose face. My jocularity with our American contacts was decidedly un-Chinese. He probably disapproved.

Ambassador Zhang spoke excellent English and treated me like a respected colleague. He arrived in Washington full of energy and purpose, immediately filling his schedule with meetings at the White House, the State Department, and Congress, and eagerly accepting speaking invitations throughout the States. He was an instant hit with audiences: relaxed, informal, and good-humored. He got the jokes, and could tell a few.

Shortly after Zhang arrived, the embassy's second-in-command, Minister Hu Dingyi, was appointed ambassador to the United Kingdom. I had been third in the pecking order, and now Ambassador Zhang moved me up to the number-two position. He also suggested that Xiangtong quit her United Nations job to work with us in the embassy, so that she and I could be together again.

Xiangtong and I saw each other only once every other month. Neither of us earned enough to afford the commute between New York and Washington, so we hitched rides with couriers driving diplomatic pouches back and forth between the U.N. mission and the embassy. People often asked me how we managed our long-distance marriage. We shared a sense of purpose. The first generation of the new China, we had survived the chaos. The rest seemed easy by comparison. Also, we respected each other as professionals and loved each other deeply.

It was often lonely. During the first twenty years of our marriage, we seemed to have spent more time apart than together, and even less time as a complete family. The prospect of setting up house together made us very happy.

Our boys were now in their late teens. They had come to visit Xiangtong in New York during the summers of 1980 and 1981, thanks to a stipend from the United Nations. The second summer, our younger son, Xiao-bin, stayed in the States and attended public high school in Manhattan. Xiaotan had a busy social life in Beijing and was preparing to go to university. When the summer vacation ended, he returned to live in our Foreign Ministry flat, where Xiangtong's cousin would look after him.

In giving up her U.N. job, Xiangtong would be sacrificing a more generous pension. We decided it was worth it. The only problem was that children of diplomats were not permitted to join their parents on overseas assignments, so my old school friend Anne Tonachel offered to have Xiao-bin live with her in her Manhattan apartment so that he could stay in school. But in the end we arranged for Xiao-bin to stay with our dear friend Mrs. Jane Shaw in Washington, D.C.

When Xiangtong arrived in Washington, Ambassador Zhang promoted her cadre rank, in part because her English was excellent, but also because it improved her diplomatic status, removing restrictions on her ability to travel and meet with foreigners. She was assigned the job of promoting sister-city relationships between Chinese and American towns. A few months later, Zhang promoted Xiangtong again, to a position normally restricted to members of the Party: once again, I was blessed with a boss who had a small ego and a big heart.

This was a happy and busy period in the embassy. I spent much of my time working with elected and appointed officials and handling press contacts. I also hobnobbed with the diplomatic corps, gleaning gossip and intelligence about the United States and its policies in relation to the rest of the world. There were few dull moments.

Ambassador Zhang encouraged Xiangtong and me to find an apartment where we would feel comfortable hosting American guests. This was also highly unusual, and a great privilege. It was a treat to be able to entertain and cook authentic Chinese meals for our American friends and associates.

One of my closest friends was David Laux, a trade expert who had been assigned to Beijing in 1981, and had worked in the Commerce Department. He was now a senior adviser on Asian affairs to the National Security Council.

Our two countries were arguing over trade. China's textile industry was booming and our exports of inexpensive goods to the United States were hurting American textile makers, who persuaded the Reagan administration to restrict imports. China retaliated with a ban on imports of American cotton, soybeans, and chemical fibers.

When talks between the two sides broke down, David's boss, William P. "Judge" Clark, the national security adviser, would tell him, "Go see your boy Ji and try to work this out." David and I would meet at a café on Connecticut Avenue and then take a walk in nearby Rock Creek Park, where we could speak freely.

One of the things I understood in dealing with American officials was how much they hated the ideological script so many of our officials brought to their meetings. David told me a story about when he worked for Reagan's first commerce secretary, Malcolm Baldridge. They had invited Ambassador Chai to meet and discuss the growing trade imbalance with China. Baldridge had a reputation for plain speaking and impatience.

David said, "The secretary and I listened to the usual propaganda for a few minutes until finally Baldridge interrupted Chai and said, 'Mr. Ambassador, come over here to the window.' Baldridge had a large office overlooking a busy street.

"He said to the ambassador, 'Look down there. See those cars? What do you see?'

"Ambassador Chai said, 'I see the cars.'

"Baldridge said, 'If you look carefully, you'll see that every other car is a Japanese car. And if you look even more carefully you'll see that every driver is wearing a Chinese sweater. We don't mind the flow of your sweaters into this country, but don't take the whole damn market! You get the message? It was good seeing you.'"

In my dealings with David and others, I skipped the ideological preambles and tried to get down to business, the way Americans like to. We each laid out our bottom-line positions without artifice. This helped cut through the diplomatic fog and allowed us to reach an understanding, which, when reported to our respective superiors, became the basis for final agreements.

In addition to maintaining close contact with current officials, I periodically met with people such as Henry Kissinger, former president Gerald Ford, and Ford's former national security adviser, Brent Scowcroft. I attended conferences on international issues, including one in Aspen, Colorado, where I shamed the host committee by pointing out that it was the Taiwan regime's flag that was fluttering in front of the conference center, rather than the flag of the People's Republic of China.

In spite of the trade tensions, relations between China and the United States continued to improve. Premier Zhao Ziyang was invited to visit in 1984 and Vice Chairman Wang Zhen was invited to visit later. Much of our time was then taken up with preparing and executing these two major visits.

Ambassador Zhang was popular in the States, but his informal, open manner raised eyebrows in Beijing. China was in the process of trying to improve its relations with Moscow, and around that time there was a shake-up in the Foreign Ministry. It wasn't a purge, but Ambassador Zhang was suddenly recalled, to be replaced by his colleague Han Xu. Our embassy staff was caught off guard. Such changes usually happen more gradually, with more notice.

The protocol was for recalled ambassadors to depart before the replacement arrived. During the vacancy, the person who held the number-two position automatically became the interim chargé d'affaires—head of mission—until the new ambassador was installed.

As soon as Ambassador Zhang received his recall cable, he announced that I would be the chargé d'affaires ad interim. It was a great honor.

Zhang's announcement of my appointment was cabled to Beijing, which immediately replied with orders that I pack my bags at once. I, too, was being recalled and reassigned.

I dispatched a cable requesting permission to stay an extra month, so that I could attend Xiao-bin's high school graduation in May 1985, as well as have time to bid farewell to my many friends and contacts.

The reply was rapid and abrupt: I must leave Washington by the end of April, *before* the arrival of the new ambassador. Han Xu did not want to find me in Washington when he arrived. That was the first and last time, in more than four decades in the Foreign Ministry, that I ever heard of an incoming ambassador's issuing such a strange order.

The reason for my urgent recall: I had been promoted to the rank of full ambassador—to Fiji!

CHAPTER 29

From Cannibals to Caviar

Ambassador Zhang was outraged. He wrote to the foreign minister pointing out that my Fiji appointment would "either give people the very wrong impression that Ji had committed some major mistake, or make people think that the leaders of the Foreign Ministry were incompetent in the judgment of their staff."

I had to get out a map, and then needed a magnifying glass to find Fiji. I was to be China's ambassador to three tiny island-states in the middle of the South Pacific: Fiji, Vanuatu, and Kiribati. Total population: less than a million. Xiangtong asked our friend Richard Holbrook, the U.S. assistant secretary of state, what they were close to. Holbrook chuckled. "They are close to nowhere," he said. "It's the craziest thing I ever heard, sending a guy with Ji's credentials to Fiji. It's just sand, palm trees, and ex-cannibals!"

The news spread quickly. A pro-Taiwan Chinese newspaper published in the United States gloated, "Ji Chaozhu has been elbowed out and downgraded to a third-class post."

Marshall Coyne, the owner of Washington's prestigious Madison Hotel and a close friend from my Liaison Office days, hastily arranged a farewell banquet for three hundred people. He invited many of the usual suspects, including Zbigniew Brzezinski, former senior State Department officials, and my Harvard roommate Herb Levin. Everyone was curious to know what was behind my reassignment, but I dared not utter a word of complaint or dissent.

"How many ambassadors can say they've been appointed to three countries at once?" I joked. "Obviously, I'm a big man in the Foreign Ministry."

My orders to depart left no time to visit Anne or any of my other childhood pals in New York. We made arrangements for Xiao-bin to stay with friends who would stand in for us at his graduation. He had been accepted to Princeton University with a generous scholarship, so we wouldn't be seeing him for a while. I managed to squeeze in a private dinner for our family at the Kissingers' home, and I had lunch with Senator Stevens from Alaska, who subsequently wrote several letters to our Foreign Ministry expressing his dismay.

But orders were orders, and Xiangtong and I had been through far worse. On our way back to Beijing, we stopped in Los Angeles to see Xiangtong's father. "I don't think I will see you again," he said mournfully. He was well into his eighties, his health declining. He pulled a gold ring from one of his fingers and handed it to me. "I've worn this all my life," he said. "You keep it now. Maybe give it to one of the boys." An inscription on the inside read, "Always keep your mouth shut."

That summed up the burden of his life, and the lives of so many others. While Xiangtong was being punished in China because of her father and her brothers, her father had been suffering in Taiwan because of Xiangtong and her mother. He'd been forced out of a good job, and required to join the Kuomintang so that he could make a living as a teacher. I appreciated my father-in-law's gesture, but the message was lost on me: I could never keep my mouth shut!

Back in Beijing, I received my ambassadorial training, and the briefing documents for my assignment—a one-page memo. The Dominion of Fiji, I learned, had been a British colony until 1970, so I wouldn't need an interpreter.

Only a handful of nations had bothered to establish embassies there, including the United States, Britain, Australia, New Zealand, France, and Japan. As in the States, Taiwan had been officially represented—until 1975, when China sent its first diplomat. Taiwan's status had been downgraded, but the representatives stayed in Fiji, paying bribes and offering other inducements to public officials to compete with us for influence.

I had been urgently recalled from Washington to rush off to a red pin on the map. I was in a miserable mood. One of my Foreign Ministry allies tried to cheer me up by assuring me that Fiji would not be the last stop on my career path. I was "only" fifty-six, he said, and could expect one more ambassadorial assignment before being turned out to pasture. He pointed out the case of another diplomat who had been sent to Papua New Guinea and then on to Venezuela. After all I'd seen and done, even Venezuela sounded like Siberia.

My ousted Ambassador Zhang was back in Beijing as well, sitting on the political hot seat. He was defending himself from claims by Foreign Ministry old guarders that he'd given me and other embassy officials too much freedom in Washington. Our shared dilemma was that we had done our jobs too well, and now Zhang was being accused of getting too liberal. But he still had some clout, and he promised that every time he saw the foreign minister he would remind him how foolish it made China look to have sent me to Fiji.

In the summer of 1985, Xiangtong and I arrived in Suva, the capital of Fiji. Our embassy was a converted motel with a swimming pool, on the beach. It was a beautiful location, but the region was humid and buggy, infested with large, fierce mosquitoes that you couldn't feel until they'd already bitten you, leaving enormous, itchy welts that took days to heal. When Xiangtong and I went to bed, we hunted and swatted as many mosquitoes as we could find. Then we lay down, wondering how long we would have to suffer this assignment.

There was little about Fiji that wasn't exotic in some way. The native Fijians, about half the population, were a mixture of Polynesians and Melanesians, beefy and strong, with a proud tribal-warrior heritage that had once included the practice of cannibalism. The other half were descendants of immigrants, mostly from India, who over the years had been brought in by the British to help harvest Fiji's principal export: cane sugar.

The armed forces were largely Fijian, and only native Fijians could legally own land. But the Fijians were unmotivated and rented out the land to the ethnic Indians at modest prices. The Indians were hardworking and, as a result, had accumulated the bulk of the wealth, running the stores and businesses, and influencing the government. The two groups were adversaries, natives versus interlopers.

Shortly after we arrived, I presented my credentials to the governor-general of Fiji. We then attended the Loloma Festival in Tavua, held outdoors under the palm trees. Standing behind Xiangtong and me was a powerfully built Fijian warrior with a painted face. Stripped to the waist, he wore a grass skirt and held a heavy wooden club.

Below the dais, in front of us, were three Fijian chiefs, also stripped to the waist, sitting cross-legged on the ground, their bodies glistening with sweat and coconut oil. One of their traditional welcoming rituals required us to drink a local intoxicant called *yagona,* made from the root of the kava plant.

The ceremony began with the chief in the center pouring some ground kava powder into a wooden vat, then adding pails of water. Next, he threw in a hemp rag, with which he swirled the brew around while loudly muttering incantations. He removed and wrung out the hemp rag, wiped it on his glistening bare chest, and tossed it to the second chief, who wiped the rag on his glistening bare chest, and then to the third chief, who did the same.

Finally, the rag was returned to the brew and the process was repeated until the liquid looked like muddy water. A painted warrior dipped up a half coconut shell of the *yagona* and, holding it in both hands, walked up to Xiangtong and me and offered us a drink! We couldn't refuse. According to the Fijians, even the queen of England had taken a sip when she visited. If it was good enough for her, it was good enough for us.

We were instructed to gulp the drink down and clap three times, after which the chiefs and warriors muttered grunts of approval. This went on until poor Xiangtong and I had each consumed six cups of the foul muck and our tongues were numb. But neither of us felt intoxicated. Later, at a similar ceremony on another island, the brew was more potent and left me feeling numb all over.

The locals treasured their cannibal past. The practice had ended a century earlier. The British arrived and, with difficulty and after a few missionaries ended up in the roasting pit, put an end to it. The Fijians maintained a small museum that included photographs showing the proper way to cook a human. The darker the skin, the better the meat, we learned—chewier, apparently.

We were treated to a reenactment of two tribes battling each other, after which the victors would have eaten some of the losers. Happily, that part was omitted. An older man I met told me that when his grandfather, a chieftain, lay on his deathbed many years earlier his last words were that he wished he could taste human flesh just one more time.

We made the best of our new home, keeping ourselves culturally nourished by spending a lot of our free time with other diplomats. The American ambassador became a good friend. He told me that he, too, had been astounded when he heard that I was being sent to the edge of the earth.

Xiangtong and I traveled to the other island-states, where we were treated to more strange aboriginal rituals, including one ceremony in which the men were naked except for penis sheaths.

As for diplomacy, when the islanders looked at us foreign officials they saw money. The governor-general received ambassadors mainly to ask for more aid. Wives of diplomats were asked to raise funds for the poor Fijians.

There were a few stabs at economic development. China sent experts to show the Fijians how to grow rice, but they thought it was too much trouble and abandoned the project when our experts left. We also sent teachers to show them how to make rattan chairs, but the students showed little interest in learning.

The aid war between the People's Republic and the Taiwan regime benefited the locals. They used this rivalry to get more than they otherwise would have. The Taiwan officials couldn't compete when it came to economic aid, and we refused to give the local officials cash. The Taiwan regime responded by doing things like sending the governor-general a free full-time cook or inviting him to Taiwan for a free vacation and for his medical treatment.

There was one bright spot. After an inspection tour by a senior Foreign Ministry official in charge of embassy operations, we received the highest praise for running an efficient little operation, better even than many of our large embassies. We were publicly cited as an "efficient and united little collective."

At the beginning of 1987, I received a letter from a friend in the Ministry telling me that he'd heard I was going to be recalled and re-posted to a European country. I slammed my fist on the arm of my chair. After Fiji, what European country would have me? Iceland? Malta? I had been hoping for a decent-size Asian country—Sri Lanka, or Burma, or even Pakistan. India would be too grand for me, but that would have been a great promotion.

Europe? Was I going to end my career on the diplomatic cocktail circuit in some easygoing, out-of-the-way country, with little to do but talk about the weather and speculate on important events taking place far away? I became as dejected as I'd ever been.

About a month later, I was sitting in my office when the phone rang. It was our communications clerk, in charge of our overseas cables. "Ambassador, could you please come to the decoding room?" he said. "There's an important message for you."

I leaped out of my chair. The traffic to and from Fiji was light. Now there was a message so top-secret that it could be read only by me in the code room. I dashed across the courtyard to the communications center, where the clerk, smiling, handed me a folded piece of paper. I opened it and read: "You are reposted effective at once as China's am-bassador extraordinaire and plenipotentiary to the Court of St. James's, London. Follow usual protocol for departing ambassadors."

I ran into the courtyard. "Xiangtong! Xiangtong! Where are you?" She emerged from one of the offices with a worried look. I rushed over and handed her the cable. I couldn't help shouting, "London! We're going to *London*!"

After a year and a half of living with the bugs and the humidity and the primitive politics, we were headed for one of the world's great cap-itals, a major hub in the diplomatic world. I couldn't wait to find out how this good fortune had come my way.

We began a hurried farewell tour of the other island-states. But be-fore we could complete our duties the Fijian army staged a bloodless coup against the recently elected pro-Indian prime minister. The situa-tion rapidly deteriorated into anarchy. We notified the home office and were ordered to return at once. We were happy to oblige.

Our return to China was warm, even triumphant. The Foreign Ministry arranged for us to tour the country and see some of the historic sights we'd never had a chance to visit. Everywhere I went, I was received by high-ranking provincial officials with great respect. I had been the man on Mao's right, and even though Mao's mistakes had been publicly acknowledged by the Party, Chairman Mao was still the founder of the People's Republic. His portrait still hung over Tiananmen Gate. I had survived all the purges and struggles, had been a close aide to a revered leader—Zhou Enlai—and was now being honored with another important overseas assignment.

I revisited one of the towns where I'd been sent to work in a cadre school during the Cultural Revolution. There were no more cadre schools. The people who had hounded me before now spoke to me of their regret, and offered their apologies, which I accepted. "I understand," I told them. "It was the two young ladies, and the times were different."

During a month's layover in Beijing, I received my new packet of documents—this time extensive, including reports on the recently concluded negotiations for the return of Hong Kong to Chinese control in 1997. The main question was how to return it in a peaceable way, so both sides would not lose face. I was going to the United Kingdom at the height of good relations between the two countries.

I learned from the Foreign Ministry that my appointment to the Court of St. James's—as the United Kingdom is referred to in diplomatic circles—was the result of a great deal of pressure, including a visit to China's head of state, Chairman Li Xiannian, by my friend Senator Stevens.

Even after Chairman Li agreed to send me to London, there were still complications. The appointment of a new ambassador is first proposed to the receiving country for approval. This is usually a formality, but the first reaction from the British Foreign Office was "Why is China sending us an ambassador from a backwater former colony?" It was, in the world of diplomacy, potentially insulting and possibly a signal of a change in relations.

It took some explaining, and a bit of diplomatic finesse on the part of the British. They didn't want to create a row by rejecting an appointed ambassador. When officials at the Foreign Office saw my résumé, they were surprised, and coyly told our embassy in London, "We had no idea you attached such importance to Fiji."

On August 29, 1987, Xiangtong and I touched down at Gatwick Airport. Our plane was met by senior embassy staff and a black Rolls-Royce with a Chinese flag fluttering from the fender, its diplomatic plate reading, "CHN 1." The indomitable ant had reached the top step.

The next year and a half were filled with extraordinary experiences and goodwill. On the work front, I spent a large amount of my time on economic issues, meeting with local officials as well as national leaders who were interested in buying from and selling to China. The Hong Kong issue was being handled by a separate group of officials from both sides, so I didn't have to navigate those waters.

I was also responsible for the success of visits from China's dignitaries. On two occasions, I prevailed on Prime Minister Margaret Thatcher to meet with Chinese officials who might not otherwise have been received. I knew, for example, that Jiang Zemin, the mayor of Shanghai, was a favorite of Vice Premier Deng Xiaoping and probably in line for an important post in the future. Thatcher met with him, and a few years later Jiang became China's president.

I also met with the media, and was pleased to find a tongue-in-cheek article rating diplomatic parties in *The Economist* on Christmas Eve, 1988, entitled "Ji Whiz":

> For Christmas parties try the Irish, for diligent lobbying take your hat off to the West Germans, for entertainment ask Iraq's ambassador about Syria's President Hafez Assad. . . . But for the most sublime mix of business and pleasure get an invitation from the Chinese ambassador. The food will be excellent, the guests chosen for their learned conversation, the host—Mr. Ji Chaozhu—chummy and relaxed in a most unChinese way.
>
> Mr. Ji grew up in America and perfected his excellent American-English at Harvard in the late 1940s. Most Chinese ambassadors have shunned Britain's disrespectful media, but Mr. Ji makes sure he gets himself on television whenever there is criticism of China's policy in Tibet.

The British love their royal ceremonies, and so did Xiangtong and I. We were invited to quite a few, beginning with my official installation. We were received by Prince Charles and the Duke of York for the presentation of my credentials. This began with a ride to Buckingham Palace in a caravan of elaborate horse-drawn carriages, and included the exacting rituals governing how one approaches and addresses the queen.

We attended a number of royal events, such as the prince's birthday, and got to meet Prince Charles and Princess Diana. We sometimes felt as though we were living in a children's fairy tale come to life.

We journeyed all over the British Isles, enjoying everything except the infamously overcooked British food. At Edinburgh Castle in Scotland, I held an ancient sword that had belonged to one of the famous knights of old. I also put an old helmet on my head. Scotland was my favorite place because of its history of revolution against oppression.

We loved our embassy building. The chancellery was the oldest diplomatic facility in the city, dating back to the Qing dynasty in the nineteenth century. The exterior had been restored to its original look, but the inside had been renovated, except for one room whose history was so important that it hadn't changed in a century.

In 1896, the man credited with the birth of modern China, Dr. Sun Yat-sen, had been living in exile in London. Dr. Sun was a physician, educated in Hawaii and Hong Kong. He'd led an unsuccessful uprising against the Qing government. With a price on his head, Sun couldn't return to China.

The Qing diplomats lured Dr. Sun into the chancellery under false pretenses, arrested him, and locked him in a small room on the second floor while they arranged to secretly ship him back to China to be executed for treason. Dr. Sun managed to slip a note through a small window to a British friend who alerted the authorities. The British forced the Qing diplomats to release Dr. Sun. Fifteen years later, after an uprising ended thousands of years of feudalism, Dr. Sun became the first president of modern China.

When the chancellery interior was renovated, the small room where Dr. Sun had been held was preserved as it was at the time of his capture. During the Cultural Revolution, some radical employees in the embassy destroyed a number of valuable relics. A few original papers survived and were preserved in glass cases, to be shown to visitors.

Ambassadors were permitted a home visit once a year, and it was during our second trip back that the infamous violence took place near Tiananmen Square, in May and June 1989. We returned to Beijing in late May to find the square filled with protesters criticizing Deng Xiaoping and demanding greater freedom. The country was in the grip of a major political crisis.

On our way home, we had stopped over in Hong Kong, where some friends asked us if the situation might escalate into violence. "Oh, no!" we assured them. "Those days are gone for good!"

The protests had started in Shanghai, in April, with the death of Hu Yaobang, a high-ranking Party official who had been an aggressive re-former highly critical of the "excesses" under Chairman Mao and an advocate of Tibetan autonomy. He'd been forced out in 1987 after being accused of sympathizing with protesting students the year before. His death sparked commemorative gatherings that led to protests in Shanghai.

The demonstrations continued to grow and spread. They became a cause of great embarrassment when students flooded Tiananmen Square in mid-May, on the eve of a welcoming ceremony for a long-scheduled visit by Soviet leader Mikhail Gorbachev, the first by a Soviet leader in thirty years. The government moved the ceremony to the airport, but the students had managed to take advantage of the presence of all the foreign press for the Gorbachev visit.

With big changes taking place in the Communist and Socialist regimes in Eastern Europe, there were rumors that the United States was hoping for, and even encouraging, similar regime change in China. Bette Bao Lord, the Chinese-born wife of the most recent U.S. ambassador to China—Winston Lord—had been seen meeting with the students in Tiananmen Square.

We had lived through terrible times, and this new movement felt frighteningly like the start of the Cultural Revolution. We thought the students were misguided in complaining about leaders who had done so much to repair the damage of the past, improve living standards, and strengthen China's position in the world. We were particularly chagrined by the vehement attacks leveled at Deng himself, the person responsible for the repudiation of the Cultural Revolution and the liberation of millions of good people who had been wrongfully accused of being enemies of the state.

But resentment had begun to surface over growing economic disparity. Booming exports were creating a small class of the newly wealthy, and there were widespread complaints about official corruption, and inflation. This was fertile soil for demagogues with ulterior motives.

Martial law was declared, but by then the students controlled Tiananmen Square so completely that the police and the military could not clear it. The protesters began a hunger strike.

The crisis was also creating trouble at the top. Zhao Ziyang, who was supposed to be Deng Xiaoping's successor as head of the Party, went to Tiananmen and, using a megaphone, made an emotional appeal to the students to leave while expressing sympathy for their complaints. Seen as too soft, he was immediately drummed out of his job by Deng. It was unclear who would succeed Deng, who was now eighty-two years old.

We were appalled at the rantings of the student leaders, especially Chai Ling, a twenty-three-year-old psychology student who had been a month-old infant when the Cultural Revolution began. In videotaped interviews with Western correspondents, she tearfully declared that her aim was to cause bloodshed at Tiananmen to arouse the Chinese people and overthrow the government. But she said she would not sacrifice her life because she was the "commander-in-chief." In the end, she fled the country like a coward after armed forces were sent to clear Tiananmen Square.

I wanted to see for myself what the demonstrators were doing, so Xiangtong and I got on our bikes and rode toward the square. But just as we turned into Chang'an Boulevard a sudden powerful headwind blew us back. We tried to walk, but even that proved nearly impossible, so we returned to our Foreign Ministry flat. In retrospect, we felt this to be a fortuitous wind that may have saved us from personal trouble. I could just imagine what the reaction would have been if we had happened to find our pictures in the paper at the wrong place at the wrong time.

We left Beijing for a scheduled visit to Shanghai, where, on May 28, 1989, we had dinner with Jiang Zemin, the mayor I had introduced to Margaret Thatcher. He was now the Party secretary for Shanghai. After some chatter about the good old days, Jiang said he'd just returned from Beijing and was convinced that steps had been taken to overthrow the government. One of the other dinner guests, an old friend of ours, disagreed with him, but Jiang told her sternly, "You are well intentioned but naïve."

On June 4, the day we were scheduled to leave Shanghai for a visit to Hangzhou, in the south, I awoke and turned on the shortwave radio that I always carried with me to listen to the BBC and Voice of America. I tuned in to Voice of America just as the announcer said, "There are credible reports of a bloody massacre in Tiananmen Square overnight. Hundreds may have been killed." Xiangtong jumped out of bed and turned on the television, but there was no signal. The screen was black.

After an anxious lunch with friends, it took us an hour and a half to travel the short distance to the railroad station. Worried that protesting students might attack us, our friends put us in an ordinary taxi instead of the official black car assigned to us. This way, I would look more like an elderly professor than a senior official. No one bothered us as we passed many overturned buses and groups of chanting students. We caught the last train out of Shanghai before the entire rail system was shut down.

The rest of our trip was equally sobering. Air travel was suspended for a time. We saw no tourists, and foreigners living in China were anxiously packing up their possessions and preparing to flee. When we finally arrived in Beijing, I phoned the Foreign Ministry to have a car sent to the airport to pick us up. We were instructed to stay at the airport hotel overnight because it was unsafe to drive after dark.

The next morning our driver told us that many people had been killed, and there were reports of rifle fire at night. Back at the Foreign Ministry, I joined a number of other senior officials to listen to reports about the Tiananmen incident and attend discussion groups about how we were to respond to questions when we returned to our posts. Our instructions were simple and vague: reassure everyone that China has not gone off the track; that we were not going backward in our policies and the disruption would soon be resolved.

Order was being restored, but, we were warned, "expect a great deal of controversy when you return to your posts." We were shown the infamous image, broadcast around the world, of the lone protester standing in front of a column of tanks.

When we'd left London for this home leave, Sino-British relations were at high tide. Prime Minister Thatcher was thinking about inviting the premier, Li Peng, to London for an official visit. Prince Charles and Princess Diana were considering an official visit to China. Sino-British trade was moving ahead rapidly. Wherever I went, I was welcomed.

Everything had changed when we arrived back in London. Protesters appeared each day in front of the embassy. One day, while riding in my official limousine, someone suddenly darted out into the street, shouting, "Stop the killings!" and spit at the car. The proposed high-level visits were put on hold. Business-development plans were shelved and the British media were full of scathing criticisms.

I plunged into the work of salvaging relations. First, I arranged meetings with British officials to reassure them that I had met personally with Jiang Zemin, who had been elevated to general secretary of the Communist Party, and that China's course toward reform and openness would not change. I met with members of Parliament with the same message, then with business and community leaders. Finally, I invited influential members of the media to the embassy and briefed them on the situation in China.

The political élite politely heard me out, but said they would need to see a period of calm before they could move ahead with the cooperative projects that had been in the works when I left.

The media were relentless in their attacks and condemnations. I chose to go on the offensive, accepting all requests for written interviews, and accepting all requests for TV and radio interviews, but only on condition that they be broadcast live, so my words could not be edited to say something other than what I meant.

It took about six months for the controversy to subside, and for my focus to return to economic development, and to articulating China's policies on the various crises that were breaking out in Eastern Europe with the collapse of the Soviet Union.

The following year, 1990, Xiangtong and I returned for our home leave and I finally had a chance to properly pay my respects to my mother, who had died just before the Tiananmen Square disaster. I had visited her the year before on home leave. Although she was getting old, I had not thought it would be the last time we spoke. She expressed admiration for my becoming "the pillar of the family."

I was caught off guard, therefore, when I got the phone call in London in the spring of 1989 from my eldest son, Xiaotan, telling me she had passed away. I felt terrible that I couldn't be with her. The best I could do was put on a black armband and remember her as the young mother teaching me the "three cleans" of making noodles. I was now an orphan.

When Father died, because he was considered a veteran revolutionary, his ashes were accepted for a special mausoleum in Taiyuan reserved for Martyrs to the Revolution. These are large marble buildings with great rooms filled with rows of shelving holding equal-size, glass-doored boxes, roughly eighteen inches wide and nine inches deep, each for a different person or married couple.

Inside each tomb, as we call them, are fancy wooden boxes—instead of ceramic urns—containing the ashes of the deceased. We also include photos, sometimes silk flowers, and other trinkets and memorabilia. My eldest brother, Chaoding, was entombed in the Babaoshan Revolutionary Cemetery in Beijing, the main resting place for the highest government officials.

When Xiangtong and I returned for our third home visit, the country had calmed down and we were able to travel to Taiyuan to visit the tomb where Mother's ashes had been placed with Father's. We performed the ritual cleaning of the tomb, removing all the contents, dusting everything off, and putting everything back. Then we bowed three times. Although I shuddered with grief, I was glad to have completed my duties as their son. My older brother Chaoli and my sister, Chin, had both settled in the United States, so I couldn't share the experience with them.

We returned to the United Kingdom from home leave in 1990, expecting to spend another year or so in London. But in January 1991, I was called to the code room to receive a top-secret cable, for my eyes only. This time I was being summoned to New York, where I had been appointed to replace another diplomat as under secretary-general of the United Nations for Economic and Social Development.

We wanted to return to China first, but my predecessor had already departed and my presence was requested without delay. Once again, we packed our bags and prepared to move on. This time, though, I felt that I was returning home.

Epilogue

Years later when I returned to New York as under secretary-general of the United Nations I went there again.

I was riding in a taxi with a dear family friend—Virginia Kamsky, an American businesswoman—when I noticed that we were headed north on Third Avenue, about to pass Twelfth Street. "Stop!" I cried out.

The driver lurched to the curb.

"This is where I grew up!" I threw open the door. My heart raced with anticipation. A half century had elapsed since the last time I'd walked on Twelfth Street.

"You can't get out here!" Virginia protested. "This is a terrible neighborhood!"

I had experienced and witnessed poverty and desperation beyond anything my well-meaning friend could have imagined in New York's East Village.

"I'll be fine," I said. "Just drive around the corner and wait for me in front of 233 East Twelfth."

I walked down East Twelfth Street with a spring in my step, looking for cues but finding none. So many blocks in New York look the same. I walked along the north side, looking at the addresses with odd numbers.

I found 233 on a building that looked luxurious compared to my memory of it. It was in a row of five identical six-story tenements, each three windows wide, that had been architecturally joined to form one long building—a cooperative apartment house. The neighborhood was much tidier and more prosperous-looking than it had been in 1950, when I had said goodbye to my mother before leaving for China.

I toyed with the idea of ringing the bell for the sixth floor but decided that it would be enough to gaze at the windows and conjure up a few memories: my father reading; my mother sewing or painting or boiling those delicious noodles; my older brother Chaoli singing some awful Chinese opera; my sister diligently poring over her homework; and me looking at the color plates in a borrowed copy of a book about King Arthur, daydreaming about knights and castles, imagining myself a courageous Han warrior fighting for his homeland. It didn't quite turn out the way I had pictured it, but my wish came true. A circle had closed.

Living in New York became a rolling reunion. I renewed my schoolboy friendships without fear of political repercussions. I recommended my old Harvard pal Herb Levin to be a special adviser to me at the United Nations.

Xiangtong and I hopped the globe during my five-year term at the United Nations, serving under two secretaries-general, attending conferences, and helping poor countries get access to development funding. We got to see many new places, and I was even able to assist my old home province, Shanxi, in obtaining a large development loan for a water project.

I completed my U.N. assignment and officially retired from active service in 1996, at the age of sixty-seven. Xiangtong and I kept an apartment in Forest Hills, Queens, where both our sons visited for a time with their wives.

In 2001, another old Harvard classmate, George Goodman—who became a famous financial author writing under the name Adam Smith—interviewed me for a documentary that he was putting together about China. He interviewed Kissinger and others who had played a role in recent history, as well as young students in Beijing, who spoke of their goals to become investment bankers or teachers.

Goodman's documentary attempted to examine China's future within the context of its past. Political relations with the United States dominated the hour-long program, and he never asked me how I thought the Chinese and the Americans viewed each other as individuals. When the interview was over, I felt compelled to add a postscript: "The Chinese know America better than the Americans know China. The risk is that we misperceive each other. My sense is that Americans see China as a mass of blue ants."

That was seven years ago. In spite of all the challenges the People's Republic still faces, especially pollution and economic disparity, I hope that impression is changing, but I suspect it still has a long way to go. Like the Foolish Old Man, I have confidence that the descendants of my descendants will keep at it, shovelful by shovelful, until the mountains have been removed and we live in a harmonious world.

Acknowledgments

It has been a great honor and a great responsibility to have this chance to offer an eyewitness account of the modern history of my native land, and to pay tribute to the America that so generously adopted my family and educated me when I was a child and a young man.

Throughout my life I have had the good fortune to enjoy the friendship of many people. I have been wealthy in my friends, many of whom played a role in assisting me with the preparation of this book or by encouraging me to keep going.

I would have been lost without my soul mate and wife of more than a half century, Wang Xiangtong, who wrote the first biography of me, published in Chinese in 1997 in my hometown of Taiyuan, Shanxi Province. Her hard work and excellent memory paved the way for this expanded, English-language version.

I have also enjoyed the wholehearted support of my elder son, Ji Xiaotan, and his wife, Wu Tao, and my younger son, Ji Xiao-bin, and his wife, Hilary Bernstein.

For sharing their memories of my years growing up in the States, I thank my old school chums—Anne Tonachel, Pierre Epstein, Peter Reich, Nick Wood, and Herb Levin, among others.

For their help in reconstructing my years in the Foreign Ministry, I am grateful to Guo Jiading, Yang Guanchun, Liang Yuhua, Zhang Hanzhi, and Chen Xiuying.

For helping me with details of my family history, I wish to thank my older brother Chaoli; my cousins Ji Chaohe, Zhang Peiji, and Zhang Jianji; and my nephew Emile.

Particular thanks go to Gregory S. Lewis, Ph.D., professor of history at Weber State University in Ogden, Utah, who devoted his 1999 doctoral thesis to an in-depth study of the life and career of my eldest brother, Chi Chaoding, and in doing so unearthed many fascinating, previously unknown details of Chaoding's underground activities in the United States.

I am especially grateful for the friendship and encouragement of Ray Dalio, Paul Dalio, Mathew Dalio, Virginia Kamsky, Julie Nixon Eisenhower, and David Laux.

I thank Ning Li, a young Chinese actor, director, and filmmaker who accompanied me and videotaped my August 2005 journey to revisit many of the locations that played a role in my life and career.

I thank my old friends and relatives from my native province of Shanxi, especially Madame Li Yue-e, former general director of the Shanxi Provincial Foreign Affairs Office, and her colleagues who took the time to travel with Xiangtong and me in 2005 as we retraced the route my family took when fleeing the Japanese in 1938. The Hubei Province and Wuhan city Foreign Affairs offices helped me locate my family's old residence and my old primary school in Wuhan.

Also helpful with their knowledge and their hospitality were my relatives in the city of Xi'an, Shaanxi Province, including the deputy mayor, Zhu Zhisheng; our nephews Zhu Hongkai, Hu Yuzhu, and Hu Yang; and our grandnephew Zhu Daqing.

Finally, this book would not have become a reality without the patient guidance of my literary agent, Al Zuckerman of Writers House, and my Random House editor, Robert Loomis.

Index

About the Author

JI CHAOZHU was born on July 30, 1929, in the Shanxi Province of China. Throughout his decorated career, he has held posts in China's Ministry of Foreign Affairs (where he was deputy director of the Department of Translation and Interpretation and deputy director of American and Oceanic Affairs). In 1982, he was appointed minister counselor of the Embassy of the People's Republic of China in the United States of America, and has served as China's ambassador to Fiji, Kiribati, Vanuatu, and the Court of St. James's. From 1991 to 1996, he served as the under secretary-general of the United Nations. He currently resides in China with his wife.

About the Type

This book was set in Sabon, a typeface designed by the well-known German typographer Jan Tschichold (1902–1974). Sabon's design is based on the original letterforms of Claude Garamond and was created specifically to be used for three sources: foundry type for hand composition, Linotype, and Monotype. Tschichold named his typeface for the famous Frankfurt typefounder Jacques Sabon, who died in 1580.

7/10 ① ¹⁰/₀₈